A Life on the Line

Dr. Pierre-Étienne Fortin, M.P. for Gaspé, aged 61.
(William James Topley/National Archives of Canada/PA33681)

A Life on the Line
Commander Pierre-Étienne Fortin and his Times

W. Brian Stewart

CARLETON LIBRARY SERIES,
Volume 188

Carleton University Press

Copyright © Carleton University Press, 1997

Printed and bound in Canada

Canadian Cataloguing in Publication Data

Stewart, W. Brian, date-
   A life on the line: Commander Pierre-Étienne Fortin and his times

(Carleton library series; #188)
Includes bibliographical references.
ISBN 0-88629-315-4

   1. Fortin, Pierre, 1823-1888. 2. Politicians—Quebec (Province)—Biography. 3. Quebec (Province)—Politics and government—1867-1897. I. Title. II. Series: The Carleton library #188.

FC2922.1.F67S75 1997   971.4'03'092   C97-900245-1
F1053.S75 1997

Cover Design: Your Aunt Nellie
Typeset: Mayhew & Associates Graphic Communications, Richmond, Ont., in association with Marie Tappin

This book has been published with the help of a grant from the Humanities and Social Sciences Federation of Canada, using funds provided by the Social Sciences and Humanities Research Council of Canada.

Carleton University Press gratefully acknowledges the support extended to its publishing program by the Canada Council and the financial assistance of the Ontario Arts Council. The Press would also like to thank the Department of Canadian Heritage, Government of Canada, and the Government of Ontario through the Ministry of Culture, Tourism and Recreation, for their assistance.

To
Gwyneth

Not least for all the meals we ate together
when I wasn't there

THE CARLETON LIBRARY SERIES

A series of original works, new collections, and reprints of source material relating to Canada, issued under the supervision of the Editorial Board, Carleton Library series, Carleton University Press Inc., Ottawa, Canada.

General Editor
John Flood

Associate General Editor
N.E.S. Griffiths

Editorial Board
Pat Armstrong (Canadian Studies)
Bruce Cox (Anthropology)
Tom Darby (Political Science)
Lynne van Luven (Journalism)
Dominique Marshall (History)
John De Vries (Sociology)
Iain Wallace (Geography)

CONTENTS

	List of Illustrations	viii
	Preface	ix
I	The Commander and *La Canadienne*	1
II	Fortin's Ancestors and his Youth	17
III	Fighting Plagues and Mobs	31
IV	The Commander and His Domain	47
V	Sellout of the Gulf	61
VI	Magistrate and Policeman	75
VII	A Company Man?	87
VIII	The War of the Candle Snuffers	105
IX	Naturalist and Conservationist	113
X	Conservation *versus* Jobs	125
XI	"Our Rivers Taken from Us"	135
XII	Fighting with the Bureaucrats	145
XIII	Fortin, the Conservatives, and Confederation	153
XIV	A Constituency Man	167
XV	Final Days	185
	Sources	199
	Index	209

ILLUSTRATIONS

1. Pierre-Étienne Fortin — *frontispiece*
2. *La Canadienne* — 8
3. Amherst Harbour — 10
4. Grosse-Île — 33
5. Fortin's Gulf (map) — 46
5. The basin at Gaspé — 49
6. Charles Robin and Co. — 95
7. Fishermen at Longue-Pointe — 110

PREFACE

The saga of the Canadian fisheries seen through the reports [to Parliament] of this loyal official, would form a notable addition to the literature of our country's development.[1]

Historian J.E. Hodgetts refers to Pierre-Étienne Fortin (1823-1888). Each summer from 1852 to 1867, Fortin crisscrossed the Gulf of St. Lawrence on the armed schooner *La Canadienne*, visiting communities on the Gaspé peninsula, the Lower North Shore, and the Îles-de-la-Madeleine. As a stipendiary magistrate, he upheld law and order and enforced the fisheries acts. As a fisheries officer, he gathered statistics and reported on Gulf fisheries and the peoples dependent on them. His reports often give a vivid account of day-to-day life in the Gulf in the mid-nineteenth century. I have used them to present a modest social history, as Fortin saw it, of that region at that time. It is a region and time that only a few Anglophone historians have explored. Fortin, however, did more than just record Gulf history; he also tried to mould it. He did this during his years on *La Canadienne*, and again as a member of the provincial and federal legislatures (1867-88). Here, he becomes controversial.

To investigate Fortin's beliefs and intentions, I could seldom refer to any personal thoughts expressed in his private letters or diaries, or in those of his family and friends. Few such letters and no diaries are extant. Instead, I have tried first to sketch with light strokes the social, economic and political milieu in which he lived. I have then used his public reports and parliamentary speeches, and his actions as magistrate and politician, to try to define his role in that milieu. Fortin is a middle-level historical figure. By that I mean that he stood between the elites, who have traditionally been the stuff of historical biographies, and the masses, who are increasingly the subject of social and economic histories. The controversial questions are: Was he a willing tool of the Jersey fishing companies, and of the Tories/Bleus of Macdonald/Cartier, simply enforcing their systems and edicts on the masses below him? Or did he struggle against the elites, trying to improve the lot of the Gulf's peoples? Then again, were he, the masses and the elites helpless in the grip of impersonal economic and social forces shaping their society? Historians mentioned in Chapter 7 have suggested or implied all three views.

The English versions of Fortin's reports vary greatly in their nomenclature for places in the Gulf. In the text I have used the official French spelling, using *Répertoire géographique du Québec, 1969* and *Répertoire toponymique du Québec, 1987*,[2] with three exceptions. When quoting Fortin directly or indirectly, I have used his nomenclature, with the French version in square brackets in appropriate places. Second, for names of Pan-Canadian significance[3] and for "North Shore," I have used the English version. Thirdly, for two places that have changed their name, I continue to use Fortin's version: the Amherst of this text is now Havre-Aubert of the Îles-de-la-Madeleine, and Pointe-aux-Esquimaux is Havre-Saint-Pierre of the Lower North Shore. Fortin sometimes applies the term "Labrador" or "Labrador coast" to the Lower North Shore as well as to Labrador proper. When his intentions are clear, I have indicated "North Shore" in square brackets. Place names are indexed by their French version, except for those of Pan-Canadian significance.

I wish to thank the following people for their help while, of course, absolving them from any of my errors: Timothy Dubé, Andrée Lavoie, and Patricia Kennedy of that excellent institution the National Archives of Canada, and Cécile Gélinas of the Musée de la Gaspésie, for their general research assistance; Josée Roy of the Musée maritime Bernier, André Bonneau of the Société du port de Québec, and Nicolas Landry of the National Archives, for their help in tracking down Fortin's *La Canadienne* from the more than two dozen vessels of that name built around this time; Olaf Janzen, editor of *Argonauta*, for help in seeking information on Canada's first navigational schools; Phebe Chartrand of McGill University Archives for information on Fortin's university career; and André Charbonneau of Parks Canada for sources concerning Fortin's sojourn on Grosse-Île. Dr. René Lavoie of the Biological Sciences Branch of the Department of Fisheries and Oceans, and an expert on the Caraquet oysters, gave me a most interesting commentary on Fortin's experiments with oyster farming, while Dr. E.J. Crossman, Curator Emeritus (Ichthyology) at the Royal Ontario Museum and

Professor Emeritus (Zoology) at the University of Toronto, kindly reviewed some of Fortin's work on Gulf fishes, and gave me his valuable comments. Two historians, unknown to me, who commented on my manuscript for the Aid to Scholarly Publications Programme, saved me from too many errors.

For the convenience of readers, the notes at the end of each chapter contain citations only. Occasional footnotes supplement the text. In the notes, a source is cited in full the first time it appears, and subsequent notations are made under an abbreviation. This is usually the last name of the author or authors, but includes other material if there is more than one author of the same name, or if an author has written more than one work. Some sources are always presented as abbreviations. These are:

Fortin, *Report*: See Sources for explanation.
HOCD: House of Commons, *Debates*.
HOCJ: House of Commons, *Journals*.
MG: Manuscript Group (National Archives).
PCA: Province of Canada, *Laws and Statutes*.
NA: National Archives of Canada.
PCA: Province of Canada, *Laws and Statutes*.
PCLAJ: Province of Canada, Legislative Assembly, Journals.
QLAD: Quebec, Legislative Assembly, *Debates*.
QLAJ: Quebec, Legislative Assembly, *Journals*.
RG: Record Group (National Archives).

I have also used "mfm" as a contraction for "microfilm."
N.B. All translations from the French are by the author.

NOTES

1. Hodgetts, J.E. *Pioneer Public Service: An Administrative History of the United Canadas, 1841-1867.* Toronto: University of Toronto Press, 1965: 148.
2. Ministère des Terres et Forêts du Québec. *Répertoire géographique du Québec.* Québec: Commission de Géographie, 1969; Commission de Toponymie du Québec. *Répertoire toponymique du Québec*, 1987. Québec: Éditeur officiel du Québec, 1987.
3. Canada, the Department of the Secretary of State. *The Canadian Style: A Guide to Writing and Editing.* Toronto and London: Dundurn Press, 1985: 227-28.

I

THE COMMANDER AND *LA CANADIENNE*

Pointe des Monts lies on the north shore of the St. Lawrence River, just over seventy kilometers east of what is now Baie-Comeau. Pointe de Cap Chat lies about opposite on the south shore. According to the joint Imperial-American Commission, appointed under the terms of the Reciprocity Treaty of 1854, the forty-eight kilometer line between the two headlands divides the St. Lawrence River from the Gulf of St. Lawrence.[1] Geography provides good reason for setting the dividing line there. Just to the east of Pointe des Monts the coast turns sharply north while the opposite coast curves away. Soon, they are one hundred kilometers apart. From either shore, you look out over an inland ocean with no coastline breaking the horizon.

From 1854 till 1866, the line marked the upper limits of where Americans could, by the Treaty, fish in the Gulf. On the Gulf side of that line, from the north came great storms; from the east came exploitative commercial houses based in the Channel Islands across the Atlantic; and from the south every summer arrived an army of thugs on hundreds of fishing schooners. They all converged to create a brutal, hazardous life for Canadian fishermen. Law and order depended heavily on one schooner coming from the west. *La Canadienne* carried a stipendiary magistrate, Pierre-Étienne Fortin, and a crew of twenty-five officers and men who also acted as police.[2]

The patrol left Québec each year as soon as the break-up in the river allowed, usually towards the end of April. It needed only a part of the crew to sail *La Canadienne*. The others, uniformed and at attention, stood on deck as the schooner glided from the wharf. A crowd of friends on the wharves cheered. Two of the vessel's four brass cannon roared in reply.[3]

Captain Louis Bernier typically plotted a course between Île d'Orléans and the South Shore, then through the Northern Channel. After crossing the line into the Gulf, *La Canadienne* sailed between the mainland and Anticosti Island. Visits followed to a series of isolated communities as far east as the Labrador border at the fifty-fourth meridian. From there the schooner crossed to Gaspé. "Gaspé" possibly derives from the Micmac "gespeg" meaning "land's end," but *La Canadienne* would sail beyond land's end into the Gulf, as far as the Îles-de-la-Madeleine.

Captain Bernier gave the sailing orders. Real authority lay with the thickset man who stood by the wheel, critically watching the actions of the crew. He wore a quasi-naval uniform, though Canada at that time had neither a navy nor even a coast guard. A skilled seaman, he lacked certification, so by law could not command sea-going vessels. However, as "Commander of the Expedition for the Protection of the Gulf Fisheries," he used the title "Commander" and wore an appropriate uniform.

This was Pierre-Étienne Fortin, a man in his thirties and forties when he sailed the Gulf. A historian referred to him, when he was in his fifties, as "the athletic Fortin."[4] A later colleague, Joseph-Israël Tarte, said of him, "Physically, he is one of the best-looking Canadians in the province. Doctor, artist, man of breeding, he is as at home in the salon as he was on the bridge of *La Canadienne*.... I have never known a man of better character, or more upright, than the honourable member for Gaspé."[5]

A report of his death far out in the Gulf appeared in the Montréal newspaper, *La Minerve*, in July 1860. The paper wrote that he was "loved and esteemed by all." He was "intelligent, a brilliant speaker, full of humour." He had "an easy manner, a generous soul, an energetic character, a delicate spirit, leaving only respect and admiration wherever he went." And this fine man was now dead "on a savage and deserted beach, far from family and friends."[6]

The report was false: a Newfoundland inspector of fisheries, not Fortin, had died. Still, the eulogies in *La Minerve* and other papers showed remarkable respect for a man just thirty-seven years old.

A graduate of McGill Medical School, Fortin had been a hero of Grosse-Île in 1847. That year, a plague killed thousands of Irish immigrants along with Canadian doctors, clergymen, and volunteers who ministered to them on the quarantine island near Québec. In 1849 he had commanded a force of mounted police in the infamous Montréal riots, when Tory mobs burned the parliament building and nearly killed the governor general and prime minister. Since 20 April 1852, Fortin had sailed the Gulf as a stipendiary magistrate for the districts of Quebec, Kamouraska and Gaspé.

Once *La Canadienne* was at sea, Fortin could go below. Climbing through a companionway just in front of the steering wheel, and then down a stepladder, he would enter the great cabin. There, amid the background sounds of creaking hemp and manila ropes, the commands of the officer on watch, and the snap of sails as the vessel came about, Fortin would write his notes about the voyage. He would list trials he had conducted and his verdicts. He would draft scientific papers on the marine life of the Gulf. And he would use his notes and the ship's log to write annual reports accounting to parliament for his stewardship. He told a parliamentary committee in 1864, "I write my general reports in English. The remainder of my correspondence is in French."[7] If he refers to his annual reports to parliament, his English was very good indeed, if sometimes ponderous.

The commander had much to write about. For seven months each year, *La Canadienne* crisscrossed the 250,000 square kilometers of stormy Gulf. Fortin's job: to uphold the law among the 30,000 Canadians who lived around its shores. He also protected them from thousands of fishermen who each season flooded into the Gulf from New England and Nova Scotia. Many were ruffians who polluted the fishing banks with ballast and offal, rammed local schooners and fouled their nets, and pillaged remote fishing stations.

As magistrate, Fortin was responsible for maintaining law and order in the wilderness. As fisheries superintendent, he enforced regulations and issued salmon licences. And as inspector of customs, he collected duties and policed the sale of liquor. His work showed rich variety within a single day:

On 6 October 1860 Fisheries Inspector Fortin was on the North Shore, somewhere near the Rivière Saint-Jean, reporting on the cod catches. Police Officer Fortin then learned that the previous night, a fisherman named Elie Debien had died suddenly, possibly by violence, in the house of one Philippe Bisson. Magistrate Fortin decided an inquest should be held, and he took the depositions of Bisson and of others in the house. He also summoned anyone who might furnish important evidence. Commander Fortin ordered his boat to return to

La Canadienne. However, the sea had got very rough. "After passing a line of breakers at great risk" he had to return to shore. The schooner, unable to withstand the heavy seas, made for Mingan. Leaving crew and witnesses to come later by boat, Fisheries Officer Fortin began walking to Longue-Pointe, arriving at 6:00 P.M. He remained long enough to visit the principal fishing establishments and take note of the codfish catches. These "had been no better in the Autumn than in the Summer." Thanks to the loan of a horse by a local farmer, ex-Cavalryman Fortin reached Mingan before midnight.

Next day, Coroner Fortin held an inquest on the body of Debien. Doctor Fortin then performed a postmortem before twelve sworn witnesses and decided "an effusion of blood on the brain" had caused death. He also gave his opinion about the injuries on the face without describing that opinion in his report. Coroner Fortin then questioned the witnesses. The jury returned a verdict at Mingan on the 15th. They found that Debien had "died from the bursting of blood vessels in the head, caused by what the evidence does not show."[8]

This account, as with most of those we have of Fortin's adventures in the Gulf, comes from his own reports. Some, however, come from independent witnesses. In a letter to the provincial secretary in 1856, an official at Baie-de-Saint-Paul described how the crew of *La Canadienne* were helping keep order during an election for the Legislative Council. Then a nearby vessel caught fire. The official wrote, "Captain Fortin was conspicuous by the light of the flames, for a full hour and a half, placing himself in personal danger." He was "not only commanding his men, but actually working with them, and by these means unquestionably saved the *Princess* from total loss." The provincial secretary wrote to Fortin expressing the governor general's thanks. Fortin included in his report both of these, as well as other, laudatory letters.[9]

Modesty did not hamper the commander. His reports often included letters from officials, clerics and businessmen thanking him and *La Canadienne*, sometimes in extravagant terms, for one service or another. A letter from the corporation of Bonaventure County said the inhabitants were pleased "at having a government vessel to protect the fisheries on this coast, and on the North Shore." The government was acting in "the dearest interest of this county" by choosing Fortin to enforce the fisheries laws. He "possesses all the necessary qualifications." He had also "performed his duty in a manner most satisfactory to the inhabitants of this coast, where fisheries abound."[10] Fortin used such letters for public relations advantage.

If Fortin's rank of commander was doubtful, discipline on *La Canadienne* was as taut as the decks were well scrubbed. Standards of training were high. His sailors were "dressed in uniform and I drill them myself in the use of arms." He wrote, "It was my constant endeavour to preserve the strictest discipline.... I aimed at all times to give to the schooner that look of a vessel of war which is absolutely necessary to impress seamen and fishermen, both British and foreign, with respect; no law but that which is enforced by an armed vessel being understood or respected by them."[11]

La Canadienne visited settlements almost daily, and parties of seamen often went ashore to arrest law breakers or quell riots. Whenever the sailors went ashore, Fortin required them to be in uniform and to act in a way that would inspire "respect and confidence." When the settlement had a church, Fortin took all seamen not on duty to Sunday mass. They wore full-dress uniform and marched under orders of the ship's gunner. "I did everything to give *La Canadienne* respectability of character."[12]

At an 1864 parliamentary committee, Captain Louis Bernier gave a glimpse into life aboard *La Canadienne*. "I was captain of the vessel, and moreover executed the orders given by the Commandant.... We sailed continually from one port to another, and we then had to visit the ports and rivers in boats.... We were often in danger when out in the boats."[13]

In his own reports, Fortin seldom refers to Bernier, or acknowledges that he was officially in command. Even in those few mentions, Bernier plays a subordinate role. In 1859 "one of my officers, Captain Bernier, whom I sent on board" a vessel, found no signs of purloined eggs. The same year, he sent Bernier to the banks of Caraquet Bay for oysters. At Pabos, Bernier and six men seized the goods and chattels of some tax dodgers. Another time, Fortin sent witnesses to Percé "in a boat, in the charge of Captain Bernier." And again, "I sent Captain Bernier ... to help the constable carry into execution a summary judgment."[14] When *La Canadienne* was wrecked in 1861, Fortin wrote that the Captain ordered the helm to be put hard up the moment the schooner struck. That is almost the only reference to Bernier during the affair. Fortin says it was he himself who finally managed to get a line ashore and save the men.[15]

If Bernier resented this lack of notice, he did not complain when he had the opportunity to do so at the 1864 committee. Some members' questions showed their hostility towards Fortin, and Bernier could have scored points. The captain, however, now a fisheries officer, told the committee he had "executed the orders given by the Commander." He spoke with approval of the economy shown on *La Canadienne*. Asked about discipline on board, he said he had spent four years on a frigate. The same discipline applied aboard *La Canadienne* as aboard the warship. During the first years, boat crews returning after long voyages in stormy autumn weather received a ration of rum, but they had stopped the practice two years earlier. His one complaint had nothing to do with Fortin. "My own salary," he said, "was not in proportion to my services."[16]

The truth is that in later years, Fortin did indeed command *La Canadienne*. No one pretended otherwise. In the first few years, however, his command may have been less secure. An undated and undocumented story says that on one occasion, the fisheries protection vessel (possibly *La Canadienne*) came upon a foreign smuggler. The schooner escaped beyond cannon range and Fortin ordered his captain, not named in the story, to make more sail and retake the smuggler. The captain refused. The angry Fortin then broke the strongest law of the sea. He allegedly shouted, "Then I am taking command," and did so. They overtook and arrested the foreigner.[17]

Fortin's reports mention no such takeover. He comes closest to doing so in 1860, but falls far short of deposing the captain. Because *La Canadienne* was then under repair, the commander had to travel on the *Napoleon III*. This government steamer supplied the Gulf lighthouses, and the captain insisted that his supply duties take precedence over the magisterial duties of Fortin. A clash came in August when the crews of several American schooners were plundering the coast. Fortin found they had pillaged a mill at Mont-Louis and had badly assaulted Canadian fishermen. Someone told him that he should go on to Mont-Louis immediately; he might find the offenders there. "I accordingly went on board [*Napoleon III*] and gave orders to set out. But the Captain of the Steamer refused to proceed thither, alleging that it was contrary to his instructions. I therefore left Montlouis [Mont-Louis] behind me and went on to Grand Valley [Grande-Vallée] at 5:45P.M. .... [to hear] fresh complaints against the American fishermen."[18]

Fortin would hardly mention in official reports his alleged takeover, but from what we know of Bernier, he would not have refused such an order. Somehow, the anecdote has an air of the apocryphal, of one of those myths that gather about popular heroes. However, a Crown Lands memorandum of 1857 shows that the first master of *La Canadienne* was a Captain Talbot. The memorandum describes Talbot as "utterly unfit" for his job because of "advanced age." He was dismissed and the younger Bernier took over. Perhaps the incident of the escaping schooner triggered Talbot's dismissal on the grounds of age and timidity.[19]

The story of Fortin in the gulf began in June 1851. In the so-called Toronto agreement, delegates from Canada, Nova Scotia and New Brunswick had agreed to acquire vessels for use in protecting British North American fisheries.[20] At that time, twenty Royal Navy ships based at Halifax were supposed to protect the fisheries from illegal foreign fishing, but wrongdoers could too easily spot the warships. They quickly stopped their activities and fled. The colonies countered by hiring schooners indistinguishable from fishing boats. These could approach foreigners unremarked until identifying themselves. Under the agreement, Canada appointed Fortin as magistrate for the Gulf. He made his first tour on the *Alliance*, a leased schooner with two three-pounder cannon and a crew of ten.[21]

In his first (1852) report, Fortin complained that the *Alliance* was too slow to catch lawbreakers. He suggested building a clipper-style schooner of about 100 tons at a cost of £1,250. Sailing six months a year with six months in dry-dock, the vessel would need no repairs to the hull for at least twelve years; only sails and cordage would need renewal. He showed that this would be cheaper than recommissioning the *Alliance*. As well, he claimed, the vessel's construction would boost Canadian shipbuilding. To help defray operating costs, he recommended that the government impose fishing licences and start collecting customs duties on the "Labrador Coast" (*i.e.*, the lower North Shore).[22] However, he did not get the right to collect customs duties there until 1858.[23]

Bureaucrats would rather spend $1.50 in operating costs than $1.00 in capital. No matter how reasonable Fortin's arguments, his superiors preferred to lease rather than build. He had proposed the new schooner in November 1852. By February 1853 he was supplying an estimate of £600 annually to rent the *Doris*. This wooden paddle-steamer, bought in England a few years earlier, performed "little better than a floating barrel."[24] The crew consisted of a coxswain and five men under Captain Talbot.[25] No reports on the 1853 and 1854 voyages appear in the parliamentary journals.

In early 1855, the Commander at last got his wish. For all but two of the next eleven years he would perform his duties on the Gulf aboard his beloved *La Canadienne*, a schooner designed specifically for the protection of the fisheries. The fine shipbuilding firm of T.C. Lee,

La Canadienne under her full suit of sails: main and foresail, two jibs, maintopsail, and fisherman. (*Canadian Illustrated News*/National Archives of Canada/C62687)

Québec, built and launched *La Canadienne* in the spring. Our only picture shows a lovely craft, heeling to windward on the starboard tack under a full suit of sails: main and foresail, two jibs, main-topsail, and fisherman. The schooner had a clipper bow. The construction, which archival records call "very sharp," required seventeen and a half tons of pig iron in ballast.[26] The foresail was "loose footed." That is to say it had no boom, allowing the canvas to stretch far back and overlap the mainsail. This rig provided a huge wind trap.

The initial survey of *La Canadienne* shows it weighed about 100 tons, New Measure.* The "length aloft" was 92.1 feet, the "extreme breadth outside" 23.7 feet, and the "depth of hold" 10.1 feet. Tamarack and oak provided a strong frame.[27] The masts were probably white pine. The "general quality of workmanship" was "Very superior." The rating of 7A1 licensed *La Canadienne* for seven years to carry perishable goods anywhere in the world, provided it received periodic sur-

---

* The Thames Measurement for calculating the tonnage of a ship replaced the Builders Old Measurement in the mid 1850s. *La Canadienne* must have been one of the earliest vessels in Canada to be measured by the new formula. See Dear, Ian and Kemp, Peter. *The Pocket Oxford Guide to Sailing Terms*. Oxford: Oxford University Press, 1976: 22, 184.

veys.[28] Of the four brass cannon, two were four-pounders. The two two-pounders were probably for signalling. The estimated operating expense for 1856 was £1,338, plus £75 for unidentified furniture and £130 for armament.

TABLE 1: CREW AND ESTIMATED EXPENSES FOR *LA CANADIENNE*, 1856

1 master pilot	£175	Magistrate	£250
1 2nd pilot	44	Provisions	300
2 coxswains	60	Clothing	100
10 1st-class seamen	220		
8 ordinary seamen	132		
1 steward	25		
1 cook	22		
1 cook's mate	10		
25 officers and crew	£688	Other £650	TOTAL: £1338

Source: NA RG 1 E1 State Minute Books, Vol. P, No. 60, 27 March 1855, armament.

In 1852 Fortin's salary was £150,[29] rising to £220 in 1853,[30] and to £250 on *La Canadienne* in 1855. This was £75 more than the master's pay, and more than ten times that of a first-class seaman. Even so, £250 was said to be £50 less than the salary of a police officer of equal status, despite the "hardships and dangers of a seafaring life."[31] When Fortin left the service in 1867, his salary had doubled to £500 or $1,200.[32] Fishing licences and leases sold by Fortin were not meant to offset the costs of *La Canadienne* and the fisheries protection. Nor did they do so, but over a three-year period, total revenue defrayed about 28 percent of total costs.

TABLE 2: *LA CANADIENNE*'s COSTS AND RECEIPTS

	Costs	Receipts
1860	$1,980.93	$ 779.75
1861	5,081.75*	939.75
1862	2,850.73	1,100.00

* "The causes for so large an amount for expenses were the census taken by Fortin; and when returning in September, the vessel was wrecked." *Source*: "Report of the Commissioner for Crown Lands," PCLAJ, 1863.

Amherst Harbour, Îles-de-la-Madeleine. In 1859, Fortin found more than 150 schooners blocking the harbour and approaches. (Thomas Pye/National Library of Canada/NL19284)

Fortin claimed that *La Canadienne* was the fastest sailing vessel in the Gulf. He needed that speed to apprehend the foreign clippers and American sharpshooters—popular, fast schooners—caught in wrongdoing. In a letter that first year, Fortin wrote, "I have the pleasure to inform you *La Canadienne* is an excellent sea boat ... steady, good against a sea, and a remarkably fast sailor. We have fallen in with some American clippers, but none of them could come up with *La Canadienne*."[33] Ten years later, Fortin described how, off the Îles-de-la-Madeleine, he had raced American schooners. These, he said, were the "the fastest sailors in the world."

My expectations were even surpassed, for in a run, close hauled to the wind, from the basin to Dead Man's Island [le Corps-Mort], we beat more than thirty of the schooners and those did not seem the slowest of the fleet. Evidently *La Canadienne* has gained much, in point of speed particularly, by the improvements and changes I had made in her masts and sails.... By beating out these vessels in working, and in outsailing them, we showed their crews that we could overtake them at any time, and we thus put them on their guard, and removed from them all temptation to violate our laws and commit depredations on our coasts, by destroying their hopes of impunity.[34]

La Canadienne was built both for speed and to withstand the violent storms that often swept the Gulf. On 1 October 1860 Fortin left Québec, having recommissioned the schooner following repairs. Soon he had to ride out a gale along the North Shore. Three other schooners had sailed the same day and all disappeared, costing thirty-eight lives.[35]

Storms often damaged *La Canadienne*'s masts and spars. In 1856 the carpenter had to work on the bowsprit, partly sprung by a sea the previous night. The schooner sailed next day in heavy seas "to test the strength of the cheeks, which were pinned and firmly lashed on each side of the bowsprit, where it was sprung." After three hours, the carpenter reported that the spar had held up even in the heaviest pitching. Fortin decided the *La Canadienne* could continue the cruise with no danger.[36]

Again, at Rivière Saint-Jean in July 1863, a large splinter fell on the deck. Inspection showed that dry rot had made both topmasts unsafe for the autumn storms *La Canadienne* would meet. Gaspésie and the Chaleur Bay had no suitable timber. Caution suggested they return to Québec, but Fortin "had not closed my first visit to our shores." To quit, he said, would mean leaving nearly 300 miles of coast without protection. He and the captain "decided to dismantle our two top masts, and to sail with great care." The schooner continued the tour by sheltering in harbours when bad weather threatened. Not till late August did Fortin order a limping return to Québec for repairs. There, work began. They lost some days in finding spars of the right size, and in making cordage for the shrouds. Finally, on 28 September *La Canadienne* returned to the Gulf to complete the autumn cruise.[37]

La Canadienne sometimes had casualties. In June 1859 in the Gaspé Basin, Fortin sent seven crewmen and an officer to examine fishing stations. A northwest squall upset their longboat. Despite prompt help from the captain of a nearby schooner, three of the men drowned. Fortin dragged the bay over the next two days for a radius of half a mile from the capsize. They found only one body, that of Calixte Fortin (no relation to the commander). They buried him next day. When *La Canadienne* sailed, the commander left instructions for burial of the two other bodies, if they were found.[38]

Just after noon on 24 November 1861, *La Canadienne* sailed from Sept-Iles into the worst disaster. The voyage started with a splendid easterly, "the most favorable wind we could expect," and fine clear weather. But thirty miles later the wind suddenly became a furious storm. The snow was so thick the lookouts could not see the dangerous

North Shore on the starboard beam. To avoid it, they altered course from southwest-quarter-west to southwest. Confident of their position, they "took all the precautions usual in such cases," Fortin wrote, including taking in all sails, except for the double-reefed foresail and the jib.[39]

Still the bow lookouts saw no breakers. Then at 6:30 P.M., with no warning, a "terrible sea" thrust the schooner on some rocks. Captain Bernier ordered the helm put hard up the moment they struck, but the vessel no longer obeyed. The storm threw the hull from side to side, tore away the keel, and *La Canadienne* began to fill. The seas striking the port side flew more than forty feet over the bulwarks. Sailors had to hold on by the rigging to stop the braking waves from sweeping them away. Each wave "lifted her and let her fall again upon the rocks." Suddenly, through the snow and the darkness, they saw trees less than 100 yards away. The cold was bitter, the wind still increasing, but by eight o'clock *La Canadienne* was off the rocks and resting on a sandy beach. "I got some of the men ashore by means of a yard that we pushed to the beach," wrote Fortin. "These helped the others, and at length all the crew were landed." After "thanking Providence," they managed to light a fire and spent a miserable night.

At daylight Fortin found they were two miles downriver from the Îlets-Caribou off the North Shore. They spent the next three days dismantling whatever they could save from the schooner. A detailed inspection showed surprisingly little damage to *La Canadienne*, now lying on its starboard side on a fine sand bed, about sixty yards from the shore. Displaced caulking and loss of the keel had allowed the schooner to fill. They then rowed to Pointe des Monts.

On 5 December they arrived in Québec, and Fortin paid off the crew. He attributed the accident to compass deviation, caused by "the electrical state of the atmosphere during the snow storm; our course having been the only right one." No blame was attached to either Bernier or Fortin.

Though *La Canadienne* suffered relatively slight structural damage, the affair was costly for the government. At first, Public Works had insured the schooner for $6,000 at 7 percent from Lloyds of London. Then two years before the wreck, the government decided to assume the risk itself.[40] Fortin knew that powerful interests disliked the expense of his fisheries protection service. Upper Canadians were interested in exporting wheat and farm products. Toronto and Montreal businessmen saw their main sources of profit in canals, railroads, lumber, and a growing secondary industry. The cod and mackerel of the Gulf were only bargaining chips for free entry into the giant American market. Why bother replacing *La Canadienne*?

Certainly the schooner required constant maintenance. In 1856 the seventeen and a half tons of pig iron used for ballast cost £149 8s 9d.[41] In April 1858 Fortin asked for new sails—granted. He also wanted the hull copper sheathed—refused, though it was painted at a cost of £90 including repair work.[42] On 18 December 1858 he submitted expenses of $1,736.80, much higher than the original estimate due to the loss of a ship's boat.[43] In September 1861, $2,499.23 had to be paid by accountable warrant for fitting out *La Canadienne* the previous spring.[44]

By the time of the 1861 disaster Fortin was an experienced bureaucrat, and experienced bureaucrats know the public relations value of reports; they know how to write them to maximize the beneficial effects of their department on the public well-being. By summarizing the achievements of his voyage and emphasizing the terrible summer weather, the commander did what he could to justify his annual cruises and explain the loss of his vessel. The approach worked. Over the fall and winter of 1861-62, Fortin convinced Québec bureaucrats that *La Canadienne* could be salvaged. They agreed that T.C. Lee should repair the vessel, the cost not to exceed $2,800.[45] In the spring, the schooner was refloated and brought back to the yards for repairs.

The people of the Gulf faced much hardship. They suffered under the hegemony of large fishing companies. They suffered from pillaging by foreign fishermen. They suffered from the neglect of the politicians at Québec. And above all, they suffered from the hazards of fishing in the Gulf, with its fogs and sudden storms. Fortin had successes and failures in ameliorating these hardships, but he invariably put himself and his vessel on the line if the Gulf fishermen required it.

Anyone watching Fortin on the deck of *La Canadienne* during those crises must have thought: Here is a man born to the sea. In fact, he was born far up the St. Lawrence River. He had no known seafaring ancestors, and he did not go to sea until he was nearly thirty. What sort of man, then, was he?

Fortin's annual voyages in *La Canadienne* took him over much of the route that Samuel de Champlain had followed two and a half centuries earlier, and for rather similar reasons. Champlain wanted "to teach the people the knowledge of God, and inform them of the glory and triumphs of Your Majesty, so that together with the French language they may also acquire a French heart and spirit." In short, he wanted to establish French law and order on the wilderness that was New France. At the same time, he was building a French economic empire.

Commander Fortin, too, had the job of establishing law and order in the wilderness that was the Gulf. And he, too, through colonization, wished to strengthen both the French-Canadian presence in, and the general economy of, the Gulf. Those three themes—law and order, economic growth, and a French presence in the Gulf—recur constantly throughout his life. When Fortin crossed the line into the Gulf, perhaps he saw himself in an old tradition. Among those heroes of New France, his own ancestors were not without honour.

NOTES

1. "Report of the Commissioner of Crown Lands," PCLAJ, 1863, App. 42d.
2. Fortin, *Report*, 1863.
3. Quebec *Daily News*, 2 May 1864.
4. Rumilly, Robert. *Histoire de la province de Québec*. 35 volumes. Montréal: Éditions Bernard Valiquette, n.d., 2: 171.
5. *Le Cultivateur*, 10 June 1882; quoted in Potvin, Damase. *Le roi du Golfe. Le Dr. P.-É. Fortin, ancien commandant de la "Canadienne."* Quebec: Éditions Quartier Latin, c. 1952: 16.
6. Quoted in Potvin, *Le roi*, 9-10.
7. "Report of the Select Committee on the Working of the Fisheries Act," PCLAJ, 1864. App. 5.
8. Fortin, *Report*, 1861.
9. Fortin, *Report*, 1857.
10. Fortin, *Report*, 1858.
11. "Report ... on the Working of the Fisheries Act."
12. Fortin, *Report*, 1857.
13. "Report ... on the Working of the Fisheries Act."
14. Fortin, *Report*, 1860: 116, 124; 1862: 124.
15. Fortin, *Report*, 1862.
16. "Report ... on the Working of the Fisheries Act."
17. "L'honorable Pierre Fortin, fondateur de la Société de géographie de Québec," Société de géographie de Québec, *Bulletin*, (Québec), Vol. 4, No. 5 (1910): 347-50.
18. Fortin, *Report*, 1861.
19. NA RG 1 E1 State Minute Books (mfm C-118), Vol. S, No. 500, 12 April 1857, Departmental memorandum, Crown Lands.
20. State Minute Books (mfm C-115), Vol. L, No. 393, 21 June 1851, Protection of Gulf Fisheries.

21. State Minute Books (mfm C-115), Vol. M, No. 130-31, 10 April 1852, Report of Committee; No. 579, 11 November 1852, Board of Ordnance, bill.
22. Fortin, *Report*, 1852-53.
23. State Minute Books (mfm C-115), Vol. S, No. 583, 14 May 1858, Captain Fortin, Authorised.
24. Dunfield, R.W. *The Atlantic Salmon in the History of North America*. Ottawa, Department of Fisheries and Oceans, 1985: 144.
25. State Minute Books (mfm C-116), Vol. N, No. 214, 12 May 1853, Protection of Gulf Fisheries.
26. State Minute Books (mfm C-117), Vol. P, No. 8, 27 February 1855, Tenders.
27. NA MG 40 J 4, Great Britain, National Maritime Museum (mfm A-935), Lloyd's Register of British and Foreign Shipping, Survey, No. 180, Quebec, 1855.
28. Cunningham, R.J., and Mabee, K.R., *Tall Ships and Master Mariners*. St. John's: Breakwater Books, 1985: 148.
29. State Minute Books (mfm C-117), Vol. P, No. 60, 27 March 1855, Fisheries Armament.
30. State Minute Books (mfm C-116), Vol. N, No. 214, 12 May 1853, Protection of Gulf Fisheries.
31. State Minute Books (mfm C-116), Vol. O, No. 159, 7 April 1854, Fisheries and Mr. Fortin's Comments.
32. Potvin, *Le roi*, 148.
33. Fortin, *Report*, 1856, Letter to Provincial Secretary Georges Cartier, 18 September 1855.
34. Fortin, *Report*, 1867-68, 12.
35. Fortin, *Report*, 1861.
36. Fortin, *Report*, 1857.
37. Fortin, *Report*, 1864.
38. Fortin, *Report*, 1860: 109.
39. Fortin, *Report*, 1862.
40. State Minute Books (mfm C-117), Vol. U, No. 12, 6 May 1859, In Reference to Insuring.
41. State Minute Books (mfm C-117), Vol. Q, No. 142, 9 February 1856, E. Michon.
42. State Minute Books (mfm C-118), Vol. S, No. 489, 8 April 1858, Captain Fortin.
43. State Minute Books (mfm C-119), Vol. T, No. 394, 18 December 1858, Captain Fortin.
44. State Minute Books (mfm C-120), Vol. W, No. 353, 14 September 1861, Department of Public Works.
45. State Minute Books (mfm C-120), Vol. X, No. 155, 10 April 1862, Protection of the Gulf Fisheries.

II

FORTIN'S ANCESTORS AND HIS YOUTH

In 1639 Christophe Crevier, a baker of Saint-Cande-le-Jeune, Rouen, France, emigrated to Trois-Rivières. He took with him his wife, Jeanne Evard, and a daughter. The Trois-Rivières parish register for 7 December 1639 shows that Crevier followed the custom for newcomers by becoming godfather to a young Algonquin from Île des Allumettes. Until his death in 1663, Christophe Crevier, Sieur La Meslée, led the hard, dangerous life of a settler in New France.

Nearly forty years before Christophe sailed, Samuel de Champlain had established Québec. By the time of his death in 1635, Champlain had begun the territorial expansion of New France by arranging for a fortified settlement at Trois-Rivières. When the Crevier family arrived, New France had about 300 settlers, with possibly seventy heads of families. Beyond Trois-Rivières lay "the wilderness."

The colony was subject to disease and often crop failure as well as Iroquois attack. Still, Christophe stayed in his new home, and between 1639 and 1651 the Creviers had at least seven more children. The youngest son, Jean-Baptiste, a fur trader at Batiscan, would later adopt an additional surname, Duvernay. Nearly 200 years after the arrival of Christophe, his descendant Julie Fortin, née Duvernay, gave birth at Verchères to a son. He would become Commander Pierre-Étienne Fortin.

Christophe lived most of his life in or near Trois-Rivières. Documents from 1654 recording land transactions in Québec show him getting a concession of Île Saint-Christophe, at the mouth of the

Saint-Maurice River.[1] However, for any prosperity Christophe achieved in his new home, the Iroquois made him pay heavily.

Iroquois hostility towards New France went back to 1609 when Champlain, with his musket, helped his Huron allies defeat their Iroquois enemies. By the 1630s the Mohawk, armed with guns supplied by Dutch traders, were raiding the Algonquin in the Ottawa valley, allies of New France. In the next decade, the Seneca destroyed the major Huron villages, while the Mohawk and Oneida attacked New France itself. The war continued off and on until 1701, when the Iroquois finally agreed not to take sides in the English-French wars.

A famous French priest and explorer, François Dollier de Casson, once wrote of Montréal, "There is not a month in this summer when our book of the dead has not been stained in red letters, by the hands of the Iroquois. No man went four steps from his house without carrying gun, sword and pistol." The story of the Crevier family throughout those eight bitter decades was quite typical of most Canadien families. In May 1653 Iroquois killed Christophe's fourteen-year-old son, Franciscus (perhaps François), near Trois-Rivières. They killed another young son, Antoine, in 1661.[2] A French captive of the "Agnieronnon [Mohawk] Iroquois," described the torture of himself and his fellow captives. "As for little Antoine de la Meslée [thought to be Christophe's son], that poor child moved my compassion deeply; for he had become the servant of these barbarians, and then they killed him too with the knife, when out hunting."

Christophe Crevier fought back. The 1657 *Jesuit Relations* reports that he had escorted some Iroquois from Trois-Rivières to Québec. Obviously they had been captured through trickery:

At nine o'clock in the evening, sieur la Meslée [Christophe] brought five Agnieronons from Trois-Rivières to M. le Gouverneur in order to learn from them who were the murderers of the three Frenchmen killed at Montréal. These five Agnieronons, with six other Agnieronons, were taken by the French of Trois-Rivières, who had obliged them all by subtlety to enter the village, and seized them there. One of them defended himself against M. le barbier, who, finding himself not strong enough to stop him, laid hold of his sword and struck the said Agnieronon with the point, which merely grazed the skin.[3]

Christophe died in November 1663. His widow showed that she too could prosper in the New World. In 1666 she was running a business at

Cap-de-la-Madeleine when she helped equip a party heading for Lake Superior. Several of the men died on the trip. When the party returned, she sued. The court ruled that of one hundred and fifty-six beaver skins belonging to the deceased, Mme Crevier should have fifty-two as her share. Again, court records for 1668 show Mme Crevier involved in a dispute over ownership of a calf. Later she went to live with her daughter in Montréal, despite the Iroquois menace.[4]

The Crevier name continued to register in the records of New France. One of Christophe's daughters, Jeanne, in 1652 married Pierre Boucher, twice governor of Trois-Rivières. Boucher's first wife, who had died, had been an Indian, an early and famous case of racial intermarriage.[5] Jeanne and he had sixteen children.[6] The Québec registry for 24 October 1663 notes that another daughter, Marguerite, had had her marriage to Jacques Fournier annulled for unspecified reasons. Annulment was unusual in New France.[7] Jean, a son of Christophe, established himself at Saint-François-du-Lac and became a famous trader. He made his home a rendezvous for the coureurs de bois. These were not very gentle men. Court records show that in 1669 a musket ball killed a young woman during a quarrel at Crevier's home, and that her father had been badly beaten. An investigation convicted a young man of the murder, but Jean was charged with complicity and fined.[8] Jean also objected to the law that banned trading liquor with the native peoples. He voted with other businessmen to support Governor Frontenac against the church in a plan to legalize the liquor trade.

Two more of Christophe Crevier's descendants died in the war between England and France (1690-97) when Frontenac waged guerrilla warfare on New England, and the colonists replied in kind. The Iroquois killed Christophe's grandson, son of Jean Crevier of Saint-François, in 1690. Then in 1693 Iroquois captured Jean himself at Saint-François. They were preparing to burn him alive when a Dutchman ransomed him, but Crevier died shortly after from wounds.[9]

Commander Fortin's direct ancestor was Jean-Baptiste Crevier, *dit* Duvernay. The 1681 census shows him, aged thirty, living at Batiscan. He owned a rifle and two beef cattle, and had forty arpents of land under cultivation. In 1684 a militia force went to Lake Ontario to intimidate the Iroquois. Among the officers was Lieutenant Duvernay of Batiscan. In 1705 Jean-Baptiste, now a merchant, set up in business in Montréal, where he was buried in 1708. He left four or five children, one of whom, Pierre, established the Duvernay family at Verchères.[10]

By 1748 Jacques Duvernay, son of Pierre and great-grandson of the original Christophe, had begun practising at Verchères as a notary. Records for 1760 show that his work included a very high proportion of marriages. It is said that, after the surrender of Montréal to the British, "All the soldiers of the vanquished army gave their word that they would contract marriage before this humble rural lawyer."[11] It is not known why.

In 1762 the British regime made Pierre Crevier, *dit* Duvernay, royal notary for all Montréal, but particularly for Verchères, Varennes and Saint-Ours. He replaced his father, Jacques, on condition that he live at Verchères, and stayed in the position until 1801.[12] Pierre's son, Joseph-Marie, was a relatively prosperous farmer and master carpenter at Verchères when his daughter, Julie, married Pierre Fortin.[13]

Meanwhile, in the early 1730s a young man named Pierre-Nicolas Fortin had emigrated from France. His parents were Pierre Fortin and Catherine LeGras of Saint-Pierre-de-Rouen, Normandy. When he arrived in New France, he could not have foreseen that he would die a British subject rather than a French citizen. True, the Treaty of Utrecht, which had ended another ten years of war in 1713, saw Nova Scotia and Newfoundland ceded to Britain. However, Fortin found a vigorous society of 40,000 compatriots and a vast empire. The future no doubt looked bright when, on 5 March 1737 at Québec, he married Françoise Lepailleur.* He had made a "good" marriage. His bride was one of the dozen children of Michel Lepailleur de Laferté, a notary.[14] The duties of Lepaillieur ranged from jail-keeper to acting lieutenant-general for civil and criminal affairs. The mother-in-law of Pierre-Nicolas, Catherine, an amateur botanist, had some fame for her search for the secrets of Indian medicine.[15]

Pierre-Nicolas had not long settled when, in 1744, another war travelled the Atlantic from Europe. He and his compatriots were shocked when the British captured Fort Louisbourg, on Cape Breton Island. But in 1748, when the Treaty of Aix-la-Chapelle returned the fort to French control, they could still believe that the essence of New France was untouched.

By the 1750s it was obvious to both sides that yet another war was inevitable over possession of the rich Ohio River valley and beyond. The odds were bad for New France. In 1755 the colony had some

---

* Variously spelled. I have used the spelling from Vachon, André, "Lepailleur de Laferté, Michel," *Dictionary of Canadian Biography*, Vol. 2 (1969): 413.

55,000 inhabitants with a militia of 8,000, some 2,000 newly arrived French regular troops, and about 16,000 friendly Indian warriors. The country depended on supplies from France, especially during poor harvests. In contrast, Americans outnumbered Canadiens by twenty-five to one. Ample grain and a strong economy, plus the might of the blockading Royal Navy, supported the British-American cause. And France sent no more than 6,600 regulars to Canada while Britain sent 23,000.[16] Despite the odds, the French and Canadian forces began the war with victories; they effectively lost it with a close-run defeat at Québec by General James Wolfe in September 1759, and because of the unlucky early arrival of British reinforcements in the spring of 1760.

The Treaty of Paris in 1763 ended the extraordinary story of New France. The British began the new regime hoping to use immigration to swamp Pierre-Nicolas's language, culture and people. Yet by choice or by economic necessity, he did not return to France. The assimilation originally planned by the British government did not happen: the immigrants never came, and succeeding governors, over the protests of local British merchants, tended to favour the French Canadian cause.

On 8 July 1765 François-Herman Fortin, second son of Pierre-Nicolas, married Angelique Maisonneuve at Terrebonne. A Catholic priest performed the ceremony—in French and under French civil law. So too at Verchères on 27 April 1820, a priest married Pierre, second child of François-Herman, and Julie Duvernay,[17] again in French and under civil law.

Pierre-Étienne Fortin was born at Verchères on 14 December 1823. Shortly after his birth, Pierre senior and Julie moved their family to Laprairie, across the river from Montréal. Here, the boy and his three sisters grew up.[18] Laprairie began as a Jesuit mission in 1647. It occupied a meadow called Laprairie de la Magdaleine. By the 1820s, American visitors travelling the traditional invasion route to Montréal via Lake Champlain and the Richelieu River usually passed through Laprairie. And they usually gave it short shrift. One traveller in 1817 said that the town, "nine miles above Montréal," was "a considerable town of long standing with a large French church and other public establishments."[19]

A Jesuit priest at Laprairie said that in the 1840s his parish was "one of the most beautiful and densely populated parishes" of the Montréal diocese. It had "broad paved streets adorned with wooden sidewalks. [They were] lined with elegant houses and prosperous shops, with a garrison in residence, a court of justice, several notaries, a population of 2,000 souls, and a place very busy with commerce and business."

The same priest, however, condemned the immorality of Fortin's home town in strong terms not unusual for clerics of that time. "Theft, fraud, usury, litigation, blasphemy, drunkenness, holidays, orgies, fights, lawbreaking, and scandals of all types, such were the excesses that forced the priests of the neighbourhood to announce in their sermons, 'My brothers, be very careful when going to Laprairie ... keep your children far from the scandals that desolate certain parishes.'" [20]

Fortin's education was exceptional in the Lower Canada of his youth. He probably learned to read and write in the Laprairie school run by the Clercs de Saint-Viateur[21] at a time when few students went on to higher education. A British official estimated that in 1838 only about 1,000 pupils in Lower Canada attended colleges and seminaries.[22]

While the large majority of Canadiens worked the land, Fortin's father belonged to the urban middle class. Trained as a carpenter, he was also a successful entrepreneur. Potvin says that at least one of the houses Fortin senior built in Verchères and Laprairie still existed in the 1940s.[23] By 1851 his status in the community earned him the position of census taker for the village of Laprairie.[24] Even by 1836 he had been successful enough to send his son, aged thirteen, to the Petit séminaire de Montréal. Young Pierre stayed there till 1841.[25]

The Sulpicians had opened the seminary in 1767. In 1837, midway through Fortin's time there, 205 students attended. The two-storeyed building that Fortin knew was built in 1806. A picture about this time shows a grim-looking edifice, softened in later pictures by gardens and trees growing in its two large courtyards. Fortin and his fellow students wore a uniform with a dark, knee-length jacket bound by the traditional French Canadian hand-woven sashes. These *ceintures fléchées* of the habitants carried colourful and intricate arrow designs.

Meals were simple, the weekday schedule severe, and the day included much religious activity. The boys rose at 5:30A.M. for prayers and study till breakfast at 7:05 ("excellent bread" made on the premises, with butter, cheese, and treacle). After mass, classes ran from 8:00 to 11:20, with a fifteen-minute break. Spiritual readings preceded and accompanied dinner (boiled beef and, when available, potatoes). Recreation was allowed from noon to 1:00P.M. when classes resumed until 4:00. A meal of bread (younger children got butter), and then study from 4:30 to 6:00. Telling beads and spiritual readings came at 6:00, supper at 6:30 (veal or beef ragout), recreation from 7:00 to 8:00, then prayers followed by spiritual readings while preparing for bed.[26]

French-Canadian colleges offered a classical syllabus. The full eight-year course included six years of grammar and literature, and two of science and philosophy. Students studied Latin, French, and English, but could substitute Greek for Latin. In 1837 the two years of science and philosophy at the college contained, among other courses, "applied mathematics, astronomy, natural history, experimental physics, chemistry, mineralogy." The syllabus also included gymnastics, and instrumental and vocal music.[27]

Anglophones often criticized the colleges for not offering the so-called practical courses given in American schools. One said, "I am told by gentlemen in the town ... that lads acquire in this institution almost no knowledge which is of any consequence to them in subsequent life."[28] Fortin's life disproves that. He later made good use of his natural history in classifying fish and birds of the Gulf, and used his applied mathematics for navigation. He was also well known for his physique, and popular in Québec salons for his piano playing and singing.[29]

The colleges had some texts and manuals, but in the main the teachers dictated lessons and the students wrote them down. All the colleges were very poor and understaffed, but "devotion and hard work" characterized the teachers, claims historian Lionel Groulx. Among them, "brilliant minds were rare; good minds abounded."[30] Certainly the colleges turned out many fine minds. The Montréal college graduates included two who would do much to restore political power to French Canada: Louis-Hippolyte La Fontaine and George-Étienne Cartier.

Fortin graduated in 1841. He then studied medicine at McGill College. The matriculation register for McGill does not start until 1843, so it is not certain when Fortin enrolled. However, he is registered for 1843 and 1844.[31] According to his biographer, Damase Potvin, he "showed brilliant qualities." His teachers said "he had uncommon intelligence, with a passion to learn, and with remarkable powers of observation."[32] No records explicitly confirm this, but Fortin's graduation, and details of his later career, suggest Potvin was right.

The matriculation register for 2 December 1843 describes Fortin as a medical student. It lists "A.F. Alexaner," probably the physician who proposed Fortin to the school, as his "parent or guardian." Next year's entry (27 November 1844) spells the name, probably correctly, as "Dr. Alexander." Curiously, both entries give Fortin's first name as Petrus. This Latin form of Pierre was not commonly used—a Peter Dease appears on the same page. Possibly Fortin wanted it stated that way; perhaps he felt the Latin form more suitable for his destiny as a doctor. The 1845 McGill graduate directory says that Pierre Fortin graduated with an MDCM (doctorate of medicine and surgery). He was the only medical graduate that year.[33]

The earliest McGill calendar, that for 1854-55, would not differ much from that of Fortin's day. A candidate for final exams must have attended at least two courses on each of anatomy, chemistry, theory and practice of medicine, principles and practice of surgery, midwifery and diseases of women and children, materia medica and pharmacy, clinical medicine, clinical surgery, practical anatomy, and at least one on medical jurisprudence. He had to attend during twelve months the practice of the Montréal General Hospital or another approved hospital. He had to prove competent classical attainments. And he had to write and present a thesis on a subject connected with medical or surgical science, either in Latin, English or French, with a private and a public defence.[34]

A mid-nineteenth century medical student needed unusual skills and a strong stomach. Dr. Edward D. Worthington tells how he and other students often had to rob graves to get a corpse for dissection. He also describes operations without anaesthetic. In one case of double amputation of the legs, two doctors operated simultaneously. One highly skilled doctor took less than three minutes to remove the leg, tie the vessels, and dress the wound. "The other amputation was not quite finished in half an-hour when some of us had to leave," wrote Worthington.[35]

Hygiene was minimal. Many doctors operated in filthy coats, often coming from postmortems. A Dr. Shepherd never saw an amputation of the thigh recover. The most common operations were amputations, legature of the arteries, cutting for stone, and removal of tumours, with the abdomen never opened except by accident. Compound fractures rarely recovered.[36]

However, breakthroughs were coming. In Europe, medical men had begun to understand the dangers of infection. About 1835 a school of Canadian doctors began insisting on hygiene in the consumption of food, water and air. They wanted city streets cleaned, and quarantine imposed for infectious diseases. One great success had come with smallpox. In 1765 inoculation, and in 1801 vaccination, had minimized its incidence.

Fortin would have learned of the stethoscope, introduced into the Canadas in 1827. He may have used a microscope, first used here around 1843 to examine urine, though not widely available for years.[37] The work of Dr. Joseph Lister, however, and the use of a carbolic spray as an antiseptic, would not be extensive in Canada for another thirty years.

Fortin graduated in 1845, aged twenty-two, and returned to Laprairie to practise. Two years later, one of the worst epidemics in Canada's history struck. The young doctor volunteered to care for the typhus-stricken Irish immigrants at Pointe-Saint-Charles and Grosse-Île. The medical education he had received, however, could do little to help the thousands of immigrants, often starving, who died in crowded and filthy sheds.

We do not know why Fortin chose to risk death. Maybe it was in part money. Potvin suggests that Laprairie was in good health and the poverty of the inhabitants meant that "a fortune, even a good honest living, was very slow in coming." This is consistent with the views of the historian Groulx. He claims that Francophone graduates were excluded from engineering, the army, the navy, and even from government administration. They had no place to go except the already overcrowded professions of church, law and medicine. The villages of Lower Canada, Groulx says, were full of notaries and doctors, more or less idle.[38]

Potvin offers another "suggestion from a vague tradition handed down to us." The young doctor, he says, may have used Grosse-Île as an excuse to escape from "a very painful love affair."[39]

This speculation is intriguing. Fortin never married, but he did acknowledge an illegitimate daughter. Suzanne-Marie was baptized on 5 September 1849, the day after her birth "of unknown parents," say the records. The godfather was Léonard Bonneau, the godmother Marie-Louise Beaubien. The registry uses the form "unknown parents" for the baptism of Marie, another illegitimate child.[40] From later records concerning Suzanne "Fortin's" marriage, it is clear that Suzanne-Marie was his daughter. The next trace of the mother and child comes in the 1851 census for Laprairie. The household of Hubert Lefebvre included his wife and two children. It also included Suzanne Bonneau, aged twenty-four, unmarried; and Suzanne, in her third year, both "non-family members."[41]

Life for Suzanne, the mother, could not have been easy. The clergy did not openly accept immorality, and certainly not its fruit. One estimate puts the ratio of illegitimate births to infant baptisms between 1800 and 1839 at 148 to 6747, or 2.2 percent. This was quite low compared with other populations at that time. As for their fate, some babies were sent to religious establishments in Montréal or Québec.

One study found that during the eighteenth century, one out of four unwed mothers defied public opinion and kept their babies. More likely, the mother secretly abandoned her child at the church door.[42] Most of these foundlings soon died, often because of the transition from mother's breast to unhygienic feeding practices.[43]

For the unmarried mother the stigma was strong and long-lasting. Society ostracized her, holding her up as a bad example to neighbours, relatives and friends. The church could impose religious penalties on the father, but the mother had little chance of legal redress. She had to prove she had had no relations with other men, and perhaps that the father had promised marriage. The "marriage of atonement" was one solution. Even here the church did not press the matter, especially if the man were of a higher social class. This, the clergy argued, would lead only to a marriage of friction, mocking the holy sacrament.[44] But Suzanne Bonneau defied adverse public opinion and kept her baby while living with family friends.

Then, on 4 July 1867, Suzanne Bonneau married Delphi Racine.[45] She would be about forty. Suzanne, the daughter, went to live with her father. In 1871 the occupants of the Fortin house were Pierre Fortin, in his forty-seventh year, his occupation listed as doctor; Julie Duvernay, widow, in her seventy-seventh year; and Suzanne Fortin, in her twenty-first year.[46] In the parish of Laprairie de la Magdalen on 1 February 1877, Suzanne-Marie Fortin married Joseph-François-Xavier Bisaillon, a lawyer of Montréal. The register describes Suzanne as "the eldest and natural daughter of the Honourable Pierre Fortin, Member of the provincial Parliament, of the city of Québec."[47]

Suzanne and her husband had three children. The youngest, Beatrice, Fortin's granddaughter, became Mme L.-J. Béique, of Ville La Salle. Potvin dedicated his book to Mme Béique. He said she was "the only surviving member of the family of Commander Fortin."[48]

Fortin left for Grosse-Île early in 1847. He took ill in the fall of 1847, went home to Laprairie to convalesce, and returned to Grosse-Île in the spring of 1848. If Suzanne's mother were the other half of the painful love affair from which he fled in the early summer of 1847, as Potvin suggests, he must have returned to her in 1848 to father Suzanne. Or were there, in these years, two women in his life? That we will never know. Nor will we know why Pierre and Suzanne did not marry. We do know that Fortin acknowledged his daughter. He brought her to live with him when illegitimacy was a social stigma for child and parents. He had given her his name by the time of her marriage. And he left her his estate.

Later in his career, during the winters between cruises, Fortin enjoyed the social life of Québec. His biographer, Potvin, archly reports, "The arrival of *La Canadienne* in port delivered for some months her fine Commander to his numerous friends in Québec and Montréal. These included the ladies for whom he knew how to lightly grace their winter salons." There he entertained with his beautiful baritone voice, his talents as a pianist and the tales of his exploits "on the bridge of his beloved schooner. It was a life full of healthy and sweet emotions, and noble occupations."[49] A contemporary, M.A. Achintre, claimed Fortin sang so well that other singers sometimes received the compliment, "He sings romantic songs as well as Fortin does."[50]

Many of Fortin's actions and writings described in later chapters will demonstrate a strong and at times rigid character. His reports, essentially bureaucratic, show no humour and tend to mask his compassion. But his relationship with Suzanne, and Potvin's picture of him, provide a rare hint of a softer side to his personality.

NOTES

1. Monière, Denis. *Ludger Duvernay et la révolution intellectuel au Bas-Canada.* Montréal: Québec-Amérique, 1987: 23.
2. Charland, Thomas. *Histoire de Saint-François-du-lac.* Ottawa: Collège Domincain, 1942: 18.
3. Thwaites, Reuben Gold, ed. *The Jesuit Relations and Allied Documents.* 73 volumes in 36. New York: Pageant Book Company, 1959. Vol. 47: 87-89, 43: 69.
4. Sulte, Benjamin. "Les ancêtres du Ludger Duvernay," *Revue Canadienne* (Montreal), New Series, Vol. 1 (April, 1908): 349-58.
5. Douville, Raymond. "Boucher, Pierre," *Dictionary of Canadian Biography.* 13 volumes and 2 indexes to date. Toronto: University of Toronto Press, 1966–. 2: 82-83.
6. Thwaites, Vol. 28: 316.
7. Leclerc, Paul-André. "Le mariage sous le régime français," *Revue d'histoire de l'Amérique française* (Montreal), Vol. 13, No. 3 (December 1959): 374-401.
8. Charland, 29-31.
9. Charland, Thomas. "Crevier de Saint-François, Jean," *Dictionary of Canadian Biography.* 1 (1966): 238-39.
10. Sulte, "Les Ancêtres," 357-58.
11. Roy, Joseph-Edmond. *Histoire du notariat au Canada.* 2 volumes. Outremont: La Revue du notariat, 1899. Vol. 1: 214-15.

12. Roy, Joseph-Edmond. *Histoire du notariat au Canada.* Vol. 2 (1900): 12.
13. Monière, 25.
14. Fortin, Cora. *Premier Fortin d'Amérique: Julien Fortin.* Québec: Société de généalogie, 1974: 56.
15. Vachon, André, "Lepailleur de Laferté, Michel," *Dictionary of Canadian Biography.* 2 (1969): 413.
16. Steele, Ian K. *Guerillas and Grenadiers: The Struggle for Canada, 1689-1760.* Toronto: Ryerson, 1969: 66.
17. Fortin, Cora, 56.
18. Potvin, *Le roi*, 23.
19. Sansom, Joseph. *Travels in Lower Canada.* Toronto: Coles Canadiana Collection, 1970: 12.
20. Cadieux, Lorenzo. *Lettres des nouvelles missions du Canada, 1843-1852.* Montréal: Bellarmin et Maisonneuve et Larose, 1973: 143, 145.
21. Chevalier, Joseph. *Laprairie: notes historiques.* Laprairie [?], 1941 [?]: 197.
22. Groulx, Lionel. *L'enseignment français au Canada, I - dans le Québec.* Montréal: Libraire d'action canadienne-française, 1931: 209-10.
23. Potvin, *Le roi*, 22.
24. NA RG 31 A 1 (mfm C-1120), 1851 Census, Village of Laprairie.
25. Chartrand, P., personal communication, 30 January 1990.
26. Maurault, O. *Le petit séminaire de Montréal.* Montréal: Derome, 1918: 41, 121, 144.
27. Groulx, 204-05.
28. Maurault, 81.
29. Potvin, *Le roi*, 24.
30. Groulx, 207-08.
31. Chartrand, P., personal communication.
32. Potvin, *Le roi*, 25.
33. Chartrand, P., personal communication.
34. *McGill Calendar*, 1854-55, in personal communication from Chartrand, P.
35. Worthington, E.D. *Reminiscences of Student Life and Practices.* Sherbrooke, 1897: 32-33, 36-37.
36. MacDermott, H.E. *History of the Montreal General Hospital.* Montréal: Montreal General Hospital, 1950: 66.
37. Bernier, Jacques. *La médecine au Québec.* Québec: Les Presses de l'université Laval, 1989: 117.
38. Groulx, 210.
39. Potvin, *Le roi*, 26.
40. Archives Nationales du Québec, Registry of Births, Deaths and Marriages, 1849, Parish of La-Prairie-de-la-Magdalen. mfm No. B-140 and Index.
41. NA RG 31 A1 (mfm C-10057), 1851 Census, Village of LaPrairie, 5.

42. Greer, Allan. *Peasant, Lord and Merchant: Rural Society in Three Quebec Parishes.* Toronto: University of Toronto Press, 1985: 58.
43. Gossage, Patrick. "Les enfants abandonnés à Montréal au 19ième siècle: la crêche d'Youville des Soeurs Grises," *Revue d'histoire de l'Amérique français,* Vol. 40, No. 4 (Spring 1987): 537-59.
44. Gagnon, Serge. *Plaisir d'amour et crainte de Dieu: sexualité et confession au Bas-Canada.* Québec: Les Presses de l'université Laval, 1990: 128-29. See also Fyson, Donald. "Criminal Justice, Civil Society and the Local State: The Justices of the Peace in the Montreal District, 1764-1830," PhD thesis, Université de Montréal, 1985: 391.
45. Jetté, Irenée. *Mariage du comté de Laprairie, 1751-1872.* Sillery, Québec: Pontbriand, 1974: 63.
46. 1871 Census, Village of Laprairie.
47. ANQ, Registry of Births, Deaths and Marriages, 1877, Parish of La-Prairie-de-la-Magdalen.
48. Potvin, *Le roi,* 24.
49. Potvin, *Le roi,* 75.
50. Achintre, M.A. Manuel electoral. *Portraits et dossiers parlementaires du premier parlement de Québec.* Montréal: Des ateliers typographique de Duvernay, frères, 1871: 63-64.

III

FIGHTING PLAGUES AND MOBS

Throughout the winter of 1846-47, Canadian newspapers abounded in horror stories from Ireland about terrible starvation and disease. The Montreal *Gazette* described how a Cork rate collector visiting one house had to push his way through a door blocked by three corpses. In another parish, a man found dead in a field was unidentifiable because dogs had eaten much of his body.[1] The *Gazette* reported that people were dying in twenties and thirties in each parish, in hundreds in each barony.

Because of such stories, Canada had set up a relief fund by public subscription for victims of the Irish famine. Then in early 1847, Canadian sympathy began changing to apprehension. A letter in the *Gazette* said the Irish immigrant ships would be arriving in the St. Lawrence immediately after the break-up. The Irish famine, said the writer, had induced "us to come forward so nobly and so generously to the relief of the sufferers." However, it would now "inundate the colony with an enormous crowd of poor and destitute emigrants."[2] He could have added, "diseased."

Epidemics had hit since the early days of New France. One of the worst occurred in 1832 when immigrants brought cholera. An act that year authorized a quarantine station at Grosse-Île, some forty-six kilometers downstream from Québec. The station was to have one or more blockhouses and "a sufficient military force, provisions, medical officers, medicines, hospital stores and attendants." The act provided up to £10,000 funding.[3]

The government rented the island and erected dormitories (called "sheds") for the sick, and housing for the staff. Approaching ships, under threat of a cannon, had to stop in an area marked by buoys. If the authorities found contagion, the river pilot anchored the ship and put the sick ashore.

At the end of May 1847, the Québec correspondent of the *Gazette* listed some of the thirty vessels and passengers detained at Grosse-Île because of the typhus they had brought with them. The government had told the authorities there to do everything needed "to secure the comfort and health of the passengers." They had converted existing sheds to hospitals and had taken the healthy to an adjacent island. The islands would be "superintended by a medical man and a military force to be sent down to preserve order among them." During the previous forty-eight hours, upwards of 3,000 immigrants had landed. "Our wharfs are crowded with strangers."[4]

The reporter was too optimistic. The Grosse-Île hospital had beds for 200 sick, an average of previous years, and could also house 800 healthy people. By 23 May, the hospital would contain 530 sick, with 40 to 50 deaths a day.[5] One contemporary wrote that the sheds, seldom disinfected, were "very miserable, so slightly built as to exclude neither the heat nor cold." He had known "many poor families prefer to burrow under heaps of loose stones" near the shore, rather than go to the infected sheds.[6]

In a series of letters to the provincial secretary, the medical superintendent of the island, Dr. George M. Douglas, pleaded for more help. The government appointed a special commission of three doctors to look into conditions on the island. The doctors recommended, as fast as possible, six more fully qualified doctors at $5 a day and rations. They thought that the pay was "by no means too high for the duties performed, and the risk incurred."[7] Although Douglas had named several doctors in previous letters, he did not mention Fortin. Indeed, the first record of Fortin on Grosse-Île came on 23 July. On that day, the Reverend Bernard O'Reilly mentioned him when giving evidence before a parliamentary committee.[8] Potvin says that Fortin had spent some weeks doctoring the sick in the sheds at Pointe-Saint-Charles, near Montréal. Then, "wishing to go to the heart of the epidemic," he left for Grosse-Île.[9] It is likely that Fortin was one of the six doctors recommended in the commission's report.

In his evidence, O'Reilly said that Fortin was in charge of two sheds. There, as in most sheds and tents, immigrants lay on bare planks

Grosse-Île from the officers' quarters c. 1838-1840, ten years before Fortin served there. (Henry H.M. Percy/National Archives of Canada/C13656)

and on the ground for days and nights. They had neither beds nor coverings. "When I remarked on this to Dr. Fortin ... [he] informed me that no straw could be procured." Fortin probably cared for some 400 patients.[10] At the same hearing, Father W.W. Moylan described how the old sheds had a double row of bunks, one above the other. With only three or four feet between them, patients could not breathe clean air. The sick on the top bunks were too weak to climb down to relieve themselves. As the planks of the top bunks did not join properly, the excreta dropped through onto the patients below.[11]

Up to 5 June, 25,400 immigrants had arrived at Grosse-Île. More than 10 percent, or 2,700, had died. Soon the disease was infecting Canadians caring for them on the island, and then the citizens of Québec and Montréal. The *Gazette* on 5 July announced that the Reverend Mr. Robson had died from typhus while serving on Grosse-Île. Other clergymen infected were now out of danger except the Reverend Mr. Horan. A young man named Giroux, a servant of the seminary, was not expected to live. Drs. Deas, Dickenson, Malhiot, Fenwick and Jamieson had left the island, sick. Dr. M'Grath, convalescing, would soon return to his duties. Mr. Symes was "in a fair way to recovery."

19 July: The abbess of the Convent of the Good Shepherd was seriously indisposed. "Sister Primeau, one of the nuns of the Grey Nunnery

died on Wednesday morning, aged twenty years." The same day, three other nuns fell sick and four lay dangerously ill with the fever.[12]

Whatever the dedication of those helping the sick, they had no idea how to treat them. Epidemic typhus results from tiny organisms, rickettsiae, carried by fleas and lice. Rickettsiae look like bacteria but have many properties of viruses. In humans, they attack the walls of blood vessels. Headaches and rashes precede temperatures as high as 40°C, resulting in delirium.[13] In a serious epidemic at that time, up to half of those taken ill would die. In 1847 medical men knew nothing of rickettsiae, and had no antibiotics, vaccines nor DDT. Speculation and ignorance substituted for sound treatment.

Despite the carnage, shiploads of sick kept coming. On 6 August the *Gazette* reported 2,460 patients in hospital on Grosse-Île, more than at any former time. The doctors had received an increase in their daily allowance, bringing it to $10, "not too much for their arduous, dangerous and disgusting duties." Drs. Dease and Allen had returned to Grosse-Île "perfectly recovered" from the fever.

Ten days later, the *Gazette* quoted the Québec *Chronicle* that Drs. Fortin and Breadon at Grosse-Île had taken the fever. Next day, the *Gazette* reported that Dr. Fortin had returned to Montréal on the *Rowland Hill*. "He is very sick."[14] *Le Journal de Québec* later gave more details. "Dr. Fortin, who has spent about five weeks at Grosse-Île, where he usually had 400 sick under his care, arrived in Québec last Friday, seriously sick with fever. He was immediately sent home to his parents in Laprairie. Letters received today tell us that he is much better, the fever has almost left him, and the attack will leave no serious results."[15]

On 16 August, about when Fortin left, Grosse-Île hospital held 903 men, 746 women, and 551 children—a total of 2,200 patients. Still, the dreadful summer had to end. In mid-October the *Gazette* reported that the quarantine establishment at Grosse-Île would be broken up within a few days. The medical staff had been reduced to Drs. Douglas and Jacques with but one hospital in use.[16]

Still the tragedy lingered. The sheds at Pointe-Saint-Charles did not close till the ice blocked more ships from ascending the St. Lawrence. In all, one source estimates that more than 20,000 migrants transported on 221 ships died of the disease that summer, nearly 5,500 of them on Grosse-Île, in addition to 4,500 dead carried ashore.[17]

Fortin's illness did not finish him with Grosse-Île. Next spring the provincial secretary wrote that he had been made medical assistant to

Dr. Douglas at the station. "It will be your peculiar duty to visit regularly the healthy division of the island." There he would attend to the medical wants of the migrants. He should "see that proper measures are taken for the cleansing and disinfecting of the passengers and their effects." His salary would be twenty-five shillings a day, starting from his arrival at Grosse-Île.[18]

Fortin's 1848 sojourn on Grosse-Île poses another small mystery. On 16 June he wrote to Captain Scott, administrator of the quarantine station. "I would like to go to LaPrairie tomorrow for a matter that absolutely requires my presence." He wanted leave from 20 June until 24 July. Scott gave his permission without prior approval from the provincial secretary's office. He said Fortin's business "appeared by his statement to be very pressing, and not to be deferred without inconvenience." The secretary approved, but hoped that "such absences, without prior approval from Montréal, will not have to happen again."[19] None of the letters say just what emergency forced Fortin's return to Laprairie. His daughter was not born for another thirteen months, so neither her conception nor her birth had any connection with this visit. Nor does the August 9 fire that destroyed Laprairie, including his father's house, account for Pierre's leave of absence.[20] The emergency that took Fortin back to Laprairie that summer remains a mystery.

This was Fortin's last year at Grosse-Île and probably his last as a full-time medical doctor. He now moved on to a very different adventure.

•

In the summer of 1849 a series of riots swept Montréal. Anglophone Tories objected violently to the Rebellion Losses Bill, designed to compensate Lower Canadians for property losses during the 1837-38 rebellions. Some scheduled for compensation had themselves been rebels, some even imprisoned or exiled for treason. In their anger, rioting Tory mobs burned the parliament building (Montréal was then the capital). They threw rocks at the governor general, Lord Elgin, and attacked the homes of leaders of the Reform government.

At one point in the riots, says Potvin, the authorities appealed to "all men of goodwill to maintain order," and in September a mounted police unit appeared in Montréal. This unit caused "a sensation among the crowds amassed all along the streets. They admired the proud and martial air of the cavalry. Above all, the unit's commander attracted general attention. His profile as of a young god, his charming and delightful presence, his fine spontaneous smile, his martial look all made a profound impression on the crowd."[21] The florid description was of Pierre-Étienne Fortin, aged twenty-six, and his troop. Potvin claims that Fortin had for five months trained these inexperienced men to protect the peace of Montréal during that riotous summer. His account moves quickly over the fact that this, one of the few visits of Fortin's unit to Montréal, occurred after the riots had finished. In fact, the authorities called on the unit to do little more than march in the final parade.

The story starts in the 1830s when depression was spreading, though unevenly, throughout Lower Canada. With the population doubling every thirty years, fresh arable land on the seigneuries was running out or being withheld by speculators. An increasing number of habitants were working as day labourers, or were leaving the valley for marginal lands or for the United States. As farm income fell, so too did the incomes of people who depended on rural prosperity: lawyers, doctors, merchants and the clergy.[22] Moreover, the Francophone middle class felt itself excluded from much of commerce and government.

Louis-Joseph Papineau and his party, the Patriotes, had used their majority in the Lower Canadian Assembly to exercise virtually the only power they possessed: they refused to authorize government salaries. The British government rejected Patriote resolutions, and removed the assembly's control over government expenditures. Unrest boiled over. On 7 May 1837 at Saint-Ours, the Patriotes in effect claimed independence for the St. Lawrence valley. The Montreal newspaper *La Minerve* published the call to "resist, by all means available to us, a tyrannical power."[23]

The owner and editor of *La Minerve* was Ludger Duvernay, brother of Julie Duvernay, Pierre Fortin's mother. In 1817 Duvernay had opened a printing shop at Trois-Rivières and founded *La Gazette*. His sister, Julie, kept house for him until she married Pierre Fortin the elder in 1820.[24] On his return to Montréal, Duvernay's journalism very soon brought problems. He went to jail in 1828 for libel; in 1832 for saying the Legislative Council was a nuisance; and in 1836 for accusing the sheriff of selecting a biased jury at an inquest.[25] He also provoked a duel with a member of the Assembly, who wounded him. In June 1834, Duvernay organized the first Saint-Jean-Baptiste fete.[26]

Duvernay was elected to the Assembly in May 1837. Soon after it opened, governor general Lord Gosford dissolved it. Discontent continued over the summer. On 16 November, Gosford issued warrants for the arrest of twenty-six Patriotes for high treason, among them

Duvernay. Warned, he escaped from Montréal and became an officer in a small Patriote battalion. The Lower Canada rebellion had begun.

One battle occurred at Moore's Corners (Saint-Armand-Station) on 6 December 1837. Some two hundred armed Patriotes, with Duvernay as one of their leaders, crossed into Quebec from the United States. Three hundred Missisquoi volunteer loyalists opposed them. After ten minutes of gunfire, the rebels fled. They left one man dead, two wounded, two cannon, and most of their rifles.[27] Duvernay escaped to America. The rebellion in Lower Canada continued sporadically, with British troops and the militia constantly defeating the Patriotes, until 10 December 1838, when four hundred Patriotes unsuccessfully defended the village of Beauharnois. The fighting was over.

The new governor general, Lord Durham, then began his famous enquiry into the causes of the rebellion. He banished eight Patriotes to Bermuda, along with another sixteen who had fled to the United States. After the rebellion collapsed, the government executed twelve Patriotes and exiled fifty-eight to the penal colony in Australia.

When the troubles occurred, Fortin, then in his early teens, was attending college. Marault, in his history of the college, makes a tantalizing non-statement about the rebellion and the students. "We will not speak of historical events such as the rebellion of 1837 ... [which] introduced into the community a certain spirit of insubordination."[28] The church had spoken against the rebellion, but probably the young men of the college demonstrated for the Patriotes. It is not hard to see young Pierre Fortin sympathizing with his uncle Ludger, especially as his mother and Ludger had been so close. But how the students protested we do not know.

The Durham Report and the 1840 Act of Union joining Upper and Lower Canada explicitly aimed at assimilating the Francophone population into the Anglophone majority. Once again, however, the French-Canadians stubbornly rejected that fate. Anglophone Reformers in Upper Canada and Francophone Reformers in Lower Canada allied against the Tories to fight for self-government. Within less than ten years they had achieved it. By 1848 La Fontaine was the first prime minister, in the modern sense, of Canada. Ten years after the rebellion, French-Canadians had more power than since the Conquest.

The Tories, furious at the rise of French power, focused on the Reform government's Rebellion Losses Bill.[29] They protested that it compensated rebels for property damage and personal losses caused by their own actions. For instance, Étienne Langlois claimed £345 for "loss of time while in exile and a £34 passage from Sydney [Australia] to Canada."[30] The Tories expected governor general Lord Elgin to kill the bill, but on the afternoon of 25 April he went to Parliament and signed it into law. As Elgin left, a mob threw eggs at his carriage. Later the mob invaded the parliament building and burned it—riots continued all night. Police charged five prominent English Montrealers with arson, but later released them. Rioting resumed the next night. In one of several incidents, the mob burned the stables at the home of the prime minister, smashed dishes and furniture, and destroyed his library.

On 30 April, protected by the Queen's Light Dragoons and the 71st Highland Light Infantry, Lord Elgin went to the Assembly to receive an address of confidence. He was leaving when the mob started throwing rocks. One rock wounded him.

Prime Minister La Fontaine disliked using British troops to suppress the rising, so the government decided to form a special police force. It consisted of a mounted constabulary of fifty men and one hundred foot police. A Captain Wetherall would organize the new force, and Pierre Fortin commanded the horse section. Wetherall's first request for ordnance for the cavalry included "50 carbines, 50 pistols, 50 scymetars, 50 sets of saddlery complete, and 500 rounds of Pistol Cartridge."[31] He was told that the governor general was very wary of the new force. His Excellency ordered him not to give the arms "to any persons whom you do not feel confident or duly qualified to be entrusted with them."[32] Wetherall replied he would not give the force arms until they could use them so "as to resist any attempt by the mob to disarm them." He wanted the force to occupy barracks at Laprairie, well out of Montréal. An officer and a few cavalry non-commissioned officers should "be permitted to instruct the force in the usual cavalry exercises and stable duties."[33]

The government appointed a rural police magistrate, R.B. Johnson, to command the overall force, but Wetherall's doubts continued. He wanted the troop trained at Laprairie as the "absence of such a force from the city would be infinitely less disadvantageous ... than its defeat by the mob." An estimated "3,000 organized and armed malcontents" roamed the city.[34]

By May's end, Wetherall had his wish. The new force was training at Laprairie under a regular officer, a sergeant of cavalry, and Royal Artillery gunners. Wetherall thought this "essential as the officer appointed to command the force is not a military man and consequently not competent to undertake these duties."[35] Whether this means Johnson or Fortin is not clear.

The new force did not much impress the Tory press. In a piece in the satiric *Punch in Canada*, the details are obscure to the modern reader, but the attitudes are obvious. "Who cometh from the town of Griffin, with a peacock's feather in his hat? Tully [a pro-Reform city councillor] of the terrible countenance, eminent in Council [saying], 'I will raise the war cry in the ranks of the Mounted Police. Come, O Fortin! Gather thy warriors for the inspection of a mighty leader!'" The piece described the troop's horses as "spavined" and "broken winded." Some dreadful poetry came in the next issue.

> Fortin! of figure fine and sinewy force,
> Fortune on thee has smiled—Captain of Horse!
> For 10 long years in leech-craft hadst thou toiled
> For town was tranquil, till the chaldron boiled.
> . . .
> Forty dragoons, I say it in deep sorrow;
> Fortin, I believe, you'll all turn tail tomorrow.[36]

A *Gazette* headline read, "Mr. Tully's Detective Police: 100 Foot and 50 Horse at the Expense of the Province." Little was known of the force, the article said, beyond the fact it had been outfitted and was drilling at Laprairie. The infantry went on duty in Montréal suburbs after midnight. "Being afraid of ghosts, they go two and two" since they had "the children's idea that hobgoblins never appear two at a time." This "useless body of men" would "cost £10,000 in hard cash before the year, besides doctors' fees."

By mid-June, the *Gazette* was glad to see the government "coming to its senses" and disbanding the foot section. "Let them also dismiss the Horse section and the future peace of Montréal is guaranteed. We really hope and trust that no sense of useless bravado or mistaken idea of duty will induce the Ministry to bring these cavalry into the city. Their services are of no use, and can be made of no use." It was absurd, said the *Gazette*, to think that a few weeks' drill could make cavalrymen. To bring them to the city would lead the men uselessly into trouble.

Through the summer, Montréal was quiet, heavily guarded by British troops. Then in August the *Gazette* carried an ominous headline, "The Madness of the Government." The paper understood police would soon arrest those allegedly responsible for burning the parliament. It added that the Fortin Dragoons—"Punch's Prairie Hens"—were coming from Laprairie to overawe the "dreadful Montréal mob."

Next day, police arrested nine Anglophones on arson charges over the burning of the parliament building. Riots followed. On 16 August the *Gazette* told its version of what had occurred the previous night. The newspaper began by deploring that "the unfortunate accident which we dreaded has happened.... The first blood has been shed by the French." It described how, as the arrests took place throughout the day, the public became more and more exasperated. By nightfall, large numbers thronged the streets amid much cheering. Between nine and ten o'clock, "the mob proceeded to La Fontaine's house in the St. Antoine suburbs for the mere purpose of hooting and groaning as evidence of [their] feelings." La Fontaine, expecting "a visit of a more hostile character, had collected a number of bullies in his house, armed with muskets and other firearms." They saw that the mob intended no damage, but though "well provided to prevent it, [the people in the house] determined to provoke the people outside to some outrage by firing among them."

The crowd threw some stones, admitted the *Gazette*, but they had no firearms or other offensive weapons that they could use against a house of solid stone. Yet "about thirty shots were fired into the crowd.... Two men who were shot, one of the name of [William] Mason, were said at a late hour last night to be mortally wounded." The paper added:

> We have just learned that a number of the beastly Fortin Dragoons amounting to fifteen or twenty were brought over on Tuesday evening from their station at Laprairie, dismounted, and in plain clothes, with their moustachios shaved off; and it was these fellows who were in La Fontaine's house and fired on the people. The feeling has always been strong against this partisan corps. Now it will be irreconcilable.

Part of this was true. A crowd did gather outside the prime minister's house. The occupants did fire on them. They did wound a young man named Mason who later died. But evidence given at the inquest into Mason's death, including a death-bed statement by Mason himself, showed the rest of the *Gazette*'s account to be false and self-serving. The mob had not been just "hooting and groaning," but had marched with fife and drum and Union Jack flying. They shouted, "Burn down the house." The early summer had set violent precedents for arson. Now, torches flaming, the mob broke down the gates to the prime minister's home. At that moment, someone inside fired. The crowd fled. Mason lay near death.

The "beastly Fortin Dragoons" were nowhere near the house but stationed miles away at their training establishment across the St. Lawrence. Instead, the defenders were prominent Reformers, including survivors of the 1837-38 rebellions. Once again they were defending themselves against the Tories. This time, however, the "rebels" formed the legitimate government; the Tories stood on the far side of the line marking the limits of law and order that Fortin and his force were formed to patrol.

The *Gazette* had not yet finished with Fortin's troop. On 18 August it carried the heading, "The Fortin Dragoons: Collision with the People." The story said, "Our Mad Ministry" having "got one half of the city under bail, thought they might bring in the Prairie Hens to take the other half." On Thursday night after dark, boats were readied at Laprairie to carry the men over the river. "A dirty looking set of blackguards they were." That evening the troop waited at the wharf for the boats. "A few boys from twelve to eighteen years of age had collected to look at them." Then the crowd increased to perhaps one hundred. The force got orders to return to quarters.

"As they marched past the scamps on Commissioner street fronting the wharves, they were groaned at most lustily," says the *Gazette*. Some of Fortin's men "had the temerity to look threatening at one or two of the lads." This "was resented by their shying a stone at them." Someone fired back but luckily hit nobody. "This roused their [assailants] and a volley of stones replied to the shot." More stones and shots followed, with no reports of casualties. Finally the *SS Transit* arrived and took the corps on board to safety.[37]

The *Gazette*'s sympathies had coloured its reporting of the mob's actions the night Mason was shot. It seems likely that there were more than just adolescent scamps in the Laprairie crowd facing Fortin. The "groaning most lustily" has the same false ring as the mob's "hooting and groaning" outside the prime minister's house. No doubt both cases involved something more sinister than boyish high spirits. Still, Fortin and his men had not distinguished themselves.

This failure to cross the river sparked a government mock advertisement in *Punch in Canada*: "Wanted for the use of the Elgin Guards, alias the Prairie-Hen Police, alias the Fortin Dragoons, alias the Forty Thieves, forty web-footed quadrupeds of the hippotamous or river horse species." They were allegedly needed to bring the Prairie-Hens across the St. Lawrence from Laprairie to Montréal.[38]

The inquest into Mason's death forced the *Gazette* to retract its story of the attack on the prime minister's house. On 25 August the paper accepted that La Fontaine had tried to get regular forces to protect his house, but they had not arrived in time. The *Gazette* now concluded that because he had tried, the public should acquit La Fontaine of shedding blood unnecessarily. Hardly a generous or comprehensive retraction, yet still a retraction.[39]

The city now calmed a little. In late August a government paper, the *Pilot*, said the city was tranquil. "Peaceable citizens can now move about without apprehension of being assaulted or insulted by the mob who have of late infested the streets."[40]

Papers supporting the government naturally saw Fortin and his troop very differently. *Le Moniteur Canadien* asked that the force relieve Montréal's overworked special constables.[41] The *Pilot* berated the government for not bringing Fortin's guards to protect La Fontaine's house on the night of the attack. They might have arrived on time and surrounded and captured the assailants, said the *Pilot*. The slower-moving foot troops actually called for had arrived too late. "With an efficient body of horse police (in Montréal), the outrages which have been perpetuated for the past few months would never have been attempted."[42]

But the Tory press kept up its scornful attacks. On 29 September the *Gazette* offered a "Notice to Parents," ironically advising them to keep their children off the streets on Monday. "Fortin's Dragoons" would be on parade. Presumably this was the parade described by Potvin. The newspaper complained that the force cost Montréal £5,000 a year, but perhaps that was worth it "to supply us with material for laughter."[43]

At about this time, *Punch in Canada* made a last, full-page attack. A cartoon shows a rather dilapidated cavalryman trying to hock his uniform and his equally dilapidated horse at Moss, the pawnbroker's. The poem, "Ballad of the Moss Trooper," begins:

> La Prairie let thy groves despair,
> Weeping their yellow leaves,
> Thy common looks uncommon bare,
> Field of the forty thieves.[44]

Lord Elgin can have the last word. In December he wrote to the British colonial secretary, Lord Grey, and quoted an extract from "an ultra-Tory paper." The newspaper reported, "By Telegraph, Montreal, 29 November, 7:00P.M.: The new constabulary force arrived [in Montréal] this morning from La Prairie. It is reported they are to be employed as a guard at the jail. The weather continues cool but pleasant." Elgin commented ironically, "The said constabulary force being no other than the Mounted Police which we were assured a few months ago by our own magistrate, Captain Wetherall, could not be introduced into the town without producing civil war."[45]

Fortin's cavalry career was now ending, and he disappeared for a while from the headlines. His force had not covered itself with glory, nor had it disgraced itself. The Montréal riots marked the end of the old Tory dominance and confirmed the reality of French-Canadian power. If not by their actions, then simply by their presence, Fortin and his men had contributed to that result. And the story was not quite over.

The 1851 census shows Fortin living with his parents in Laprairie. Their house was one story and made of wood, typical for the town at that time.[46] The census does not state Fortin's occupation, but presumably he was practising as a doctor. If so, he at times broke away from his practice to ride with his cavalry force, this time against a different type of mob.

The Canada East education acts of 1845-46[47] had established a school system supported by property taxes. The taxes applied whether or not children in a household went to school. The strict measures for collecting the taxes were highly unpopular in rural Quebec. Especially from 1846 to 1850, the acts caused many riots in what was known as *la guerre des éteignoirs* (the war of the candle snuffers.) The rioters were said to be snuffing out the light of learning.

In 1850 people at Saint-François—the seigneury of Fortin's ancestor, Jean Crevier—were beating up school commissioners and burning their houses. The government responded in late April by sending a detachment of sixty men plus a dozen of Fortin's mounted policemen to establish order. In June, more violence threatened. "This time," says an historian, "thanks to the presence of magistrate Johnson and of the Fortin cavalry, great tranquility reigned."[48]

The government then disbanded the mounted police. In October the force placed its arms in the Montréal military stores.[49] Fortin's taste for adventure had, by now, fully displaced any desire to practise medicine. Soon he would set out on his greatest adventure. And not the least of it would be more skirmishes in the war of the candle snuffers.

NOTES

1. Montreal *Gazette*, 3 March 1847.
2. *Gazette*, 19 April 1847.
3. Lower Canada, *Acts*, 2 Wm. 4 c.16 (1832).
4. *Gazette*, 28 May 1847.
5. O'Gallagher, Marianna. *Grosse Île: Gateway to Canada, 1832-1937*. Sainte-Foy, Québec: Carraig Books, 1984: 50.
6. De Vere, Stephen. "Report on emigrant shipboard conditions in 1847," Arthur G. Doughty, ed. *The Elgin-Grey Papers, 1846-1852*. 4 volumes. Ottawa: King's Printer, 1947. Vol. 4: 1341.
7. PCLAJ, 1847: App. L.
8. PCLAJ, 1847: App. RRR, 23 July.
9. Potvin, *Le roi*, 28.
10. *Le Journal de Québec* (Québec), 19 August 1847.
11. PCLAJ, 1847: App. RRR, 13 July.
12. *Gazette*, 11 June; 5, 19 July 1847.
13. "Typhus." *Collier's Encyclopedia*. 18 volumes. Chicago: Field Enterprises Educational Corporation, 1970. Vol. 18: 444.
14. *Gazette*, 6, 16, 17 August 1847.
15. *Journal de Québec*, 19 August 1847.
16. *Gazette*, 16 October 1847.
17. Occhiette, Serge. "Grosse Île." *The Canadian Encyclopedia*. 3 volumes. Edmonton: Hurtig, 1985. Vol. 1: 777.
18. NA RG 8, I, C Series, No. 323 (mfm C-10471), Provincial Secretary to Fortin, 4 May 1848.
19. NA RG 4, Vol. 223, PSO File 2003, Captain Scott to Provincial Secretary, 19 June 1848.
20. *Le Canadien* (Québec), 10 August 1848.
21. Potvin, *Le roi*, 34.
22. Armstrong, Robert. *Structure and Change: An Economic History of Quebec*. Toronto: Gage, 1984: 84.
23. Monière, 111-12.
24. Tessier, Yves. "Ludger Duvernay et les débuts de la presse periodique aux Trois-Rivières," *Revue d'histoire de l'Amérique français*, Vol. 18 (1964-65): 387-404.
25. Lebel, Jean-Marie. "Duvernay, Ludger," *Dictionary of Canadian Biography*, Vol. 8 (1985): 258-63.
26. Monière, 99.
27. De Celles, Alfred D. *The 'Patriotes' of '37*. Glasgow: Brook and Company, 1920: 91.
28. Maurault, 159.
29. PCA 12 Vic. c.58 (1849).

30. PCLAJ, 1846: App. X.
31. RG 8, Vol. 80, No. 13, Charles Wetherall to Captain Vesey Kirkland, 19 May 1849.
32. RG 8, Vol. 1303, Kirkland to Wetherall, 21 May 1849.
33. RG 8, Vol. 80, No. 15, Wetherall to James Leslie, 21 May 1849.
34. RG 8, Vol. 1303, Kirkland to Wetherall, 21 May 1849.
35. RG 8, Vol. 80, No. 10, Wetherall to Kirkland.
36. *Punch in Canada* (Montreal), 1 (1849): 96, 99.
37. *Gazette*, 9, 15 June; 14, 16, 18 August 1849.
38. *Punch in Canada*, 1: 124.
39. *Gazette*, 25 August 1849.
40. *Pilot* (Montréal), 25 August 1849.
41. *Gazette*, 5 September 1849.
42. *Pilot*, 25 August 1849
43. *Gazette*, 29 September 1847.
44. *Punch in Canada*, 1: 140.
45. *Elgin-Grey Papers*, 2: 552.
46. 1851 Census, Village of LaPrairie.
47. PCA, 8 Vic. c. 41 (1845) and 9 Vic. c. 20 (1846).
48. Charland, *Histoire*, 307-09.
49. NA RG 8, Vol. 80, p. 79, William Ermatinger and R.B. Johnson to Captain George Talbot, 10 October 1850.

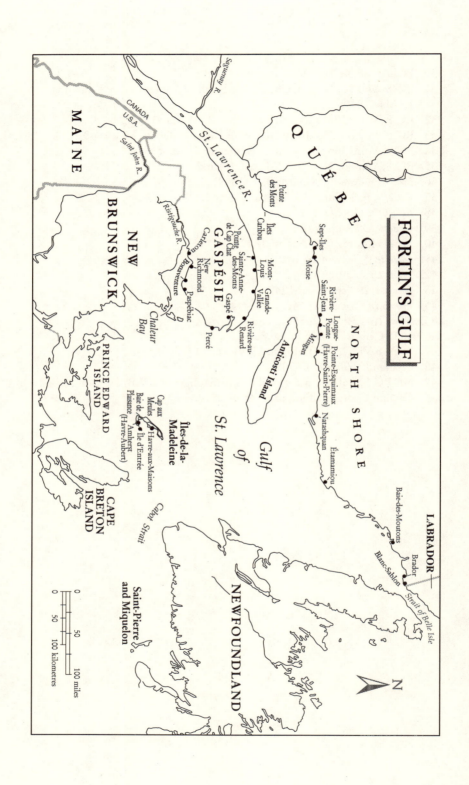

IV

THE COMMANDER AND HIS DOMAIN

Some 13,000 years ago, in the area now known as the St. Lawrence Lowland, the last of the glacial ice broke up. Great floods formed the Champlain Sea that covered much of the region. Relieved of the weight of ice, the land rose and reduced the sea to a lake. Then the St. Lawrence River eroded a path to the Atlantic, draining the lake and leaving the present geographic formation.

The Gulf of St. Lawrence covers nearly 250,000 square kilometers. British North America, as Fortin knew it, almost wholly surrounds the Gulf. The main channel flows south of Anticosti Island, past the north of the Îles-de-la-Madeleine and Cape Breton, then through the Cabot Strait to the continental shelf and the open Atlantic. The northern channel reaches the Atlantic via the Strait of Belle Isle, between Newfoundland and Labrador.[1] Fortin's domain was bounded on the north by the North Shore from Sept-Iles to the Labrador border; on the south by the south shore of the Gaspé peninsula (Gaspésie) and Chaleur Bay; and, far to the east, by the Îles-de-la-Madeleine. He himself estimated a permanent population of some 30,000.

European contact with the Gaspé peninsula goes back to 1534, when Jacques Cartier's ships escaped "a contrary and violent wind" by sailing into the Gaspé basin. Champlain also went to Gaspé in 1603 while mapping the Gulf. By 1634 European fishermen were not only visiting the peninsula for the summer, some also lived there permanently. English and/or American naval forces on their way to raid Québec increased the hardships faced by French fishermen and their

Micmac allies on the peninsula. The Kirke brothers spent some days in Gaspésie, plundering and burning, in 1628. Sir William Phips did much the same in 1690. Admiral Hovenden Walker again burned Gaspé on 20 August 1711, before he wrecked his fleet on Île aux Oeufs.[2] In September, 1758 Wolfe and Admiral Sir Charles Hardy destroyed all fishing craft, houses and fish in Gaspé.[3] With the Conquest, commercial companies from the Channel Islands arrived and soon dominated the Gulf cod-fishing grounds. Later, a wave of Loyalists fleeing the American revolution took up much of the scarce agricultural land, but fishing remained the staple industry.

The wooden buildings of a typical Gaspé fishing post looked from the sea like a small village. They often stood at the mouth of a stream. The house of the agent occupied the high ground; from there he could overlook the establishment and watch boats fishing. Stores housed goods and provisions, salt, rigging and spars. They stood alongside workshops for the carpenter, sailmaker, and blacksmith. Other buildings lodged fishermen and employees. Some housed dried or salted fish. Last came the stage, placed near the beach. This large wooden building was covered with boards or shingles. From one end, a wharf or stagehead extended out into the water. The larger villages were attractive. A fine 1860s sketch looking down from the hills on Gaspé shows its charm. The artist identifies the schooner seen at anchor as "*La Canadienne* ... under the command of Pierre Fortin, esq."[4]

Much of the coastline consists of cliffs with striking rock formations. Even in the 1860s, Gaspésie scenery stimulated a tourist industry. Two steamers, *Lady Head* and *Arabian*, carried mail between Québec, Pictou, Nova Scotia, and intermediate ports "with much regularity and without accident," wrote Fortin. In summer they brought crowds of passengers from Upper and Lower Canada and the United States, "visiting the highly picturesque coasts ... and enjoying the eminently salubrious and temperate climate of these places." Weekly steamer trips had developed commerce between these remote villages on the peninsula and upstream cities, but steamers, Fortin felt, could much improve travel by touching at Carleton, New Richmond and other ports.[5]

Gaspésie is a peninsula about 240 kilometers long and 97 to 144 kilometers wide. The interior of the peninsula, rising 1,269 meters to the peak of Mont Jacques-Cartier, has high tundra lands and forested river valleys. In Fortin's time, few people had settled away from the coasts. In 1861 Fortin described the seventy-five mile Grande-Rivière

The basin at Gaspé (c. 1866) with *La Canadienne*, "under the command of Pierre Fortin," at anchor. (Thomas Pye/National Library of Canada/NL19282)

Cascapédia, sprinkling his prose with superlatives and boosting the locale. "The water is very clear and limpid. Numerous islands [are] covered with the finest trees of the country, such as elm, ash, maple, white and red birch, and beech, all growing on alluvial soil." Its shores, "sometimes steep, sometimes gently sloping, and covered with rich grass, contribute to make this river one of the most picturesque in Canada." Its banks carry excellent timber, and "the salmon exported from the river is the finest in Canada."[6]

Acadians, facing land ownership problems in Prince Edward Island, had settled on the banks of Rivière Matapédia. The area, Fortin said, had "splendid forests, rich lands, and a climate favourable to every branch of agriculture." He wanted the government to open more roads so settlers could clear land. From Lac-Matapédia, they would form an unbroken line of agricultural settlements linking the communities bordering Chaleur Bay to the parishes on the St. Lawrence.[7]

This was highly desirable, he said in his reports, because winter isolated the peninsula. True, mail came from Québec, but the mailman had either to carry it on foot or on a traineau (a type of sleigh) drawn by dogs. Regular vehicles could not travel through the woodland roads. People on the Gaspé coast with business in Québec or Montréal had to travel via New Brunswick and the United States.

Fortin spent his life fighting for the prosperity of the peninsula. As early as 1863 a writer paid tribute to him and another fisheries officer. The fisheries of "this great peninsula are growing more and more valuable" due to the work of Richard Nettle and Commander Fortin in "protecting these immense reserves of public wealth."[8] Years later, *l'Opinion Publique*, a Montréal newspaper, said that Fortin, then a legislator, always wanted to make a prosperous Gaspé, a county depending equally on fishing and agriculture. He spared nothing: trips, visits to the county, patriotic discourses. "Happily, it is succeeding."[9]

Some 250 kilometers southeast of Gaspé lie the Îles-de-la-Madeleine, perhaps the most romantic region of Fortin's domain. This series of hilly islands is mostly linked by a double line of sandbars. If the weather were fine as *La Canadienne* approached, Fortin would first see a patch of cumulus cloud lying ahead. Under that, the higher peaks of the crescent-shaped archipelago would grow on the horizon, with the highest, Île d'Éntrée, rising to nearly 600 feet. Closing in, he would see the remarkable red and grey sandstone cliffs, and miles of white sand beaches. Cartier had named them *les Araynes*, from the Latin *arena* meaning sand. The islands had fine harbours, crowded with schooners fishing for the abundant herring, cod, plaice, halibut, mackerel and scallops.

Fortin loved the islands and their people. Many inhabitants could trace their ancestry to ten Acadian families who escaped there after their expulsion from Nova Scotia. The first settlers subsisted mainly on fish, supplemented with homegrown potatoes and vegetables. In 1798 the one hundred families were still mainly Acadian. By 1831 about 150 families totalled 1,057 people; by 1844, 1,738 people; and by Fortin's first visit, the population numbered about 2,200, predominantly French-speaking.

At one time the islands had belonged to Newfoundland, but the 1774 Quebec Act had returned them to Lower Canada. Prince Edward Island and Nova Scotia both wanted to annex the islands.[10] During the 1852-53 session of the Canadian legislature, a special committee recommended that the islands remain Canadian.

The superintendent of education, Pierre-Joseph-Olivier Chauveau, claimed that Fortin had helped keep the islands in Quebec. The inhabitants, "discouraged by the lack of success of their demands, were inclined to join Prince Edward Island," but "Happily, the passionate initiative of M. Christie, longtime representative of the Gaspé constituency, and later, the reports of Captain Fortin, superintendent of fisheries, have drawn the attention of our public men to these precious possessions."[11]

The committee discussed several problems that plagued the islands, and preoccupied Fortin, for many years. The first of these was the doubtful land titles of the islanders. In 1798 the British government had granted the islands to Sir Isaac Coffin in "free and common soccage." This meant that the one hundred families who had farmed the land for nearly a generation found themselves living on another man's land in near feudal conditions. They had none of the rights, nor the proprietor any of the obligations, associated with Lower Canada's seigneurial system of land ownership. By Fortin's time, many were paying rent to J.C. Coffin, descendant of Sir Isaac. One witness told the committee that half the property "owners" had no clear title, though some had occupied the land for up to forty years.[12] They lived in great poverty. Over the years, many had migrated to the North Shore and founded small communities.

As Gulf magistrate, Fortin could not do much about the land question. Some twenty-five years later, as a legislator, he became chairman of another parliamentary committee looking into the problem. He found little improvement. In a typical Fortin drive for information, some fifty islanders answered twenty-four questions. His 1875 committee report said that an "active, laborious, robust" people inhabited the island. They wanted to get all the benefits of a soil "well adapted to cultivation," but because of lack of title and sometimes exorbitant rent, many abandoned the land and often emigrated.[13] No action followed this or subsequent reports until 1895, when the islanders finally won the right to own their land.

Fortin first visited the islands in 1852. They were then one of the few areas of British North America where the Convention of 1818 gave Americans the right to fish within the three-mile limit. Too often they abused the right, but even without criminal activity, schooners caused major traffic jams. In the spring of 1859 Fortin, as usual, found the harbour at Amherst crowded. More than 150 schooners, anchored haphazardly, blocked the channel and entrance. Some captains had been trying to get out for a week. Somehow Fortin had to free the harbour entrance from the clutter of 1,500 mainly foreign fishermen and their more than 3,000 nets. By law, the nets could be set no closer to one another than 200 yards. This distance assured mackerel free passage to the spawning grounds near the shore. Fortin ordered "thirty or forty schooners entangled in a narrow space, and a greater number aground at half-tide, to move from their berths."[14]

Next year, *La Canadienne* returned to Amherst to find the harbour again crowded. Most of the schooners came from Nova Scotia, the rest from Prince Edward Island, the United States, and the islands themselves. Fortin sorted them out and left an officer to prevent further clutter. Returning to Amherst three weeks later, he found that his officer had kept order satisfactorily. *La Canadienne* cruised among the schooners distributing copies of the fishing regulations. He especially warned them against dumping offal in the harbour and on the banks.[15]

Fortin's reports show none of the enthusiasm for the Lower North Shore that they show for Gaspésie and the Îles-de-la-Madeleine. The North Shore coastline was rugged. Steady cloud cover badly hampered cod drying; summer fog and rain made navigation hazardous. The interior was even more desolate. In 1857 Fortin went inland from Brador at the eastern end of the Canadian Shield. He found the country completely cut up by ravines and lakes, making the route very difficult. The land was quite unfit for agriculture.

[It was] a succession of ranges and living rock and sandy plains covered with a little of different kinds of moss and lichens. In the bottom of the ravines alone can we find any vegetable soil, and there in so thin a layer, that the stunted pine and dwarf white birch can hardly take root in it. Near the rivers we find fir, white birch and a few tamarack trees ... but everywhere else there is nothing but the living rock covered with moss. There is neither tree nor shrub. I know of no place which has so desolate an appearance.[16]

Innu people had visited Sept-Îles for centuries. Then came the Basque fishermen. And in 1535 Cartier named it after the seven islands guarding the bay. East of Sept-Îles lay small, isolated communities reachable only by boat. In the 1850s émigrés from the Îles-de-la-Madeleine colonized the coast with settlements including Blanc-Sablon, Pointe-aux-Esquimaux and Natashquan.

With agriculture a near impossibility, fishing for seal, cod and herring became almost the only industry. Some years fish were plentiful. When *La Canadienne* anchored at Brador in 1864, a Captain Jones had captured 270 seals, fifty herring schooners had left earlier with full loads, and some Jersey vessels were still waiting to load their cargoes of dried codfish.[17] In other years, famine struck. In 1863 at Baie-de-Mouton, the cod fishing failed entirely. Fortin found the resident fishermen "in the poorest state," some of them without food. He gave them meat and also fed some starving native families.[18]

Trapping provided some income on the North Shore, but Fortin seldom discussed it. At Mingan, he reported that trappers had taken many foxes, silver and black, with prices as high as £20 to £35 a skin. Halifax traders sent them to the Leipzig fair in Germany. There Russians bought them for domestic use, or for resale in China, where they were highly prized.[19]

In 1861 Fortin and *La Canadienne* crisscrossed as usual this vast region. His report concludes with "Some Remarks" showing the nature and extent of his domain. He wrote that in his seven years on *La Canadienne*, the trip was "one of the most active and productive of happy results." It was also "one of the severest in labour and hardship.... Never were there seen such frequent storms, so much rain and so many fogs, and never did the Fall set in so early."

The voyage lasted 186 days, from 23 May to 24 November, the day *La Canadienne* foundered near the Caribou Îlets. The period had seventy-six days of rain, snow or fog. One fifty-five-day period saw thirty days of rain or snow. Nevertheless, *La Canadienne* visited eastern Labrador once, the North Shore three times, Anticosti twice, the Îles-de-la-Madeleine three times, Chaleur Bay three times, Percé ten times, and Gaspé five times. All this sailing totalled 4,821 nautical miles plus "many hundred miles" in a boat visiting more than 300 fishing stations. Add to that, Fortin recorded, some 1,000 miles of tacking or lying-to due to head winds, or when it was dangerous to anchor. In all, the schooner sailed about 6,000 miles.

From May to July, Fortin visited thirty-one salmon rivers, seventeen on the North Shore and fourteen on Gaspésie. Along 900 miles of coast he issued 264 salmon licences at more than 100 fishing stations. He also took a census of 4,000 North Shore inhabitants from Bersimis to Blanc-Sablon. As magistrate, Fortin heard forty-three complaints during the journey. He committed fourteen men to jail. Nevertheless, he found the Gulf comparatively peaceful. "With few exceptions, public order and peace have not been troubled on the North and South Shores.... There was no renewal of the fights and quarrels which so often occurred between our fishermen and strangers."[20]

The names of villages, coves and rivers on the Gulf coast fill Fortin's journals. He describes angry rioters, dedicated school teachers, marauding foreigners, starving Montagnais-Naskapi. His accounts of chasing smugglers, delivering mail, issuing fishing licences, arresting lawbreakers, giving free medical services, clearing rivers, and planting oyster beds, give a vivid picture of life in the Gulf.

Percé, 2 June 1856: At the request of the manager of Charles Robin and Company, a local fishing business, Fortin anchors *La Canadienne* near an American schooner. He wants to stop her enticing deserters from Canadian schooners. The American sails next day with no Canadians aboard.[21]

Paspébiac, 1 October 1858: The collector of customs asks Fortin to retrieve goods stolen by rioters and kept in the storehouse of the local merchants, LeBoutillier Brothers. Fortin and his men land and retrieve the goods.[22]

L'Anse-aux-Cousins and l'Anse-aux-Morts, 29 May 1859: Fortin explains the fishing regulations to the Montagnais. They object to the prohibition against spearing salmon by torchlight. Fortin questions whether the regulation can be enforced, but he will continue trying to do so.

Bonaventure, 24 August 1859: Fortin sets fifteen of his men to clear the eastern channel of the Bonaventure, blocked by fallen trees. The changed current is silting up the other channel, making navigation impossible.

Gaspé Basin, 19 October 1859: A storm at high tide strands the schooner delivering mail between the Îles-de-la-Madeleine, Percé and Pictou, Nova Scotia. Fortin's men cannot refloat the vessel, so *La Canadienne* delivers the mail.

Pabos, 3 November 1859: Fortin sends six sailors ashore. They seize the goods and chattels of tax dodgers "without meeting any resistance."[23]

Mont-Louis, 5 August 1861: In this small parish Fortin finds an excellent school kept by Mlle. Blais, with forty-five children. He notes that the mistress "has a superior method" and "the scholars were intelligent and generally proficient."[24]

Amherst Harbour, 16 May 1864: Usually the harbour can hardly contain the hundreds of fishing vessels wanting anchorage. Now he finds only nine schooners. Ice fills the Gulf from the Gut of Canso to Prince Edward Island, and even quite near to the Îles-de-la-Madeleine. It completely obstructs navigation.

L'Anse-au-Griffon, November 1864: "A fever of a serious character and of a very contagious description" rages. The many suffering families have no physician to treat them. Fortin uses his medical training to visit the sick and distribute medicines. He advises those not yet affected on "the best means to be employed to arrest its progress." And he leaves with the priest of Rivière-au-Renard some "febrifuge powders with directions as to their administration."[25]

Fortin spent much time and effort describing the fishermen and their fishing methods, and his work remains a standard reference. In his 1860 report he described the cod fisheries at length. The fishing boats, he wrote, were shaped like whaleboats: "pointed at the stem as well as the stern" and built very sheer. They were eighteen to twenty-two feet long with a five- to seven-foot beam, and with either two spritsails or two gaffsails, four-sided, fore-and-aft rigged sails. Boats from the Îles-de-la-Madeleine were smaller and lighter so they could be easily hauled ashore when the wind blew hard. North Shore fishermen used boats with sixteen-foot keels and cotton sails "very high but narrow aloft."

A typical fishing day, long with immensely hard work, started at 2 or 3:00A.M. The fishermen first raised nets set the night before to catch herring or caplin for bait. Without a favourable wind, they had to row for several hours to the fishing grounds. Off the Gaspé coast, each of two fishermen to a boat had two lines, usually with two hooks on each line, and a sinker of from one to four pounds. As Fortin described it, they had to haul in from 120 to 240 feet of line carrying maybe two fish with a total weight of twenty-five pounds or more. On the North Shore, they often fished with four lines of thirty feet. When fish were plentiful, action never stopped. As the fisherman hauled up one line, the other was going down.

If fishing was poor at one anchorage, they raised the anchor and went looking for a better place. It often happened that they had to sail or row fifteen to twenty miles in a day, then return in the evening with no more than fifty or sixty fish. When fish were plentiful, a boat could take from 756 to 1,260 pound weight. "On the North Shore, boats manned by two men only have been known to take from 1,500 to 2,000 cod fish in a single day during the time they most abound on the banks."

The fishermen stayed out until 4 or 5:00P.M. Then they hurried home to ensure that the cod were split and salted before they could heat or soften. Storms often kept them ashore for weeks. Sometimes when they reached the fishing grounds, the wind rose or a fog forced them to return quickly, often with no fish. A season seldom passed without squalls and hurricanes so violent and so sudden that fishermen had to scud home under bare poles. They might have to remain indoors, with no income, for days at a time. "And every year a score of fishermen are lost in boats which founder at sea, or capsize among the breakers in attempting to gain the shore."

Fortin's description of the fish processing is detailed. Three men on the stage, called the cutthroat, the header and the splitter, began. The cutthroat seized the fish by the eyes, cut its throat, opened it down to the navel with a single stroke, and passed it to the header. The header detached the liver and threw it into a barrel. With the same hand he tore out the entrails while his other hand cut off the head. The splitter now took the fish by the left side of the neck. He opened it from neck to tail, cutting from left to right. Then he placed it by a batten nailed to the table, and with one stroke removed the backbone from the navel upwards. The men threw the heads, entrails and other offal through a hole under the table into the sea. The ebb tide carried off the waste unless the angler fish and plaice swarming around the stages ate it first.

From there, the salter sprinkled enough salt on each fish to make it keep well, but not enough to burn it. When the fish were cured, workers washed off the salt. They then spread the fish, flesh side up, on hurdles called flakes. Sun and circulating air dried the cod to the point where they would keep for several years. "The faster the cod is dried, the whiter and more transparent it is, and the dearer it sells on foreign markets."

The beachmaster had to watch constantly both his barometer and the sky for any threat of rain. If "the rain seems very near and there is much fish out, all go to work from the chief to the smallest cabin boy." They turned the cod skin side up on the flakes to protect them from the damp.

In the dry season when westerlies predominated, cod was of the first quality. However, when easterly and southeasterly winds prevailed, bringing weeks of mist and rain, the situation grew serious. Despite all precautions, fishermen frequently saw spoiled the fish that had cost them so much toil and danger. "For once the fish has been washed and is exposed upon the flakes, it cannot be taken into the stores until it is perfectly dry." Ordinarily, from five to six percent of the dried codfish was of secondary quality; in rainy seasons, some fifteen to twenty percent.

Canadians, except for some on the North Shore, fished in this way. Americans and Nova Scotians, however, flooded the Gulf in schooners. These vessels were expensive but yielded "the finest fish," said Fortin. Manned by from ten to thirty fishermen, a schooner anchored in water up to fifty fathoms using hemp or manila cables. After netting bait, the fishermen used handlines "often by night as well as by day, in spite of wind and storm, until the hold of the vessel is filled with fish, all split and salted." When the vessel returned to port, the cod was washed and dried, ready for export.[26]

Storms played a major role in the lives of Gulf fishermen. Tides, river currents and many islands added to the navigation hazards. Fortin constantly refers to vessels wrecked and lives lost. Such disasters had occurred long before his time. The greatest was in 1711, when a British fleet sailing to blockade Québec lost eight ships and 900 men.

Gulf weather varies greatly. During summer, many cyclonic disturbances pass to the north. For the rest of the year, however, shipping often faces gale to storm-force winds. When the centre stalls, the storm can last for days. Occasionally in late summer, tropical storms arrive violently from the West Indies, with little warning from the barometer. Sudden squalls, often on summer evenings, can occur with very little cloud. Heavy fog is most frequent in late spring and early summer. Waterspouts are not uncommon. The Gulf is fully calm for only two to three percent of the time. In open waters in summer, southwest winds prevail, but coastal effects make navigation tricky. In the passage between the Gaspé peninsula and Anticosti, for instance, a southeast wind prevails in summer.[27]

Storms were often disastrous for fishermen. On a September afternoon in 1859, a violent storm forced *La Canadienne* to drop two anchors in the harbour at Mingan. Six schooners had already sheltered there. The wind redoubled that night, and *La Canadienne* dragged its anchors for about 200 feet, said Fortin, so the captain dropped a third. A schooner to leeward broke its cables and drifted onto a sand bank at the mouth of the Mingan, suffering no damage.

The storm was still raging on the 15th. Almost all the fishing boats at anchor at Longue-Pointe had snapped their cables and were drifting away, some outside of the harbour, others inside it. "I rescued some of the latter, but with the greatest difficulty, for at times the wind was so violent that the men could hardly hold their oars," Fortin wrote. In the afternoon, the schooner *Bee*, at anchor at Longue-Pointe, broke both its cables and went on shore.[28] On the 16th the wind diminished early but later strengthened. Two more schooners entered harbour. By noon next day it was calm enough for *La Canadienne* to sail to Longue-Pointe. Not much damage had occurred there, but the storm had carried away twenty boats. About twelve were saved at Mingan, the others lost.

Tragedies shine through Fortin's matter-of-fact prose. Later that day, he landed at l'Anse de l'Indien. The seas had shattered the *Mary Jane*, fifty tons, on the rocks. Just recently built, the schooner did not leave enough timbers to build a boat. All hands survived except one seaman. Her owner, Captain Fabien Fourgères, had not insured her.

Another storm on 1 July 1856 drove twenty-nine schooners onto a sandy beach at Île Vert. All the crews got ashore, about 300 men. Some badly damaged vessels were raised, but fourteen, totalling 616 tons, were lost. Nine came from the Îles-de-la-Madeleine, two from the United States, and one from Nova Scotia. Fortin gave what help he could to crewmen not taken onto other vessels. He promised to return for any islanders unable to get passage home.[29]

In the fall of 1864 storms wrecked twenty-five vessels on the northern coast of the Îles-de-la-Madeleine. In one wreck, a captain and four sailors died trying to land in their jolly boat. Such accidents, said Fortin, were "commonly the fault of inexperience or carelessness" by the captains. They created the impression that navigation of the Gulf was more dangerous than it really was. This kept insurance rates for ships sailing from Canada higher than those sailing from other British or American ports, and worked "to the great detriment of the Maritime commerce of our country." Richibucto and Miramichi vessels often ended their lives, sometimes just off the stocks and newly launched, on the sandy shoals.[30]

The Gulf claimed not only sailing vessels. In July 1867 the steamer *North American* went ashore on the south point of Anticosti, without loss of life. When *La Canadienne* arrived, the 300 passengers, including some women and children, were "all onshore, more or less well camped." At the request of her captain, Fortin hurried to Percé to call for a steamer from Québec. From Percé he sent a special messenger 110 miles to the nearest telegraph station at Dalhousie.[31]

Fortin illustrated the dangerous life of a fisherman in an 1883 House of Commons speech on tariffs, while pleading for the removal of duties on ships' cordage and other fishing tools.

What are the tools of the fisherman? They are the boat with its sails and rigging and hawser; and a very important part of the equipment of the boat is the hawser, because on its strength depends the safety of the boat and crew. Let me tell this House that during a great tempest in the month of August 1858, which caused the death of 100 fishermen, mostly all fathers of families, the only man of a fleet who saved himself by his boat owed his safety to his hawser which was new and very strong, and by means of it he was able to ride during the gale on the banks.[32]

Seal hunting was equally dangerous. In 1864 Fortin reported that Amherst had fitted out nine schooners for seal hunting, and Havre-aux-Maisons had sent sixteen. That totalled 1,046 tons with 250 hands. Of these, two vessels sank with all hands. Twenty men drowned, leaving thirteen widows and forty-five orphans.[33]

Sometimes hundreds of hunters pursued the seals out onto the pack ice as far as two leagues (six miles) from the shore. If winds drove the ice off the shore, canoes had to bring the men back. Any caught on the ice soon died. In the spring of 1857 Fortin reported that two seal hunters had gone too far out on the icefields. They were "unable to return before the land wind carried the ice out to sea, and thus cut off all communications with the land."[34] This had occurred in the islands many times "to poor unfortunates who could not be got ashore, and disappeared forever with the banks carrying them away." They were "soon doomed to death from exposure and hunger." This year, one of many cases of frozen feet had proved fatal. The hunt lasted only a few days, but islanders collected about 2,500 young seals valued at about £1 each.[35]

Unfortunately, dangers facing Canadian fishermen in the Gulf were not confined to natural disasters. The invasion of foreign fishermen each summer brought its own hazards.

NOTES

1. Smith, P.C. and Conover, R.J. "St. Lawrence, Gulf of," *The Canadian Encyclopedia*, 3: 1624.
2. Roy, C.E. *Gaspé depuis Cartier*. Québec: Moulin des lettres, 1934: 68, 90.
3. Knox, John. *An Historical Journal of the Campaigns in North America for the Years 1757, 1758, 1759 and 1760*. 3 volumes. London, 1768. Vol. 1: 296-97, cited in Stanley, George F.G. *New France: The Last Phase*. Toronto: McLelland and Stewart, 1968: 175.
4. Pye, Thomas. *Canadian Scenery, District of Gaspé*. Montréal: Lowell, 1866: 21.
5. Fortin, *Report*, 1861.
6. Fortin, *Report*, 1862.
7. Fortin, *Report*, 1861.
8. Drapeau, Stanislas. *Études sur les developpments de la colonisation du Bas-Canada depuis dix ans (1851-1861)*. Québec: Léger Brousseau, 1863: 16.
9. *L'Opinion Publique* (Montréal), 23 December 1875.
10. Landry, Frédéric. *Laboureurs du Golfe*. Québec: Le Marteloire, 1985: 94.
11. Drapeau, 29.
12. "Report of the Special Committee on the Magdalen Islands," PCLAJ, 1852-53: App. ZZZ, 33-36.
13. "Report of the Select Committee on ... the Magdalen Islands," QLAJ, 1874-75: 234.
14. Fortin, *Report*, 1859.

15. Fortin, *Report*, 1860: 107, 109.
16. Fortin, *Report*, 1858: 13.
17. Fortin, *Report*, 1865.
18. Fortin, *Report*, 1860: 110.
19. Fortin, *Report*, 1861.
20. Fortin, *Report*, 1862.
21. Fortin, *Report*, 1857.
22. Fortin, *Report*, 1859.
23. Fortin, *Report*, 1860: 119, 121, 128, 129.
24. Fortin, *Report*, 1862.
25. Fortin, *Report*, 1865: 6, 19.
26. Fortin, *Report*, 1860: 134-38.
27. Canada, Department of the Environment, Canadian Hydrographic Service, *Sailing Directions for Gulf and River St. Lawrence*. Ottawa, 1975: 115-18.
28. Fortin, *Report*, 1860: 122.
29. Fortin, *Report*, 1857.
30. Fortin, *Report*, 1865: 7.
31. Fortin, *Report*, 1867-68.
32. HOCD, 17 April 1883, 670.
33. Fortin, *Report* 1865.
34. Fortin, *Report*, 1858.
35. Fortin, *Report*, 1864.

V

SELLOUT OF THE GULF

Canadian sovereignty in the Gulf touched on the fishing activities of two other countries, France and the United States. France caused only minor problems in the nineteenth century, but Fortin believed that Canada sold out the interests of the Gulf fishermen to the United States.

The 1763 Treaty of Paris had ceded the islands of Saint-Pierre and Miquelon to France. The French also got fishing but not settlement rights on long stretches of the Newfoundland coastline. This included a part of the northwest coast almost down to Channel-Port aux Basques. Newfoundland increasingly challenged France's fishing rights on what became known as the French Shore. Canada, however, was concerned only when French fishing vessels crossed into Canadian jurisdiction.

On 3 August 1863 Fortin found seven small French schooners fishing for cod at Baie de Brador. "This being forbidden by the treaties, I ordered them to leave, which they did on the next day," he wrote. *La Canadienne* then moved to Blanc-Sablon. That evening Fortin met Commander Cosse of the French war schooner *La Fauvette*. Cosse had left the job of protecting the French fisheries off Newfoundland to make a goodwill visit to the Canadian shore. Fortin missed no chance to rebuke his political masters. He pointed out that besides *La Fauvette*, another schooner, *La Mouche*, and two steamers were protecting the French fisheries. These four ships patrolled "an extent of shore barely one half of the Canadian fishing shores."[1] Canada in effect had only *La Canadienne* to protect her much longer shoreline. Fortin felt this was no way to maintain Canadian sovereignty.

The problem of illegal French fishing schooners recurred the next year. At Île Vert and Baie de Brador, Fortin met French schooners from Miquelon. "On the complaint of our fishermen, [I] obliged them to quit our coast and to carry on their fishing in the open sea."[2] However, incidents with French fishermen at that time were rare.

During 1863 Fortin recorded three foreign men-of-war visiting the Gulf besides *Fauvette*. A French steam-powered corvette, *Le Marceau*, eight guns, Commander Vavin, came in July to pick up the French consul, Baron Gauldrée Boilleau. He had been studying the resources of the land bordering the St. Lawrence and hoped to develop trade with Saint-Pierre and Miquelon. He also wanted to educate French merchants and outfitters on the kinds of supplies available in Canada and the other British provinces. His Majesty Victor Emmanuel's frigate, the *San Giovanni*, 28 guns, Commander Faà di Bruno, had a crew of 360. For a month in August-September the Italian warship stayed at Gaspé, where people welcomed it "with pleasure." They felt a special relationship with Italy, "where so great a quantity of our dried fish is consumed." A third vessel was an American armed schooner. Fortin recorded her as the *George Magnum*, Commander Collins, with seven guns and a crew of seventy.[3]

Since the Revolutionary War, relations between Britain and the United States had been poor. During the war, two American armies had invaded the St. Lawrence valley, captured Montréal, and laid siege to Québec. On the east coast a quasi-war flared off Nova Scotia, where many rebel privateers harassed the Loyalist coasts and shut down British fishing in the Bay of Fundy and Chaleur Bay. However, by 1779 the British had cleared the rebels from the Bay of Fundy, and Jersey fishing firms had begun returning to Chaleur Bay.

Before the revolution, New Englanders had had the right to fish anywhere off the North Atlantic coast. After independence, Americans wanted to retain those rights. The loyal colonists objected, but Britain had more important problems and gave the Americans what they wanted. The fisheries question festered until the War of 1812. Again American privateers sailed against British North America. Three years after war's end, Britain and the United States signed the Convention of 1818. By the first article, Americans could dry and cure fish on unsettled parts of the western half of Labrador's southern coast. They could fish, but not dry or cure, on the entire western coast of Newfoundland and on the shores of the Îles-de-la-Madeleine. And they could enter any bay or harbour of British North America for shelter, repairs, supplies, etc. In return, Americans renounced the right "to take, dry or cure fish" within the three-mile limit other than in places explicitly listed. Canadian fishermen were not at all happy with the agreement.

Over the years, Britain and the United States occasionally clashed about other matters in and around Lower Canada. They squabbled over American sanctuary for the Canadian rebels of 1837-38 and incursions into Canada by secret societies known as Hunters' Lodges. They came near to blows over the Maine-New Brunswick border in 1842. And fishing rights in the Gulf remained a chronic sore on Anglo-American relations.

By 1839 the two powers were arguing over the interpretation of the convention. The United States claimed that the three-mile limit twisted in and out exactly parallel to the coast. Britain said it extended from a line drawn between headlands and therefore preserved the bays for Canada.[4] Again, American fishermen claimed they could land for wood, water and supplies any time they wanted. Britain counterclaimed they could do so only in untoward circumstances. Their vessels should be properly provisioned beforehand.

In the early 1840s, Britain and the United States had their navies patrolling the disputed waters, and tension ran high. But neither country wanted war, and they began to negotiate. By the time Fortin came on the scene, British imperialism was more and more switching from Canada, Australia, and New Zealand, to India, Asia and Africa. American imperialism also turned away from British North America's eastern flank, moving on to Indian lands of the midwest, to Mexico and Texas, through to California and the Pacific northwest. The French were no longer a factor, and Canadian expansionism would not push into the Prairies till later. It seemed that on the east coast only the fisheries of the Gulf remained an international irritant.

Until 1851 the Royal Navy had the main responsibility for enforcing the 1818 convention. It was ineffective. Fishing schooners breaking the law could too easily spot the warships on the horizon and quickly flee. Paul Crowell, a member of the Nova Scotia Assembly, described one type of American schooner called the sharpshooter. They ranged from 60 to 130 tons, "very sharp built, well fitted in every respect ... varying from 12 to 24 men." They often threatened to run down Nova Scotian vessels. "They are usually prepared for this, their bowsprits are fitted large and strong and the end well ironed." Some arrived with guns in case of opposition from local fishermen.[5]

According to Fortin, the American fishing vessels were "easily distinguishable by the sharp hull and large white sails."[6]

Nova Scotians had talked about armed action against the Americans as early as 1836, when James Boyle Uniacke introduced a bill for the protection of the fisheries. Another member suggested that half a dozen small cruisers, "well officered, with a couple of guns, and twenty to thirty-five men" would do the trick. "Each of the Colonies having a Gulf coast ought to contribute to this purpose."[7]

By the Toronto agreement of 21 June 1851, Canada and the other British North American colonies agreed to cooperate in protecting the Atlantic fisheries. Each would provide vessels to cruise in the Gulf of St. Lawrence and along the coasts of Labrador.[8] Nova Scotia commissioned two vessels to protect her waters, New Brunswick another, then Canada and Prince Edward Island one each. Under this agreement, Fortin received his commission in 1852 as Commander of the Fisheries Expedition.

Soon after, Britain suggested reciprocity, or free trade in natural products, with the United States. The Americans protested this was an attempt to use fishing rights to force reciprocity. Senator Lewis Cass said that the American people would not "submit to surrender their rights." The convention was now thirty years old, and he claimed it recognized clearly the right of Americans to fish within three miles of any shore. Another influential American, Senator William Seward, also protested. He said it was well known that any attempt to drive American fishermen from these fisheries would involve the whole country in a blaze of war.

The new protective schooners also brought a protest from Daniel Webster, American secretary of state. He said the United States would protect her fishermen "hook and lines and bob and sinker." The fisheries "have been the very nurseries of our navy." The 1818 convention was made with "the crown of England." If the British arrested an American vessel, "the crown of England is answerable, and then we'll know whom we have to deal with." He added, "But it is not to be expected that the United States will submit their rights to be adjudicated upon by the petty tribunals of the provinces. Or that we shall allow our vessels to be seized on by constables and other petty officers, or condemned by the municipal courts of Quebec and Newfoundland, New Brunswick or Canada."[9] The president replied by sending a frigate to protect "the rights of American fishermen under the convention of 1818."

The squabble dragged on until 1854. Then the Reciprocity Treaty solved the problem, satisfying the Americans and most Canadians. Canada gained free trade in natural products with the United States. This benefitted the farmers and traders, but Gulf and Atlantic fishermen were again most unhappy. For them, the treaty had sold out their livelihood.

An Imperial Act ratified the Reciprocity Treaty. It permitted Americans to take any kind of fish, except shellfish, on the coasts and shores and in the bays, harbours and creeks of British North America; in other words, inside the three-mile limit. They could also land on the coasts and on the Gulf islands, including the Îles-de-la-Madeleine, to dry their nets and cure their fish, but they could not interfere with private property or hinder British fishermen peaceably using the beaches.[10] In exchange, British North American fishermen could work in American coastal waters down to thirty-six degrees north latitude. This concession had little value to Gulf fishermen; their methods did not suit the distant New England coast.

The Canadian Assembly's special committee report on the Îles-de-la-Madeleine in 1852 contained the fishermen's view of reciprocity: it was fine, provided it was fair and equal, but it was neither fair nor equal. Worse, a witness, John Fontana, said that between May and July each year, up to 200 foreign fishing vessels brought 1,000 fishermen to the island. Many of them would go ashore and commit "whatever depredations they choose."[11]

When Fortin first patrolled the Gulf in 1852 on the *Alliance*, he found that cod, mackerel and herring fisheries attracted 1,000 schooners from the United States and from other British colonies, as well as those from Lower Canada. The visitors, he said, consisted mostly "of the scum of the seaport towns." They harassed Canadian fishermen and destroyed their nets. Fortin also complained that in the spring they took possession of small islands in the Gulf. They then raided nests for the eggs of penguins and small divers, destroying thousands of birds. Those two complaints—foreign mistreatment of local fishermen and foreign mistreatment of the environment—became dominant themes in Fortin's public life.

"Robberies had been committed in many places," he wrote. "The fishermen had forced entrance into houses in order to pass the night in dancing and the commission of every species of insult." They had no fear of having to answer for their actions in a Court of Justice. They were well aware that the authorities "cannot find throughout their entire population any force whatever to carry their orders into effect."

Reciprocity, Fortin reported, brought more problems. American fishermen were using the agreement to fish on Canadian coasts, then to sneak into the bays and rivers to smuggle rum. A coast guard officer had confiscated "a tun of molasses," but because he had no armed support, the smugglers took it back. At Amherst, Fortin apprehended an American schooner thought to be smuggling. The captain pleaded ignorance and "submitted to the collector [of customs's] orders."

Still, by now matters were improving. Fortin was not too modest to take some credit—he had bureaucratic battles to win:

I am happy to be able to announce that smuggling has for the most part ceased. [This is] thanks to the firmness and sang froid displayed on many occasions by the first Collector of the Port of Amherst, but more particularly to the aid which I have been able to give since 1852 by means of the force placed under my control.... Ever since the arrival of the Government vessel in the Gulf, our coasts and seaports have enjoyed the most perfect tranquility.[12]

This claim perhaps weakened his case when, that same year, he recommended that two more vessels patrol the Gulf coasts. His recommendation was turned down.[13]

Unfortunately, Fortin was also overoptimistic about the effectiveness of *La Canadienne*. In 1859 he reported violence increasing again. In July at Amherst, "a great number" of American schooners were fishing for mackerel. Complaints came from all over the islands of depredations committed by their crews: stolen nets, stolen timber, and fish taken from nets.[14]

In May 1860 Fortin could not sail in *La Canadienne* because its keel and standing rigging were under repair. Instead he had to return to the *Napoleon III*. This move brought him into conflict with the captain, whose primary responsibility was the maintenance and supply of lighthouses.

Fortin's unhappy voyage on the *Napoleon III* lasted from May to September 1860. In a long series of incidents, he was unable to capture foreigners who had violated Canadian law. Then in October he recommissioned *La Canadienne* and, once again with Bernier, completed the fall cruise. Now, he reported, foreign violations had ceased. This result would have been in good part because American fishing in the Gulf slackened off in the fall; only in part because *La Canadienne* frightened off transgressors. At any rate, Fortin used the situation to strengthen his case to Parliament for *La Canadienne*'s annual cruises. This "will shew how necessary it is" that *La Canadienne* should cruise the waters as soon as the American and Nova Scotia schooners arrived for the mackerel fishery. He could then "protect our fishermen from the depredations and insolent behavior of these unprincipled foreigners."

That same year on the South Shore, Fortin met many complaints about marauders behaving with "great rudeness and violence." He reported complaints that Americans caused much mischief at sea. Worse, in mobs of fifteen, twenty or thirty men, they trampled on growing crops, forcefully entered houses and often insulted inhabitants "in the grossest manner. Unfortunately, our fishermen had on no occasion been sufficiently numerous to bring them to reason."[15]

Fortin had to chase wrongdoers across hundreds of square kilometers of Gulf waters. In 1861 in the Baie de Plaisance, Joseph Bourque told Fortin that the previous night eight or ten foreign sailors had broken into his house. They threatened his life with a dagger, and stole clothing and other goods worth about £200. He could not identify their schooners.

After taking the deposition, Fortin boarded the schooners *Stacey*, *St. Lawrence* and *Village Belle*, but their crews were innocent. The *Sarah and Julia* also lay at anchor. Fortin suspected that several of her crew were among the robbers, so he delayed her till next day and searched her rigorously. No results. "Mr. Bourque and his son, who were on board, examined all the men of the crew, one after another, but could not identify any one as having committed the robbery." The captain told Fortin that two small schooners had also lain at anchor at Cap-aux-Meules. He did not know their names. They had left at first light under full sail towards Cape Breton and a fine west-north-west breeze had long taken them out of sight.

La Canadienne sailed to Havre-aux-Maisons seeking more information. The day after the robbery, the schooners had left Cap-aux-Meules between 4 and 5 A.M. They were soon out of sight, going towards Cape Breton. Fortin strongly suspected them of the robbery. However, "I neither knew the name, nor the place to which they were bound. During my stay at the Magdalen Islands [Îles-de-la-Madeleine], I used every exertion to discover a clue to that robbery, but without any result."[16]

The livelihood of the fishermen depended on their expensive fishing nets. Too often foreigners, usually Americans but sometimes Nova Scotians, wantonly destroyed the Canadian nets. On one occasion in

1861, Noel Cloutier of Grande-Vallée reported that the keel of the Gloucester schooner, *Isa*, had carried away one of his herring nets. Germain Dionne complained that on the same morning an American schooner had torn one of his nets, and Narcisse Dugal said that another American schooner had torn three of his herring nets, making them unserviceable. Pierre Dery also complained of the schooner *Commerce* of Southport. While getting under sail to leave the bay of Grande-Vallée, the vessel had carried away a net set to catch herring for bait and had torn another. He had cautioned the schooner's crew beforehand. He showed them the damage they would cause and pointed out that they could easily avoid his nets. They paid no attention. That stopped him fishing until he could get new nets from Gaspé Basin.

Canadians living in isolated coves usually found themselves outnumbered by marauding foreigners. August Richard told Fortin that American fishermen had stolen fish oil to grease their boots, and had taken some cod fish drying on the stages. He did not resist because there were ten of them.

When the Canadians had a fair chance, they fought back. The cutwater of an American schooner caught and carried off one of François Joncas's nets. Next day, Joncas found the net so torn it was valueless. Later, a Nova Scotia schooner, the *Front of Chester*, fouled its cable in another of his nets. The net would have been torn to pieces if Joncas "had not induced the captain to give a turn on the capstan to release it, by threatening that if he did not do it himself, he (Joncas) would fetch men from the shore who would do it for him."

The same year, American schooners at Grand-Étang were fishing very near shore. When standing out to sea, they would have surely destroyed the herring nets Mr. Esperance had set for bait. "He went immediately to remonstrate with the masters of the vessels, telling them their schooners were anchored in a manner contrary to the law. They refused to listen." Unfortunately, Esperance "could expect no assistance from the government vessel [the *Alliance*] which was cruising elsewhere." So he told the offenders he would return with 150 fishermen in his employ. They would "shift the [American] vessels from their present berths and moor them further offshore." The threat was effective.

Fortin used such complaints to justify *La Canadienne* to his political and bureaucratic superiors. He also sought allies wherever he could find them. Again in 1861, the priest at Rivière-au-Renard, describing more American depredations, was "anxiously solicitous" about his parishioners. He asked Fortin to advise the government of the great need for *La Canadienne* to cruise in the Gulf each summer to protect the fishermen. Fortin adds, "In speaking of American fishermen, I do not intend to allege that all of that nation who frequent our coast deserve reprobation." No doubt there were many exceptions. It was still true, however, that "a great many of them have conducted themselves in a most outrageous manner in places where they had always met with a kind reception."[17]

On 12 April 1861 the American Civil War began. Britain's commercial ties with the South, especially in cotton, promoted Confederate sympathies there. This helped lead to a series of naval incidents bringing Britain and the Union close to war. On 8 November 1861 the USS *San Jacinto* stopped and boarded the British ship *Trent* in the Atlantic, taking off two Southern diplomats. War seemed close until in late December the Union returned the diplomats.

In December 1863 Nova Scotians welcomed a Confederate crew on a highjacked Union ship, the *Chesapeake*. They then harassed the crew of the Union ship *Dacotah* which had retaken the *Chesapeake* and escorted it to Halifax. In 1863 a Confederate warship, the *Alabama*, was built in Britain and (claimed the Americans) illegally allowed to leave there. The *Alabama* took seventy prizes in the Atlantic until she was sunk by a Union ship in June 1864. These incidents made Americans very bitter, and could have easily drawn Canada into war.

It was in this tense climate that Fortin reported the arrival at Gaspé of the Northern armed schooner, *George Magnum*. The warship, under Commander Collins, had seven guns and a crew of seventy. Rumour had it, said Fortin, that the *George Magnum* was seeking Confederate cruisers in the Gulf.[18] He had, however, mistaken the name. The vessel was a wooden schooner, the *George Mangham*, acting master John Collins. Built in 1854, the *George Mangham* was 110 feet long with a speed of ten knots. Its mortar and two thirty-two pounders had bombarded rebel land forces in various Civil War battles. After taking four prizes on the Potomac River, the warship had refitted in the Washington dockyard. Assignment: to search for rebel raiders in the Gulf of St. Lawrence. Leaving Washington on 5 August 1863, the *George Mangham* cruised off the Îles-de-la-Madeleine and Prince Edward Island, and made at least the one visit to Gaspé, without sighting any Confederate vessels. On 5 November the warship left Georgetown, P.E.I, for New York.[19]

Fortin must have been aware of the earlier threats by American officials against the protective schooners, and of the tensions caused by the

Trent and *Alabama* crises. We can only speculate on his actions had he met the *George Mangham* violating Canadian sovereignty by attacking a Southern vessel sheltering in some Canadian bay.

The St. Alban's raid in the fall of 1864 turned out to be important to Fortin and the Gulf fishermen. A Confederate gang based in Quebec raided St. Alban's, Vt. and robbed a bank, killing a man. When Union troops chased them back to Quebec, Canadian authorities arrested some of the gang, but then released them. The infuriated Americans threatened to (but did not) abrogate the Rush-Bagot Treaty regulating the number of warships on the Great Lakes. Instead they (for a while) required passports from Canadians crossing the border. And they (permanently) abrogated the Reciprocity Treaty in 1866.

Fortin did not regret the end of reciprocity, since American fishing rights in the Gulf reverted to the much more limited rights of the 1818 convention. Still, the problems continued over the years. Finally, Fortin could tackle them from the government benches in the House of Commons.

On 18 May 1868 Prime Minister Macdonald moved third reading of a new fisheries act. It licensed foreign fishermen in Canadian waters at a fee of $2 per registered ton. Canadian officials could board vessels and search them. If the master lied about his cargo or destination, he could be fined $400. If he were fishing or preparing to fish without a licence within three miles of the coast, the officials could seize the vessels, their stores and their cargoes.[20]

Fortin, now member for Gaspé, regretted the lack of bounty for Canadian boats, though he supported the increase in licence fees specified by the act:

This increase ... has created a good deal of excitement among our neighbors ... as shown in the House of Representatives of the United States, and a large majority of that body has even voted a proposition calling on the President to send an armed force into the Gulf of St. Lawrence for the protection of American fishermen, under the supposition that they would be molested by British cruisers. Now the American fishermen have never been molested in the gulf, by British or Provincial cruisers, and there is no danger of it ever happening.

As magistrate and civil servant, Fortin could not question government policy; as member for Gaspé he had no such restraint. The Atlantic fisheries were essential to Canadian sovereignty in face of growing American power. They were, he said, closely connected with national defence. "The gulf is the doorway of our country," he told the Commons. "As long as Britain owned the fisheries of British North America, there was no danger of her losing her Maritime power. But if they were to pass into the hands of the Americans, and with them the Maritime population of the Provinces—well, ... the United States would be in the position to wrest from England the naval supremacy that she has enjoyed so long." The Americans would become "the first naval power in the world." Macdonald assured Fortin he was "alive to the importance" of the fisheries. The licence fee had been doubled, and doubled again, but it was now set for the season "lest a restrictive course might be pursued by the United States."

Again, larger considerations had overridden the fisheries' interests. They would yet again the following year, when a member asked in the Commons how many licences had been given in 1868 to American fishermen in Canadian waters. He also wanted to know the government's position on fishing rights in the Bay of Fundy, where one headland was Canadian, the other American. The Americans claimed they had the right to fish anywhere in the bay, while Canadians claimed they could not fish within three miles of the Canadian shore. American "bullies," the member said, had been very active in the bay.

Fortin joined the criticism of his government. Protection of our fishermen "had been very ineffective," he said. Royal Navy ships in the Gulf could seize American vessels within the three-mile limit, but only after a warning. This made the measure "a farce." He wanted "real and adequate protection," especially for Gulf fishermen, who were at a great disadvantage. Canada had only one schooner with a crew of twenty-four against 200 American vessels, each as strongly manned. He understood even the twenty-four-man crew of *La Canadienne* was to be cut to seventeen.

Macdonald replied. With the end of reciprocity, the government had decided to license American fishing vessels, not for the revenue but in order to assert Canada's rights to these waters. Four British warships were patrolling Canadian shores and another two were coming. As well, *La Canadienne* and Nova Scotia's *Druid* were active. If the United States kept on refusing reciprocity, he would favour stronger measures against American fishermen. At the moment, however, the Americans appeared interested in reciprocity. "It would be unwise on the part of Canada to abolish the present system." For Fortin, they were still selling out the Gulf in the interests of free trade.

The following year, Fortin again took on the prime minister. Why did *La Canadienne* not go to Chaleur Bay in the mackerel season to restrain the nearly 800 American schooners fishing without licences? Why did the Royal Navy spend only a few days there protecting our shores? Did the prime minister know of the "depredations" there by Americans? Macdonald replied that *La Canadienne* had twice visited the bay. He could not say why the Royal Navy had not stayed longer.

Then came Fortin's key question. Would the government refuse further licences and organize a force to protect the fisheries? He liked the answer. "It was not the intention of the government," said Macdonald, "to issue licences during the ensuing season (cheers), and it was the intention of the government to take steps to protect the rights of Canadian fishermen in Canadian waters (cheers)."[21] Victory came for Fortin on 8 January 1870. An order-in-council said that the following year "all foreign fishermen shall be prevented from fishing the waters of Canada." That year, government vessels boarded 400 vessels and condemned fifteen for illegal fishing.[22]

The victory was short-lived. In 1871 Britain and America signed the Treaty of Washington, effective in 1873. Macdonald, one of the five commissioners who signed, had little influence on the outcome. The treaty solved some problems that Britain and Canada had with the United States. But once again it admitted the Americans, this time for twelve years, to the Gulf's inshore fisheries. One historian has described this as "surely the worst blow of all." The fisheries "were to have been Canada's trump card in negotiating a renewal of reciprocity in natural products."[23] Instead, Canada got free entry for fish only, and unwanted fishing rights off the New England coast.

Fortin must have been bitter on two scores. First, Canada had been willing to barter Gulf fisheries for reciprocity. This would once again have yielded agricultural benefits for farmers and commercial benefits for traders, but sold out Gulf fishermen. Second, the actual treaty sold out the fishermen without even achieving reciprocity. In debate Fortin claimed that if the treaty were ratified, Americans would gain 2,000 miles of fishing coast, Canadians only 300 miles. Canadians, he argued, should get compensation for that imbalance. In contrast to the Canadian government's lack of interest, the American government had spent $7,000,000 encouraging and developing its fishing industry. The treaty would make things worse, and "would injure in a very material way" the interests of the Maritime population, including Gaspésie's 2,500 fishermen. On 16 May Conservative Fortin joined the Liberals in voting against the bill. But the treaty was accepted: 121 in favor; fifty-five against.[24] Fortin had lost his long battle. The Gulf fisheries and fishermen had been betrayed, in part by Britain for the sake of "higher" imperial interests, in part by Upper Canada and the commercial and agricultural interests of Lower Canada. The fisheries were a pawn to be sacrificed for other interests.

But Fortin would see some victories later. The Treaty of Washington had set up an international commission to decide on compensation for the loss of British North America's exclusive fishing rights off its coasts. Fortin collected and presented expert evidence to the commission, and his expertise helped secure the $5.5 million compensation awarded. He also helped compel the government to reinstitute bounties for Canadian vessels. These successes must have given him satisfaction, but the sensible exploitation of Gulf fisheries by Canadian fishermen, a cause he advocated all his life, eluded him.

NOTES

1. Fortin, *Report*, 1864.
2. Fortin, *Report*, 1865: 13.
3. Fortin, *Report*, 1864.
4. Kerr, William Hastings. *The Fisheries Questions: Or American Rights in Canadian Waters.* Montréal: Daniel Rose, 1868: 9-13. For an opposing version, see Isham, Charles. *The Fisheries Question: Its Origin, History and Present Situation.* New York: Putnam, 1887.
5. Cited in Innis, Harold A. *The Cod Fisheries: The History of an International Economy.* Toronto: University of Toronto Press, 1954: 332.
6. Fortin, *Report*, 1861.
7. *Gazette*, 20 February 1836.
8. NA RG 1 E1, State Minute Books (mfm C-115), Vol. L, No. 393, 21 June 1851, Protection of Gulf Fisheries.
9. Elliott, Charles Burke. *The United States and the Northeastern Fisheries.* Minneapolis: University of Minnesota, 1887: 69.
10. Great Britain, *Acts*, 18 Vic. c.3 (1855).
11. "Report of the Special Committee on the Magdalen Islands," PCLAJ, 1852-53: App. ZZZ, 20.
12. Fortin, *Report*, 1856.
13. State Minute Books (mfm C-118), Vol. R, No. 209, 14 February 1857. Captain Fortin.
14. Fortin, *Report*, 1860: 118.
15. Fortin, *Report*, 1861.
16. Fortin, *Report*, 1862.
17. Fortin, *Report*, 1861.
18. Fortin, *Report*, 1864.

19. United States Navy Department, Naval Historical Division, *Dictionary of American Fighting Ships.* 8 volumes. Washington: 1959-81. Vol. 3: 79; Silverstone, P.H. Warships of the Civil War Navies. Annapolis: Naval Institute Press, 1988: 135.
20. Canada, *Acts*, 31 Vic. c.61 (1868).
21. HOCD, 18 May 1868, 729; 3 May 1869, 161; 3 March 1870, 207.
22. Elliott, 79.
23. Beck, J.M. *Pendulum of Power: Canada's Federal Elections.* Scarborough, Ont.: Prentice Hall, 1968: 14.
24. HOCD, 4 May 1872, 579; 16 May, 647.

VI

MAGISTRATE AND POLICEMAN

The threat to law and order in Fortin's domain did not come only from foreigners. During his 1857 tour, Fortin received a petition from the municipal council of Rivière-au-Renard, Gaspésie. "A party of fanatics, excited and authorised, as they declare, by John de St. Croix, Esq., one of her Majesty's Justices of the Peace" were threatening the councillors. If the council were to meet on public business, the mob would "turn them out and beat them without mercy." Fearing for their lives, the members could not discharge their municipal duties.

Bullies had already beaten the councillor entrusted with assessment accounts. He had obtained a warrant for the arrest of one assailant, but he could neither serve the warrant nor bring the delinquent to justice. Some thirty or forty men had gathered at the councillor's house, "armed with guns, sticks, pikes, and other dangerous weapons, and with frightful yells, prevented his arrest." Council members suffered "grievous and continual insults of riotous persons." The "appointed guardians of the public peace" had not done their duty for many years. The council said that the mere appearance of *La Canadienne* always brought respect everywhere, and Mayor G. Lavergne and six councillors begged Magistrate Fortin to come. They wanted "disturbers of the public peace" brought to justice, and "suitable means adopted to ensure respect to the laws."

Commander Fortin could not ignore the appeal. He promised the mayor he would be there on 1 June to keep order while the council passed its unpopular ordinances. However, *La Canadienne* was then at

Paspébiac, and Fortin found that the new jib he had to install would not be ready in time.

He therefore set out for Rivière-au-Renard on 28 May in *La Canadienne*'s boat with six of his best seamen. He hoped for a fair wind, but they had just embarked when rain began. Next day was worse, with strong head winds as they travelled along a dangerous coastline. However, with "the goodwill and strong arms of my six oarsmen," they reached Gaspé Basin by the evening of 31 May after a ninety-five-mile journey. The men then walked from Penouille to l'Anse-aux-Griffons. Finally, they rowed a whaleboat to Rivière-au-Renard, arriving at 5:00P.M. on 1 June. The council, said Fortin laconically, held its meeting "without the least interruption or hostile demonstration."

Fortin's report stressed the value of *La Canadienne* to the people of the Gulf. The Council's letter, he said, showed "the disorderly and agitated state" of Rivière-au-Renard before his visit. Fortunately, his presence "was the means of restoring order and tranquillity for the remainder of the season." However, he guarded against charges of false boasting. Some, he wrote, may think he exaggerated a little the effect of his visit to Rivière-au-Renard. However, anyone who had seen a riot "knows the impression which the presence of a few disciplined men produce on a crowd when they are resolute and acting under authority." Those likely to offer resistance "were well aware that I might come back in a few days with *La Canadienne*." Then no resistance would be possible.[1]

Fortin stopped another potential riot over taxes in Gaspé South in 1863. The School Corporation also sent him a letter of "warmest thanks."[2]

The crew of *La Canadienne* often provided muscle when local authorities needed it. The reasons were both serious and trivial. At Carleton, Deputy Sheriff Freer asked Fortin to serve a writ against a man who threatened to kill him. He at once went there with some of his men, and Freer executed the writ "without any opposition." The justice of the peace at Pointe-Saint-Pierre asked for help serving a warrant against Peter Rail, who had refused to stop cutting grass and hay on the common. Fortin sent three men to serve the warrants.[3]

Canada had formed its first modern police force only fifteen years before Fortin's marine force. Before that, in Montréal a mix of full-time constables, bailiffs, night watchmen, and administrative inspectors had carried out police work under the authority of justices of the peace.

Small-town and rural communities had similar elements, more sparsely distributed. Complaints about these quasi-police were common. Militia officers also had police responsibilities.[4] The rebellion prompted the first centralized police force, in Québec, and a Montréal force soon followed. In 1839 a mounted police force, supervised by fourteen newly appointed stipendiary magistrates, began working the countryside around Montréal.[5]

As a stipendiary magistrate backed by twenty-five armed men, Fortin had much power. He could summons or arrest anyone suspected of treason, felony, indictable offences or misdemeanours. In the case of felony, he could dismiss the charges for lack of evidence. If the evidence warranted, he sent the case to a higher court. With simple larceny, assault, keeping or being an inmate of a bawdy-house, and misdemeanours, he had to ask the accused whether he wanted a summary trial or have his case go to a higher court. If the former, and if the accused pleaded guilty, Fortin could convict and impose a sentence of up to six months in prison and/or a fine of up to $100. Should the defendant deny the charge, Fortin could call witnesses, examine evidence, and then pass judgment. Among other powers that he reports using, he could grant a warrant to search a building on the evidence of a credible witness. He could give bail for misdemeanours, and in some cases for felonies.[6] He could also proceed summarily with alleged violations of the fisheries act.[7]

Fortin presided over forty-three cases in 1861. The most common charge was breaching the fisheries act (eighteen cases). Seven men were charged with theft from a wrecked vessel, five with assault, and four sailors with insubordination on a vessel. There were two robbery/burglary charges, two for receiving stolen goods, one rape, and one manslaughter charge. One man also succeeded in an action to recover his wages of $3.

The manslaughter charge arose on 13 August at Gaspé. Mr. Tilly, coroner, laid a complaint against George Girard of Malbaie, who had allegedly shot and killed Joseph Gauthier. The inquest found accidental death, but public opinion, strongly against the verdict, compelled Fortin to investigate. He arrested Girard. Witnesses gave depositions before the grand jury in Percé. They showed that Girard had killed Gauthier when a gun "accidentally went off and struck the latter." Previous to the fatal accident, "there never had been any quarrel or hatred between Girard and Gauthier." The jury found no bill against Girard, who was freed.[8] Had he been convicted, the penalty would have been death.

Criminal laws in Fortin's early days were grim. By the 1774 Quebec Act, the criminal courts had continued to use English penal law in Lower Canada. That law, infamous for its cruelty, listed more than 200 offences warranting the death penalty. The legislature of Lower Canada did little to amend the British legislation, though in 1824 it abolished the death penalty for many kinds of larceny. One historian has shown that many ordinances, often enforced at the level of the magistrates, defined new offences punishable by imprisonment or fines.[9] In 1833 Upper Canada reduced the number of capital offences to eleven. After the Act of Union, promulgated in Montréal in February 1841, the Upper Canadian law was extended to Lower Canada.[10]

In 1859 codification of the criminal law changed little of substance. The statutes stated that anyone guilty of murder or of being an accessory before the fact would "suffer death as a felon." However, killing someone was not a prerequisite for the death penalty. Hanging could also follow poisoning, stabbing, cutting or wounding, or any action causing "any bodily injury dangerous to life" with intent to commit murder. It could also follow rape; unlawful and carnal knowledge of, and abuses to, a girl under ten years; and "the abominable crime of Buggery committed either with mankind or any animal." Some crimes against property and person also warranted death. They included injuring someone while breaking and entering a dwelling, deliberately setting fire to a house or ship with someone in it, and showing "a false light" to endanger a vessel.[11] Most capital offences remained until Fortin had almost finished his career as magistrate. An 1865 act, however, abolished the death penalty for all crimes except murder, rape and treason.[12]

Such serious crimes came before Fortin. At Point-aux-Outardes in May 1864, he heard preliminary proceedings against an unnamed man accused of assault and battery with intent to commit murder. Such a charge could still lead to capital punishment. He ordered the accused to appear before the next session of the preliminary court for the District of Saguenay, at Malbaie.[13]

But much of his work involved settling small disputes. Sometimes persuasion worked. In 1857 two North Shore fishermen were quarrelling over a beach where both wanted to build processing facilities. Solomon-like, Fortin persuaded them they had room to split the beach between them. Other cases required the full court process. The same year, a Hudson's Bay Company agent on the North Shore accused two men of killing a horse. One of the men had evaded capture. Fortin heard the agent's deposition, questioned the other man, and also questioned the only witness, a Montagnais named Pierre Petarhoo. He dismissed the case.[14]

The magistrate knew a guilty man when he saw one, even if he could not touch him. When he searched a Sainte-Anne trading post for salmon taken illegally, his men emptied several puncheons of fish. About half were unmarked whole fish. The others had been divided in the middle, just where a spear would have marked them. Fortin knew the mutilation concealed illegal spear marks, but he had no proof. The owner claimed he had divided them so they would pack more easily in half barrels. "I could neither seize them, nor bring him to trial for the offence."[15]

Fortin's job was to try and to punish the guilty. In 1859 at Gaspé, he convicted two sailors of assaulting their captain. They refused to pay the fine, so *La Canadienne* carried them to the county jail at Percé. He could also show compassion. The same day, the captain of the *Atravida* told Fortin that his first mate was deranged and had tried to drown himself. "Thinking that the fit would only be temporary," Fortin kept the man on *La Canadienne* before sending him to jail. "As I had suspected, after a few days he was quite well and I discharged him."[16]

At other times his mercy was strained. "The next station belonged to a poor woman of eighty-nine years of age, Mme J.B. Beaudin." For ten days her nets had "not quite" met the legal requirements, but confiscation of her nets and fish would have deprived her of her livelihood. "Therefore I thought it right to make use of the discretionary powers entrusted to every Justice of the Peace in such cases." He simply warned her not to repeat the offence. If she did, "no excuse that she could make would prevent the law from taking its course."[17]

Sometimes Fortin's police work failed. In 1860 at Godbout, he could not find the men who had robbed a store and taken fishing gear. Nor could he trace the man who took from the same storehouse a canoe and fishing gear seized earlier from an Indian. At other times, his detective work paid off. At Natashquan a man accused Edgar Quigley, his five brothers, and others, of stealing goods from a wrecked vessel. Fortin searched and found the goods in Quigley senior's vessel. He arrested the men and took them on *La Canadienne* to Percé jail to await trial.[18]

Wrecks, common enough in the Gulf, sometimes involved Fortin as a magistrate. In September 1856 he went to Île aux Oiseaux, where the *Lochmaben Castle* had recently run aground in a gale, and broken up. A Mr. Sutherland of the Îles-de-la-Madeleine, who had bought the wreck, "burned it to the waters" to get at the ironwork. Fortin boarded the schooner *Victoria* of Argyll, N.S., and recovered "six chests of linen and wearing apparel" owned by passengers of the *Lochmaben Castle*. He also found the schooner, *Silver Key* of Boston, salvaging property from the wreck. The captain was working without any authority of the owner. "I carried him into Amherst harbour to restore to Mr. Sutherland the property recovered." Later Fortin recovered from the schooner *Shylock* eleven sails, twenty-nine boxes of soap, five chests of linen and the *Lochmaben Castle*'s medicine chest. Other captains "voluntarily" returned goods taken from the wreck.[19]

Liquor often caused problems for Fortin. From the earliest years of British rule in Canada, the government had controlled the production and sale of liquor, but heavy drinking was common in nineteenth-century Canada. Protests at the evils of liquor mounted. In 1828, at a Montréal temperance meeting, thirty took the pledge. The temperance movement grew rapidly. In 1850, the Order of the Sons of Temperance began exerting political pressure for reform. That year an act aimed at "the suppression of intemperance" deplored "the great evils arising out of the abuse of spirituous liquors."[20] Only the senior magistrate, senior officer of the militia, and churchwarden in a parish could issue certificates qualifying people for licences to sell liquor. Anyone found drunk could be fined not more than twenty-five shillings nor less than five, plus court and jail costs. The most interesting clause concerned drunken people who died "by suicide or by drowning, or perishing from cold or any other accident." Any innkeeper who had sold that person liquor was liable to a misdemeanour charge. A guilty innkeeper risked imprisonment for not less than two or more than six months. He also had to compensate heirs with £25 to £100.

Fortin saw what alcohol could do around the poverty-stricken Gulf coasts. An 1860 act, directed specifically to the Gulf and other "unorganized" sections of the province, had similar provisions.[21] At Moisie in 1863, Fortin fined a man $25 and costs for selling liquor without a licence. He paid the fine at once. Fortin wrote, "I have been determined" to enforce the act on the Gulf shores. Liquor could have "the worst effect on the morals of the fishermen, and is most injurious to the fishing industry." He hoped the well-deserved fine would prevent other parties from selling liquor illegally.[22]

Smuggling was widespread. The Americans used reciprocity to bring in contraband. French smugglers operating out of Saint-Pierre and Miquelon took brandy, wine, and other French products to the Îles-de-la-Madeleine. There they found schooners ready to take their cargoes. Some went to the lower parishes, the rest to the port of Québec. The smugglers "took care to conceal with codfish and barrels the casks containing the contraband articles."[23]

The Canada/Labrador border posed yet another problem. In 1859 the Fruing store at Blanc-Sablon paid duties on foreign goods. When the commander crossed to Île à Bois, he asked the agent for LeBoutillier Brothers also to pay duties. The agent demurred because two years ago he had had to pay duty to a Newfoundland customs officer. He would not pay Fortin until he got "proof positive" that the island belonged to Canada and not Newfoundland. Fortin decided to await instructions from headquarters.[24]

The problem recurred in 1863. Fortin "was surprised to learn" that two armed schooners of Newfoundland customs had anchored at Blanc-Sablon. Local merchants had initially refused to pay Newfoundland duties but then did so. Until now, they said, they were recognized as occupying Canadian territory. Fortin reported this to the collector of customs for clarification.[25]

But Fortin's first duty was to protect the fisheries. By law, fishing nets could not block navigation for other fishermen or for fish returning to their spawning grounds. Enforcing this law among the tough fishermen who swarmed over the Gulf sometimes led to violence. In the early summer of 1861, Fortin arrived at the Baie de Plaisance in the Îles-de-la-Madeleine. Finding many nets contravening the law, he removed some and reset them legally. Other parts of the bay that should have remained free and open were cluttered. He could not discover who owned the offending nets so his men then removed them and marked the legal limits with a buoy. "This labour was difficult and very toilsome." His men had to haul up nets fifty to sixty fathoms (300 to 360 feet) long, held to the bottom by stones weighing up to 100 pounds.

They began to remove the nets of a Nova Scotia fisherman named Joseph Hunson. Suddenly Hunson threw a stone that struck Bernier's head, causing serious loss of blood. Fortunately "I was there to dress the wound in time and in a fitting manner." A boatman hit by another rock was unharmed. Fortin arrested Hunson and one of his crew, and kept them under guard on *La Canadienne*. Next day he freed the accomplice on lack of evidence, but Hunson admitted the charge.

The case came up on 13 August at Gaspé before a judge. The result was not to Fortin's liking. Bernier and the sailors gave evidence, and the grand jury found a true bill against Hunson. "But the Petty Jury," said Fortin, "in spite of the most convincing proof, the judge's charge, and the prisoner's own confession before me at the Magdalen Islands ... acquitted the man." This surprised all who had heard the depositions.[26]

Desertion and other violations of the master-servant laws formed a continuing theme in Fortin's court. The labour laws he had to enforce heavily favoured the employers. And the courts used common law to penalize unions. In Lower Canada in 1841, seven journeymen painters had been found guilty under English common law of conspiracy for forming a union. Despite this, several unions had operated in Upper and Lower Canada during the 1830s and 1840s, but they were usually local and very short-lived.

In 1847 a union began to organize seamen. The organizers, called crimps, soon antagonized the shipping companies, which complained of a closed shop and of exorbitant wage demands.[27] The crimps provoked an 1847 act appointing a Quebec shipping master to register all seamen. To prevent "abuses," ships could hire crews only through the shipping master, and no third party such as a union could be involved.[28] The act proved ineffective. Another imposed penalties on anyone who encouraged seamen to desert or who sheltered deserting seamen.[29]

More labour legislation fell under the Fisheries Act of 1857. Anyone engaged to fish should not abandon his employer's service during the terms of his engagement. Transgressors could be fined up to £10 or imprisoned for not more than one month. Anyone found guilty of luring away a fishermen already engaged could also be fined or imprisoned. As a sop to the fishermen, the act allowed them to recover their wages before the nearest tribunal, and gave them first claim for their wages before any other of their employer's creditors. Nor could anyone seize the boats or equipment of fishermen during the fishing season.[30]

Fortin, as magistrate, often had to enforce these laws. At Gaspé he tried cases of desertion from the English schooner *Electra*. Four of those found guilty refused to return to their vessel. Fortin sentenced three of them to six weeks and the other to four weeks imprisonment in Percé.[31]

In June 1856 *La Canadienne* arrived at Percé, where the agent of Robin's, the local fishing company, asked for Fortin's help. The agent believed that several of Robin's people, engaged for the season, had taken money to desert to an American schooner. He asked Fortin to prevent their desertion because the cod fishery was at its height. Fortin anchored *La Canadienne* near the schooner and ordered the watch to advise him if any canoe or fishing boat should approach the American during the night. Next day the suspected schooner made sail for Cap Gaspé. The American had not "succeeded in seducing any of the fishermen."[32]

Fortin could be merciful within the law. In 1859 the owner of a fishing station at Rivière-au-Tonnere complained that Frederick Obus had deserted. Fortin took the deposition, issued a summons, and sent one of his men after Obus. But the accused appeared that evening and pleaded guilty. "As he promised to go back to his work, I imposed but a very slight fine on him." The punishments, however, continued. At Rivière-au-Renard he gave a $10 fine to Louis Fournier who had "deserted the service of his master." At Percé he fined two fishermen $10 each with costs of $1.15, or eight days, for desertion. Both paid the fines.[33]

Fortin did not back away from a fight when it was necessary, but he preferred reason to force. One day in October 1861, he reported, the *Royal Middy* out of Montréal was bound for Liverpool with 30,000 bushels of Indian corn. A storm off Anticosti took away the schooner's mizzen mast and *La Canadienne* helped tow the vessel into Gaspé Basin. The following afternoon the mate came to see Fortin and lodged a complaint of assault against a crew member. Fortin brought the man on board by warrant. The situation worsened next day, when Captain Davidson of the *Royal Middy* told his men that he would take the disabled schooner into winter quarters, then discharge the crew. Some of them threatened open mutiny. Davidson also came aboard *La Canadienne* for protection. Fortin first found the sailor guilty of assault against the mate, and fined him $10. Then Fortin, Davidson, and a Lloyd's agent boarded the *Royal Middy*. "After much talking," they made arrangements satisfactory to all parties, with Fortin promising to give the crew passage to Québec. That night they were paid, discharged, and taken on board *La Canadienne*.[34]

Fortin's strict interpretation of the labour law was quite consistent with his generally conservative views on law and order. But it brought him into disrepute with some who declared him to be "a company man."

TABLE 3: CASES HEARD BY FORTIN IN 1861

DEFENDANT	DATE	NATURE OF COMPLAINT	RESULT: fine or jail
Pierre Loiselle	29 May	damaging a house	$5 damages
unknown sailor	5 Jun	burglary	bound over
Pierre Briant	7 June	assault	acquitted
Alex Belau		obstructing municipal officer	died
Joseph Hunson	11 June	assault and battery	acquitted
Abraham Coffin	24 June	breach of fisheries law	$5, net confiscated
P. Beliveau	8 July	"	$12 fine
Prudent Nicol	9 July	"	$8 fine
Edward Quigley	13 July	theft from wrecked vessel	prison
Ed. Quigley jnr	"	"	"
Michael Quigley	"	"	"
Daniel Quigley	"	"	"
Jason Quigley	"	"	discharged
William Welsh	"	"	"
Wm. Hamilton	"	"	"
John Vigneault	15 July	assault and battery	$10 fine
Peter Rhynard	6 July	breach of fisheries law	$20, fish confiscated
Samuel Foreman	"	"	$20 fine
Hegwick Wager	23 July	insubordination on a vessel	6 weeks in prison
David Collis	"	"	"
Robert Hobson	"	"	"
Henry Enderby	"	"	"
Peter Glasgow	27 July	breach of fisheries law	$8 fine
David Têtu	"	"	referred to court
Thomas Picard	"	"	$5 fine
D. Lepage	"	"	acquitted
Daniel Holmes	"	"	sick
James Gillis	"	"	acquitted
John Renouff	"	"	absent
George Sennett	5 Aug.	"	acquitted
M. Coulomb	"	"	$5 fine
Wm. Knowles	"	"	$5 fine
George Girard	12 Aug.	manslaughter	acquitted: grand jury
Jean Giroux	17 Aug.	breach of fisheries law	absent
A. Guimette	"	"	"
John Bodman	25 Aug.	recovery of wages	settled for $3
Michael Kenty	9 Sept.	breach of fisheries law	acquitted
James Brophy	"	rape	bound over
Charles Miles	03 Oct.	assault and battery	8 weeks in prison
Albert Mouett	18 Oct.	robbery	prison
Michael Ryan	"	assault and battery	$20 fine
Ricard Ranger	"	receiving stolen goods	prison
Henry Haywood	12 Nov.	"	$10 fine

Source: Fortin, *Report*, 1862.

NOTES

1. Fortin, *Report*, 1858: 57.
2. Fortin, *Report*, 1864.
3. Fortin, *Report*, 1860: 121.
4. Fyson, 207-55.
5. Greer, Allan. "Birth of the Police in Canada," Allan Greer and Ian Radforth, eds. *Colonial Leviathan: State Formation in Mid-19th Century Canada.* Toronto: University of Toronto Press, 1992: 17-49.
6. Province of Canada, *Consolidated Statutes*, 22 Vic. c.101, 102, 103, 105 (1859).
7. PCA, 21 and 22 Vic. c.86 (1858).
8. Fortin, *Report*, 1862.
9. Fyson, 48-49.
10. PCA, 4 and 5 Vic. c.24 to 27 (1841); see Brown, Desmond H. *The Genesis of the Canadian Criminal Code of 1892.* Toronto: University of Toronto Press, 1989: 56-57, 87.
11. *Consolidated Statutes*, 22 Vic. c.91-93 (1859).
12. PCA, 28 Vic. c.13 (1865).
13. Fortin, *Report*, 1865.
14. Fortin, *Report*, 1858: 23-24.
15. Fortin, *Report*, 1858, 1861.
16. Fortin, *Report*, 1860: 127.
17. Fortin, *Report*, 1867-68: 7.
18. Fortin, *Report* 1861.
19. Fortin, *Report*, 1856, Letter to Provincial Secretary Cartier, 18 September 1855.
20. PCA, 13 and 14 Vic. c.27 (1850).
21. PCA, 23 Vic. c.6 (1860), 320.
22. Fortin, *Report*, 1864.
23. Fortin, *Report*, 1856.
24. Fortin, *Report*, 1860: 117.
25. Fortin, *Report*, 1864.
26. Fortin, *Report*, 1862.
27. Forsey, Eugene. *Trade Unions in Canada: 1812-1902.* Toronto: University of Toronto Press, 1982: 15.
28. PCA, 10 and 11 Vic. c.25 (1847).
29. PCA, 16 Vic. c.165 (1853).
30. PCA, 20 Vic. c.21 (1857).
31. Fortin, *Report*, 1862.
32. Fortin, *Report*, 1857.
33. Fortin, *Report*, 1860: 120-21.
34. Fortin, *Report*, 1862.

VII

A COMPANY MAN?

Auguste Béchard, a Gaspé school inspector, wrote that Fortin had once stopped a mob from hanging him. He said, "Commander Fortin has been reproached, perhaps not without reason ... for having been too friendly, much too friendly, with the Jersey merchants." These merchants, Béchard claimed, were "leeches on the fishermen and the born enemy of all progress on the coast." He then added, "However that may be, Commander Fortin did fine work in quelling the mob launched against me by the Robins."[1]

Potvin repeats but softens Béchard's criticism. "Naturally, when Fortin found himself in a conflict between merchants and fishermen, the task of the magistrate was very delicate and not always easy to judge."[2] Other historians make the same point.[3] Yet another, is much more critical. She says that Fortin "became a notorious ally of the companies; he was soon elected deputy."[4] She gives no evidence to support her assertion.

The story behind these criticisms goes back to 1765, when a small brig, the *Seaflower*, sailed from Jersey in the Channel Islands to Cape Breton. The captain, John Robin, and his younger brother Charles, were investigating the old French fishing grounds off Louisbourg. Aunts had raised John and Charles and an elder brother, Philip. Their uncles, fishing captains, told the boys of great cod banks off the coasts of Newfoundland. The boys founded the firm of Robin, Pipon Company, later Charles Robin and Company. Of the brothers, Philip stayed at home and operated the family store, John remained a ship's captain, while Charles became chief executive of the firm. In the next two years, the Robins bought more vessels. They began fishing Chaleur Bay in 1767, with a base at Paspébiac. Soon the firm had a virtual fishing monopoly from the Ristigouche River to Percé. By Fortin's time, Robin's had expanded to Gaspé.[5]

In the 1830s other Channel Island firms followed the Robins in buying cod from the Gulf fishermen. First came the Janvrins, then John LeBoutillier, the LeBoutillier Brothers, and John Fauvel. By the 1840s Hyman's, owned by a Jew of Russian background, was one of the few non-Channel Island companies in Gaspésie. In 1855 William Fruing, a Jerseyman, bought out the Janvrins at Grande-Grave. The Fruing Company often frightened or blackmailed any local fishermen who did business with Hyman or other competitors.[6] Settlement increased, and with it the number of small fishing posts, but the Channel Island companies continued to dominate the fisheries. Contemporaries charged that the big firms virtually controlled the price of fish through an understanding among themselves.[7]

At first the Robin family members lived on the peninsula and managed the firm. By Fortin's time, the family members had died, left for Ontario, or returned to oversee the company from Jersey. A series of well-trained managers, often sent from Jersey to start their apprenticeship at about fourteen years of age, carried out day-to-day operations. These employees had to be unmarried or to leave their wives at home. Strict, detailed rules governed their conduct, down to the plates to be used at table. Though not well paid, they were loyal. A contemporary, Abbé Jean-Baptiste-Antoine Ferland, said, "They are motivated to feel that their own interests and the interests of the company are identical."[8]

Until the depression of the 1930s, Robin's brought indentured workmen from Jersey to fill clerical and trades jobs. In the 1800s these men contracted not to "commit fornication, nor contract matrimony"; not to play cards or shoot dice; and not to "haunt ale-houses, taverns, playhouses, or any other place of debauchery."[9]

The Channel Island firms practised what today is called vertical integration. Their activities ranged from building their own vessels to carrying their own fish to market in Europe. Fortin noted an example of their shipbuilding when he anchored at Paspébiac on 26 September 1859. Two of Robin's ships, named by Fortin as *Blanchard* and *Mackerel*, had just arrived from Rio de Janeiro after delivering cargos of dried codfish.* The *Blanchard* with 3,000 barrels had taken eighty-

---

* These were probably the *O Blanchard* and the *Markwell.*

five days to complete the round trip, the *Mackerel* with 2,000 barrels had taken rather longer. These two "splendid" ships, wrote Fortin, were built at Paspébiac with timber from Chaleur Bay.[10]

For all their hard and often dangerous work, most fishermen lived in near poverty. In the early days, the Robins began a system of credit, sometimes called a truck system, and other companies followed. Under this system, most fishermen were nominally independent. However, credit usually bound these "independents" to the company stores. The company supplied the fisherman with equipment (from nets to salt), food (flour and meat), clothing (mainly work clothes), hardware and building materials (from tools to gunpowder), and various household needs.[11] In return, the fisherman tied himself at least for that season to supply fish to his creditor.

Money was usually only an accounting tool to set how much merchandise was worth how much fish. To maximize profits, the company tried as far as it could to raise the price of merchandise it sold, while minimizing the price of fish it bought. "The fisheries keep busy all the men, women and young girls, and all children able to do a little work," wrote a contemporary, Abbé Nerée Gingras. "As happens everywhere, fishing has both rich and poor." Those who built in the coves, where they could anchor their boats, were well off. "The rest are only poor wretches who cannot get a living from the sea." He adds, "The life of a fisherman is a life of misery; always malnourished; always on the water."[12]

Fishermen often hated what they called "The Company." In good years they might carry over a small credit. In bad years they either paid the debt by labouring in company yards, or carried it over till next season. The constant debts fishermen incurred through the credit system often gave the company immense power. In some areas it had the right to secure any land held by debtors, making it more difficult for families to amass property. Sometimes fathers could bequeath their debts to their son, but not their houses.

Still, necessity tended to restrain the company's use of its power. It could not push fishermen to the point of starving them or of forcing them to move away, since that would damage the company itself. Some historians see the credit system, based on a social ethic accepted by both merchant and fisherman, as at least providing a basic standard of living.[13] One historian concludes that, even allowing for "isolation and transportation difficulties," high markups by Robin's "clearly reduced the fisherman's real wage below the nominal wage." The system was "a deliberate means of defrauding the workers of a part of their wages."[14] From a Marxist perspective, it was an impersonal and inevitable stage, determined by external conditions of the time, in the development of merchant capital.[15] Either way, the life of fishermen and their families was hard. Even Robin's agent in Paspébiac recognized the fact in an 1867 letter to Jersey:

As I stated in my last, the misery and destitution along the coast is fearful and I am afraid that some will die of starvation before the Spring—many are actually starving or next thing to it at present and we must absolutely give them something to eat to keep them alive. I mean our fishermen. Many of them are certainly in a pitiful state. I shall be glad when the Spring arrives so that we may have work to give them and ennable them to earn something so as to keep them alive.[16]

Two weeks later, a Paspébiac letter to Jersey is almost apologetic. "When you examine the copy of the Caraquet cash accounts, you will see that I did not draw unless absolutely necessary. In some instances it is impossible to refuse cash to good dealers who give a great deal of fish and pay their accounts. If overdue, we charge interest." Apparently, only a few of the most reliable of the dealers got any sort of help from Robin's that miserable late winter and spring. The following November, conditions among the fishermen and their families must have been as bad. Relief did not come from the agent at Paspébiac who wrote home, "The Government, through Dr. Fortin, have sent down 300 barrels of flour and Indian meal for the County of Gaspé poor, all distributed in each township."[17]

The Robins were extremely conservative. In 1836 Ferland wrote that they "forbid any innovations whatsoever." They once nearly fired a shipwright for suggesting designs for a round-sterned schooner rather than the company's usual square stern.[18]

The Jersey companies had much political influence and encouraged Quebec politicians in their natural inclination to ignore the peninsula. The Robins were at least scrupulously honest. "The inhabitants have unlimited confidence in the Robins, for they control the electorate and all public affairs," wrote Gingras. Company officials were Protestant, but they were very friendly towards Catholic priests. "They come often to the Presbytery and the missionary has no need to genuflect to get whatever he needs. They have magnificent homes."[19] These, then, were the Jersey companies that Béchard referred to when he wrote,

"Commander Fortin has been reproached, perhaps not without reason, ... for having been too friendly with the Jersey merchants."

Fortin's reports show how this perception could arise. As magistrate-commander of *La Canadienne*, he had real power. Many years later he commented on this. The commander of a government vessel with twenty-five seamen could spend large sums of money. Such a man, he said, could exercise "a great deal of influence over the populations."[20] The obvious example of his power came when Fortin, as a magistrate, strictly imposed the labour laws. As discussed earlier, these gave the advantage to the fishing companies. An 1864 case illustrates Fortin's attitude. In a Percé court he and another justice of the peace found five fishermen guilty of breaking their engagement. They sentenced them to a fine of $10 each or imprisonment for twenty days. Since the men did not or could not pay their fine, they went to jail Fortin comments, "Such an example as this could not fail to produce a salutary effect among the people of the coast." It warned them not to break their engagement after accepting advances in fishing tackle and provisions. If they did, "Justice would overtake them and punish them for their bad faith." But the law "would also protect them against any unworthy treatment from their employers."[21]

Fortin was not alone in his strict interpretation of the master/servant laws. One historian studying seamen in the 19th century found that stipendiary magistrates "clearly favoured capital in its legal battles with labour."[22]

In 1868 Fortin introduced a private member's bill in the Quebec Assembly. It showed the same balance between enforcing contracts and protecting fishermen against "unworthy treatment." The penalty for desertion remained. Anyone "engaged by written agreement" to fish, but who deserted his employer, could be fined up to $40 or imprisoned up to three months. No reference to an oral agreement occurred in this section of the bill. However, anyone "engaged either by written agreement or otherwise" (orally) would have a first lien on the produce of his employer's fishery to secure his wages or share. This clause slightly favoured the fishermen. Also, between May and November no one could seize any boat, tackle or provisions needed for a fisherman's livelihood. That again gave the fishermen some minimum protection from arbitrary seizure. The bill became law later that year.[23]

The perception of bias could also arise because Fortin and the senior company men often worked together. They all belonged to the establishment. This relationship recurred in Fortin's annual reports. At

Percé in 1856, he wrote, "I sat with Mr John LeBoutillier on a case of assault and battery." [24] Again, in 1857 he owed his "warmest thanks to M. Briard, the general agent for the house of Robin and Company at Paspébiac for his obliging attention and readiness." Briard had placed his workmen at Fortin's disposal when the repairs to *La Canadienne* were required.[25] Elsewhere Fortin shows admiration for the efficiency of the companies. In September 1855 he took John LeBoutillier to visit Îles-de-la-Madeleine, "of which that gentleman is the intelligent representative."[26] In 1856 he visited Robin's establishment at Grande-Rivière and admired "the order and neatness" in every department. This, he said, characterized the Jersey fishing establishments.[27]

In the elections of 1867 the Jersey companies strongly supported Fortin's candidature. The Robin's representative in Paspébiac, Moses Gibaud, wrote to his Jersey headquarters that he hoped Fortin would be returned for both the federal and provincial houses. "I saw Mr Martel yesterday and after hearing from me that we supported [Fortin], he [Martel] retired from the contest.... I promised him [Fortin] our support. Collas and LeBoutillier Bros. do the same."

A month later Gibaud again wrote. "The Government Schooner *La Canadienne* arrived here 4th instant, put in by bad weather. Mr Fortin saw his friends along the coast of Gaspé. He is supported by Fruings, Hyman, Savage, Collas and several others. John LeBoutillier is also in favor of him but will remain neutral." Another candidate, he said, did not have a chance. "I think he [another LeBoutillier] will resign like Martel, and Fortin be elected by acclamation."[28] And that's the way it worked out. Fortin, supported by the fishing companies, had no opponent for the Gaspé seat in either house.

This support continued in the 1871 provincial elections. The Robin's head office in Jersey instructed the Paspébiac agent, "In the coming election, you will support our friends Théo Robitaille [Bonaventure] and Fortin. We cannot have two better men to represent us, so we must do our utmost to get them returned. You will write our other agents to use their best endeavours to carry out this." After the election, headquarters wrote, "Dr Robitaille and Fortin being elected gives satisfaction."[29]

Fortin's relations with Robin and Company, as expressed in this correspondence, were clearly very cordial. In 1868 Fortin went to Europe. He first attended the Maritime Exhibition at Le Havre, France, and watched an international yachting race. He then visited fishing ports and shipbuilding centres in France and Britain.[30] Before sailing, Fortin wrote, "I hope that this trip will be profitable to my constituents as I will be able to learn many things that will be of interest.... I will not fail to go to Jersey and visit Mr Robin and the other gentlemen who carry on business on the coast." A letter from Jersey showed that Fortin had indeed visited, and that the Robins valued his opinion. They wrote that the use of bottom lines "should have our attention. If it destroys the mother fish, a stop should be put to it or we shall have no fish left. We understand Fortin is not of that opinion, but he should be consulted on the matter. He had left [here] when we heard of it, or would have asked him about it."

In 1867 Pierre Fortin had become not just the representative for Gaspé but its Conservative representative. As such, the companies would inevitably support him rather than the Liberals. Equally, he would see it as his duty to press for the interests of the main commercial houses of his constituency, on whom the prosperity of the region largely depended. The most interesting questions are, first, is there evidence of improper conduct on his part in favour of the companies? Second, is there evidence that he sacrificed the well-being of the fishermen for that of the companies?

As to the first, the Robin's correspondence shows that he never received money from the company. With the approach of the 1872 federal election, Robin's headquarters wrote, "Drs. Fortin and Robitaille will come forward for reelection. These gentlemen can be supported, given all our influence possible, but without being put to any expenses whatever. Pray note this." Nor did he get himself in quite such dubious circumstances as did Robitaille, Conservative member for the neighbouring constitutency of Bonaventure. "Dr Theo. Robitaille should pay up his election debt," wrote Robin's headquarters, "It will not do to leave this stand behind. If it is politics that makes him contract debts, why does he go in? If we are to pay for getting a man returned into Paliament, better abandon such a scheme—enough to give our influence."[31] A series of letters from Robin's Jersey to Robin's Paspébiac constantly complained about Robitaille not paying his 1867 debts, and the complaints continued until at least 1876.* Robin's then began legal action for repayment.

---

* See for instance NA MG28 III 18, Robin Correspondence, Letters Incoming, Vol 76: Robin's Jersey to Théodore Robitaille, 17 July 1876. Robitaille is flayed for mortgaging his home with a bank. This left Robin and Company without security. A medical doctor, Robitaille worked for Robin's as a medical consultant prior to and after his election.

During his years as the Gaspé representative, Fortin inevitably had dealings with Robin and Company, an important and powerful constituent. Just after his first election, he wrote a long and rather excited letter to the Robin's agent at Paspébiac. He congratulated himself for overcoming political and bureaucratic roadblocks in the Quebec legislature during passage of a bill dividing the municipalities of Percé and Grande-Rivière. Another letter that year assured the company that he was trying to get a lighthouse for Paspébiac, something he had argued for when on *La Canadienne*. A third letter went to Robin's representative at Paspébiac and to other firms on the coast. He asked for "the probable amount of business that a telegraph office, opened in your locality, would be likely to get." The letter included a long and detailed list of questions about how their businesses might be affected.

Routine letters on other projects crop up occasionally over the years. In 1872 he told Robin's agent at Paspébiac that he would support the proposed improvement of the habour at Chetichan (sic). "I understand so well the importance of harbors for fishing vessels." For that reason "I am striving so much to improve the harbors of the Magdalen Islands." He was also "taking steps to have a larger and faster vessel as a packet for the North Shore postal service.... I believe firmly that postal communications are essential to the development of the resources of the North Shore."[32] Other letters between the company and Fortin concerned posts for a telegraph line around the Gaspé coast. He also asked if the company would take charge of the post office at Magpie on the North Shore.[33]

A more vexed question concerned the location of the administrative capital (*chef-lieu*) of Gaspésie. In 1868 it was still Percé, but the Consolidated Statutes of Lower Canada ordered that when the council or the county of Gaspé had provided a site for a jail and courthouse, and the government had built them, then "for all purposes for the administration of justice" Gaspé Basin would become the capital instead of Percé.[34] The Robin's agent Paspébiac several times lobbied Fortin to keep the capital at Percé. The municipal councillors there and in the surrounding districts were "preparing resolutions, and subscriptions are on foot to raise funds to repair or help to build a new gaol there— we are very anxious to keep it there having a majority of the population on our side."[35] The letters do not say what site Fortin supported, but the capital eventually moved to Gaspé.

This correspondence seems no more than routine business any member of parliament or of the assembly would conduct with an

The Charles Robin and Co. establishment at Paspébiac c. 1866, a century after its founding. (Thomas Pye/National Library of Canada/NL19283)

important constituent. In January 1873, however, a month before Fortin became commissioner of crown lands, Robin's agent at Percé sent Fortin a letter whose peremptory ring suggests a less innocent relationship.

We enclose you herewith [said Robin's] a diagram of the timber limits which we would like to secure on the Grand River [Grande-Rivière], say, four miles in breadth and twelve miles in depth. Please secure this for us if possible, without delay. Please send us a regular form of application which we would fill up or perhaps you might do the needful yourself. We will be glad to know what this timber limit will cost per square mile.

Unfortunately, we do not have Fortin's side of the correspondence, but perhaps he gave this letter a cool welcome, for a month later Percé wrote again, this time more circumspectly: "We propose lumbering on the Grand River shortly. We therefore would like to secure timber limits, say, 12 square miles, in rear of the Grand River Seigneury, as in the enclosed diagram. Would you be kind enough to have these limits advertised for sale, and secure them for us if possible for 20 years?"[36] An accompanying note, marked private, tried to justify the request. "There is not much valuable timber on the land in question, little or no pine, but plenty of [illegible] and Spruce which is especially what we want for manufacturing tubs [illegible] for Brazil and West Indian markets. There is no other timber fit for actual lumbering purposes which I daresay you are aware of. I hope you will succeed in getting these limits for us at cheap figures." The letter insisted that the company had applied as soon as possible. Presumably Fortin had said the application was too late. Its fate is not known.

After Fortin joined the Quebec cabinet as commissioner of crown lands, Robin's agent at Paspébiac wrote, "I was much pleased to receive telegrams announcing your appointment, upon which I wish to congratulate you. All your well wishers here are highly delighted to think that your services are so highly appreciated. No doubt this is equivalent to a defeat to your political enemies."[37]

However, the company was not above making indirect threats. At one point it was unhappy because the dominion government considered a wharf at Barachois to be a local government responsibility. Merchants and fishermen alike, said the agent, would benefit from it:

Though we have always been staunch supporters of the government, we fear that a feeling that we are all slighted is gaining ground. And if treated unjustly, a day may come when this feeling of neglect may produce undeniable effects; people are more determined than ever to think and act for themselves; and should they find themselves badly treated, not even our influence could secure their support to the Conservative interest.[38]

The relationship between Fortin and Robin and Company became a little more murky in three 1875 letters. Here patronage is at work. In May their representative at Percé, Mr. deVeulle, wrote to Fortin in the Commons. He said that "three good Conservatives" would be tendering for the mail contract at Percé, "viz. Archie Kerr, James Enwright, and Greg Grenier.... Now these three are going to understand each other so that it does not matter which one gets it, he will divide it between the three. In that way, three good Blues will be pleased instead of one." The man who earlier held the contract had "lost it thro being a Conservative" during the Liberal regime in Ottawa.

A search of the correspondence did not reveal Fortin's response, but again he seems to have been cool. DeVeulle takes exception to Fortin's replies. "My dear doctor, yours of 31 May and 3 June received. I think you are a little out in saying [they are] my protégés. I need not enter into explanations concerning the men. Enwright is a good Conservative and as to Kerr, well, he lost the contract because he was a Conservative.

I leave the matter in your hands." DeVeulle then moves on to another matter which brutally illustrates politics at that time:

I am pleased to see the stand you are taking for Dr Wakeham. It must be as great a surprise to you (knowing how we have treated Dr. Robitaille) to see him acting as he is doing. I cannot explain it at all. What is the matter with him. Even as late as last winter, in his own county, I did him a great deal of good by punishing some who had voted against him the previous election, and now instead of helping you, he opposes the nominations you wish to make.

He then asks, "What about our friend, Mr. Gibaud. Is there any chance of success for him. I wired you this afternoon, asking you to write. I hope you will excuse my troubling you so often. I myself do not like bothering you so often, but having known him for so long a time, it grieves me to see him idle when he wishes for work."

The records do not show whether or not Fortin pushed for the appointments for Wakeham and Gibaud. However, two weeks later deVeulle wrote, very formally:

Percé, 16 June 1879. Hon. P. Fortin, *Minerve* Office, Montréal.—Dear Sir, I consider it fair to yourself to let you know that by papers that have been seen and read, a considerable portion, and in fact all the blame attending the non-appointment of Messrs Wakeham and Gibaud is thrown upon you and exculpates Dr. Robitaille. For fear you might suspect the innocent of setting this abroad, let me say they do not come from either of the parties [Wakeham and Gibaud] here named. Yours truly, Henry M. deVeulle.[39]

Two key letters in 1872 and 1873, however, show Fortin explicitly keeping a distance from Robin and Company. The first letter concerned incorporation of the Labrador Company. He had sent all the Channel Island companies on the North Shore two copies of the bill of incorporation—as introduced, and as passed. The bill as passed eliminated sections which Fortin and others felt dangerous to fishing interests there. However, he said, he could not advise Robin and Company on the legalities of the matter; the company should consult its lawyer.

Fortin followed this with a second letter, marked private, to the Paspébiac agent, written from Québec on 7 July 1873. He acknowledged receipt of a letter concerning Robin's fishing establishment at

Magpie on the North Shore. Fortin writes, "On account of being Commissioner of Crown Lands for the Province of Quebec, I do not feel at liberty to give you any advice or opinion on the matters you refer to in your letter." He again advised the company to consult its lawyer.[40] These letters suggest that Fortin was fully aware of the line between legitimately serving the interests of a constituent and giving that constituent undue favours.

Given these interests and pressures, did Fortin sacrifice the interests of the fishermen for those of the Jersey companies? In his days on *La Canadienne*, he sometimes criticized the Jersey companies and their policies. In the main, the companies were interested only in inshore cod fishing. As a result, Canadian fishermen largely ignored herring, except as bait. Based on figures from the Îles-de-la-Madeleine, foreigners in 1861 took 40,000 barrels of herrings, locals took 1,500. In 1865 the ratio was 27,000 to 3,000.[41]

One historian sees Robin's general conservatism as no more than staying with a profitable system that provided high-quality, marketable fish.[42] Fortin, however, fought this conservatism: all fish were a God-given resource. It was wasteful and stupid, he argued, to leave valuable species such as herring and mackerel. In his 1856 report he castigated Canadians, in effect the big companies, for not taking mackerel off the North Shore coast and leaving them to Americans.[43] In 1858 at Restigouche, he again complained that Canadian fishermen would not go after mackerel. He also said that herring and caplin used as manure could provide extra funds. Nor would this harm the numbers coming in to spawn since the fish were so numerous.[44]

In 1859 in the Îles-de-la-Madeleine, Fortin discussed herring taken early in spring, when they came into shallow water to lay eggs. Admittedly, they were small and lean, not so valuable as those taken in autumn. All the same, they formed an important article for possible export to warm climates such as the West Indies, where fat fish could not be preserved. Canadians should not leave them to foreigners, he said.[45] All this was aimed against the companies' policy of cod fishing only.

When the law demanded it, Fortin could act against the interests of the companies. In 1858 the Paspébiac collector of customs asked for help to get back goods "forcibly taken from me out of HM warehouse at Paspébiac." The LeBoutilliers disliked paying duties on imports and had illegally appropriated them. He accused Martin Shepphard, sheriff, "agents and clerks of Messrs LeBoutilliers Bros, and a very large number of other rioters." Fortin landed with nine men and took back the goods from the LeBoutilliers' store. He stayed a few days to see there was no more trouble. For whatever reason, however, he does not mention charging the firm or its agents for the illegal acts.[46]

Fortin well knew the misery that the credit system could bring when it broke down. In 1864 "Great destitution prevailed" along the coast of Labrador [North Shore]. Cod fishing had failed. So too had fur trapping the previous winter. Only the herring season had been successful. Without that, he did not know how many would have been able "without great suffering, to struggle through the long winter in that inclement region." The traders had suffered heavy losses for many years past, and they were now determined to make no advances of provisions to the poorest of the fishermen. If the herring season had not provided "providential aid," the fishermen would "have been absolutely destitute of provisions."[47]

Public charity in Quebec later sent the *Napoleon III* to the North Shore with flour and other provisions. However, on the Labrador coast controlled by Newfoundland, "the distress was still greater than on ours." Many were already destitute. If not helped by autumn, "a large portion of them will perish by starvation during the winter."

In his 1865 report Fortin harshly criticized the Jersey hegemony. Cod prices on the peninsula were high, and Fortin credited this in part to the scarcity of fish. As well, however, Gaspé had become a free port in 1860. This, Fortin claimed, led to increased "rivalship and competition between the many commercial houses at the Basin." And that too favoured the fishermen. "The old mode of doing business is gone, never to return." Previously two or three large firms had fixed the price of fish on their own terms. They paid for the fish in "provisions or goods, almost never with money. Now I have personal knowledge that ... sales of fish" have amounted to "many thousands of pounds, ready cash. This is an auspicious change in our fish trade, presaging for the future the most beneficial results."[48] These were not the words of a slavish company man.

Many did not share Fortin's optimism about the free port, and they argued it had failed because the big merchants were simply too powerful for small businesses to compete. Whatever the merits of the free port, the government abolished it a few years later.[49]

Fortin also attacked the stranglehold of the Jersey companies on fish shipments overseas. Gulf fish were carried to Europe and South America "almost entirely" by Channel Island vessels. Meanwhile, Canadian schooners and brigantines lay idle for months since their commanders lacked training in deep-water navigation.[50] As the next chapter will show, Fortin wanted to establish schools to teach navigation to the fishermen. They could then export their own produce, breaking the hold of the Jersey companies.

North Shore fishermen had their own problems with the Hudson's Bay Company. The king's domain or king's posts, he said, stretched 270 miles from near Québec to Cap Cormoran. For years, the Hudson's Bay Company held exclusive rights over these 72,000 square miles. A North Shore sealer claimed that the company had "locked up and held as a desert" the huge area and its major harbors. It had "the single objective of permitting a few adventurers to exploit the miserable aborigines" living there.[51]

An 1853 fisheries act took away the exclusive rights of the HBC. The act said "a strong hand" had prevented fishermen erecting buildings necessary for their trade. It permitted any British subject to take possession of part of an unoccupied beach to build a fishing station.[52] Fortin used this authority in 1859 to move against the company. On 21 June at Mingan, a senior company official complained to Fortin that British sports fishermen were illegally fishing the rivers of the seigneury of Mingan. Fortin refused to act against the fishermen. He said his instructions were to issue licences for North Shore rivers, just as he did on the South Shore.[53]

Fortin gave credit to *La Canadienne* for prising much of the North Shore from the grip of the HBC. Years ago, he wrote in 1865, the abundant cod attracted many Gaspé shippers and fishermen. However, they could not build fishing posts without protection. The HBC employees claimed they had exclusive right to the coast and its attached fisheries, and drove the fishermen away. They were "without mercy." Several times they burned and destroyed the fishermen's vessels and buildings. Then the 1853 law had defined the rights of the fishermen on this ninety-mile coast. Now several thousand fishermen worked hundreds of cod-fishing posts. "But it is well known that [the law] would have remained a dead letter but for the Service for the Protection of the Fisheries."[54]

Opening the North Shore to the Jersey companies, however, brought its own problems for fishermen from the Îles-de-la-Madeleine. In June 1863 a brigantine arrived to hire about 100 cod fishermen. The company operating the vessel took the fishermen to the North Shore, gave them good, well-fitted fishing boats, and supplied fresh bait when available at a cost to the fishermen of $6 to $8. For each hundred codfish delivered, the company paid the fishermen 5s. 6d., half in money, half in goods and provisions. At those prices and with plenty fish, Fortin estimated they could earn from $5 to $20 a day. After six to nine weeks, they might bring home from $80 to $120, sometimes more. However, they owed the company for provisions left for their families. They also owed for their own board, and for the cost of their lines. A poor catch meant the loss of most of their earnings, and "They very often return to the Magdalen Islands with empty pockets."

The experience of many years had shown Fortin that fishermen would be better off fishing on the shores of their home islands than hiring on with the Jersey companies on the North Shore. "They might not find as many fish, but they might at least work upon their farms on days when bad weather would prevent them from going to sea."[55]

Fortin also recognized that the fisheries had benefited the Channel Island firms more than the fishermen of the St. Lawrence. He told the legislature that the fisheries "were founded in the main by shipbuilders, British subjects it is true, but foreigners to Canada; and to this day, the principal owners of the big companies live in the Channel Islands. It is there that the great benefits from the Canadian fisheries accumulate."[56]

The two questions asked about Fortin remain. First, is there evidence of improper conduct on his part in favour of the companies? Second, is there evidence that he sacrificed the well-being of the fishermen for that of the companies?

As to the first, the letters confirm that Fortin did push for the interests of the Jersey companies. He was, after all, their representative. Both he and they were Conservatives, and they saw him and their party as most likely to help their cause. In that he was no different from any other politician using patronage for his and his party's advantage. The letters also show, however, that he had no financial backing from the companies. We do not have his responses, but the Robin's letters suggest that he replied coolly when his support was taken for granted. When warranted, he drew a clear line between his duties as a minister and his work as a representative of his constituents.

On the second question, in key matters such as restrictive fishing practices, education, navigation schools, and the excesses of the truck system, Fortin spoke out for the fishermen against the companies. Béchard had no love for Robin's and other Jersey merchants in Gaspésie, and no doubt overstated the case against them. They were, he claimed, "a race of vampires, with no compassion or moral character." He goes on, "They and they alone fed on the sweat and blood of the Gaspésie fishermen.... [They] have kept them in misery, far from schools, from agriculture and from all ideas of progress.... These fat merchants, having received the profits of their infamous trade, justly receive all the shame and all the maledictions."

These were the firms with whom Fortin may have been "too friendly." Yet at Fortin's death, Béchard wrote, "Gaspé was long represented by a man distinguished by his devotion to the interests of his electors. In effect, Commander Fortin ... has by himself achieved more than all his predecessors in Gaspé."[57] If Béchard regarded Fortin as the crony of "leeches" who "sapped the blood and sweat of Gaspésian fishermen," he nevertheless wrote a generous tribute to him.

Perhaps Fortin should be judged not by who among the politically powerful supported him and his party. Perhaps, as Béchard implies, he should be judged by what he pushed for, and helped achieve, for the people of the Gulf. One of the most important of those goals was better schooling.

NOTES

1. Béchard, Auguste, *La Gaspésie en 1888*. Québec: L'Imprimerie Nationale, 1918: 119.
2. Potvin, *Le roi*, 66.
3. Morissoneau, Christian. *La société de géographie de Québec*. Québec: Les Presses de l'université Laval, 1971: 49.
4. Grandbois, Maryse. "Le développement des disparités régionales en Gaspésie," *Revue d'histoire de l'Amérique française*, Vol. 36, No. 4 (March 1983): 483-506.
5. Lee, David. *The Robins in Gaspé, 1766 to 1925*. Markham, Ont.: Fitzhenry and Whiteside, 1984: 14-15.
6. Samson, Roch. *Fishermen and Merchants in 19th-century Gaspé*. Ottawa: Parks Canada, 1984: 12, 23.
7. "Report of the Inspector of Free Ports," PCLAJ 1865. App. 37: 21.
8. Ferland, J.-B.-A. *La Gaspésie*. Québec: Nouvelle Édition, 1877: 117-18.
9. Lee, 97.
10. Fortin, *Report*, 1860: 123-24.
11. Samson, *Fishermen*, 68-69.
12. Gingras, Nérée. "Impressions de Gaspésie en 1857," *Le Canada français* (Québec), Vol. 26, No. 5 (January 1939): 483-97.
13. See for instance Samson, 73-74, 83-84.

14. Ommer, Rosemary E. "The Truck System in Gaspé, 1822-27," *Acadiensis* (Fredericton), Vol. 19, No. 1 (Fall 1989): 91-104.
15. See for instance Lepage, André. "Le Capitalisme marchand et la pêche à la morue en Gaspésie: La Charles Robin and Company dans la Baie des Chaleurs, 1820-1870." Ph.D. thesis, Université Laval, Québec, 1983: part 1.
16. NA MG 28, III18, Robin Correspondence. Paspébiac Letter Books, Vol. 1: Robin's Paspébiac to Robin's Jersey, 13 March 1867.
17. Paspébiac Letter Books, Vol. 6: Robin's Paspébiac to Robin's Jersey, 26 March 1867; Vol. 1: Robin's Paspébiac to Robin's Jersey, 12 November 1867.
18. Ferland, 370.
19. Gingras, 492.
20. HOCD, 19 March 1879, 560.
21. Fortin, *Report*, 1865: 9
22. Fingard, Judith. *Jack in Port: Sailortowns of Eastern Canada.* Toronto: University of Toronto Press, 1982: 188.
23. Quebec, *Acts*, 32 Vic. c.37 (1869).
24. Fortin, *Report*, 1857.
25. Fortin, *Report*, 1858: 7.
26. Fortin, *Report*, 1856.
27. Fortin, *Report*, 1857.
28. Paspébiac Letter Books, Vol. 1: Robin's Paspébiac to Robin's Jersey, 15 May, 6 June 1867.
29. Robin's Correspondence. Letters Incoming, Vol. 67: Robin's Naples to Robin's Paspébiac, 19 January 1871; Robin's Jersey to Robin's Paspébiac, 7 August 1871.
30. NA MG 29, D61, Henry James Morgan papers, 3071-78, handwritten biography of Fortin by Morgan.
31. Letters Incoming, Vol. 61: Fortin to Robin's Paspébiac, 1 July 1868; Vol. 61: Robin's Jersey to Robin's Paspébiac, November 28 1868; Vol. 71: Robin's Jersey to Robin's Paspébiac, 20 February 1872; Robin's Naples to Robin's Paspébiac, 22 March, 1872.
32. Letters Incoming, Vol. 61: Fortin to Robin's Paspébiac, 1868; Vol. 70: Fortin to Robin's Paspébiac, 1872.
33. Paspébiac Letter Books, Vol. 6: Robin's Paspébiac to Fortin, 26 December 1870; 19 January 1871.
34. Canada. *Consolidated Statutes*, Vic. 28, c.109 (1859).
35. Paspébiac Letter Books, Vol. 3: Robin's Paspébiac to Fortin, 14 April 1868; Vol. 4: Robin's Paspébiac to Fortin, 23 February 1869.
36. Robin's Correspondence, Percé Letter Books, Vol. 28: Robin's Percé to Fortin, 6 January 1873; 3 February 1873.
37. Percé Letter Books, Vol. 28: Robin's Percé to Fortin, 22 November 1875.

38. Paspébiac Letter Books, Vol. 9: Robin's Paspébiac to Fortin, 18 March 1880.
39. Percé Letter Books, Vol. 29: Robin's Percé to Fortin, 10 May, 6 June, 16 June 1879.
40. Letters Incoming, Vol. 71: Fortin to Robin's Paspébiac, 7 July 1873; Vol. 70: Fortin to Robin Paspébiac, 20 January 1872.
41. Geistdoerfer, Aliette. *Pêcheurs acadiennes: pêcheurs madelinots.* Québec: Les Presses de l'université Laval, 1987: Annexe 10. See also Fortin, Report, 1857.
42. Lepage, 81.
43. Fortin, *Report*, 1857.
44. Fortin, *Report*, 1859.
45. Fortin, *Report*, 1860: 106.
46. Fortin, *Report*, 1859.
47. Fortin, *Report*, 1865: 18.
48. Fortin, *Report*, 1865: 19.
49. Innis, 359.
50. Fortin, *Report*, 1858: App. 2.
51. Chambers, E.T.D. *Les pêcheries de la province de Québec: 1ère partie, introduction historique.* Québec: Département de la colonisation, 1912: 143.
52. PCA 16 Vic. c.92 (1853).
53. Fortin, *Report*, 1860: 110.
54. Fortin, *Report*, 1865: 23.
55. Fortin, *Report*, 1864.
56. Ommer, Rosemary E. "Nouvelles de mer: The Rise of Jersey Shipping, 1830-1840," Eric Sagar, ed. *The Enterprising Canadians.* St. John's: Memorial University of Newfoundland, 1979: 177.
57. Béchard, 22, 51.

VIII

THE WAR OF THE CANDLE SNUFFERS

Abbé Ferland, writing in 1836, quoted Philip Robin on the Gulf fishermen. "There is no need of instruction for them. If they were educated, would they be better fishermen?"[1]

Perhaps not, but Fortin believed passionately that education was essential for their well-being. He wrote in 1861 that the people of Natashquan had started a school, but lack of funds had closed it. The community could defray the cost of a school house if aided by the government; it would also do its part in paying a master. The fishermen, "in their rough calling, [are] inferior to none for strength, courage and skill." He deplored that they "should be doomed to the darkness of perpetual ignorance." They should not, in their education, "remain inferior to fishermen with whom they are in daily contact or intercourse."[2]

Schools were scarce on the Gulf coasts. In his reports, Fortin many times stressed the need for more of them, from elementary to adult schools in seamanship and navigation.

If Philip Robin and the Jersey companies saw no good in educating fishermen, they were even less pleased at having to pay property taxes in order to subsidize that education. Many fishermen themselves were no more enthusiastic. In the short run, schools struck a double blow at family finances: they incurred taxes when few families had money, and children attending school could not gainfully work. Child labour often made the difference to a family between destitution and mere poverty.

Years earlier, Fortin and his mounted police had met the same problem in the St. Lawrence valley. Habitants, hating the new school taxes, had rioted, encouraged by wealthy landowners.[3] Now the fishing companies were allegedly using the same tactics. In short, the war of the candle snuffers had spread to Gaspésie. Fortin found himself again fighting, as he saw it, for education and enlightenment.

In November 1859 Fortin anchored at Percé. He found a letter from August Béchard, inspector of public schools and justice of the peace. Béchard complained that two ratepayers at Pabos were refusing to pay their school taxes. Judgment had gone against them. "But owing to the repeated threats of these two individuals, no bailiff or constable can be found to take charge of the writs of execution." Fortin took on board the Percé bailiff and on 3 November, *La Canadienne* anchored at Pabos. There Bernier and six men seized the goods and chattels of the tax dodgers, "this time without meeting any resistance."[4]

La Canadienne returned to Percé five days later to find a riot brewing. Béchard, hating the Robins, later described the scene. The old school system had depended on voluntary contributions. The Robins, said Béchard, owned most of Percé, but they had never contributed more than four piastres* a year and often nothing. He charged that the company provoked hostility among the fishermen towards education. As a result, the schools were miserable and often had to close.

Finally, the Lower Canadian superintendent of instruction ordered Béchard to establish and collect a school tax. Béchard began his task, but the inhabitants of Irishtown objected violently. According to Béchard, officers of Robin and Company circulated among the Irish. They gave them whisky, and shouted "No taxes!" and "Down with the school tax!" Fighting broke out. Signs on walls threatened to hang Béchard if he did not back off. Then late that evening, *La Canadienne* and Commander Fortin arrived. "It was," wrote Béchard, "Providence who sent him."[5]

Fortin now takes up the story. Many people in Gaspésie, he wrote, had refused to pay their share of school-operating costs. The school commissioners found it impossible to pay their schoolmasters and keep their schoolhouses in repair. The minister, Chauveau, had instructed them to remedy that: they must enforce the system of taxation.

---

* In his book, McCullough makes only a brief reference to piastres as a Spanish coin, one among many foreign coins circulating about this time. Béchard may have meant simply that Robin's contributions were trivial. See McCullough, A.B. *Money and Exchange in Canada to 1900*. Toronto and Charlottetown: Dundurn Press, 1984: 211.

Arriving at Percé, Fortin learned of a meeting of those opposed to paying the taxes. Violence could easily have broken out. The meeting took place next day "for the avowed purpose of opposing the imposition of School Rates." At one o'clock Fortin and his armed sailors went to the courthouse to meet about 200 people. They "seemed all very well disposed to listen to me," Fortin, with his armed men beside him, wrote laconically. He spoke to the crowd for two hours, explaining the most important clauses of the school laws. At 3:00 P.M., "I had the satisfaction of seeing the crowd disperse in the most orderly manner." The majority had given up any idea of violent opposition to the school rates.[6]

Four years later the war of the candle snuffers still thrived in Gaspésie. On 4 November 1863 at Gaspé, the school commissioners again called on him to enforce the tax law. He told his constables to arrest many who had refused to pay the tax. Brought before him, they either paid or agreed to make some arrangement. He hoped there would be no more difficulty in the future.[7]

But some fishermen and communities strongly supported education for their children, even at much sacrifice to themselves. When visiting Havre-aux-Maisons in 1859, Fortin wrote that education, so long neglected, was now attracting attention. "The inhabitants spare no exertion nor expense for maintaining the old schools and establishing new ones." Unfortunately, many inhabitants were so poor they could not afford to pay suitable salaries to their school teachers.[8]

In 1860 he visited a Baie-au-Saumon missionary station. Residents and visiting sailors used the two large halls. A school for boys and one for girls also used the halls. Teachers and servants had apartments there. "Such an institution has been long wanted on this part of the coast of Labrador [North Shore] ... where the population [could] furnish thirty or forty children fit for school." He said that nearly fifty Acadian families had settled at Natashquan and Pointe-aux-Esquimaux. He hoped they would open schools and the children learn both French and English. English would be very useful to them "now that they have so much intercourse with the fishermen of Nova Scotia and the United States." Their principal trade was with Halifax.[9]

In the Îles-de-la-Madeleine, he wished one of the teachers at Amherst or Havre-aux-Maisons could instruct his pupils "in the elementary branches of the art of navigation." More than that, in winter the teacher could also instruct fishermen in that "science so useful to them." Fishermen had little else to do in the off season. After a few years of instruction, captains of Gulf fishing vessels "would be competent to cross the seas with their vessels, laden with the proceeds of the fisheries." They could sell their cargoes in foreign countries where they would get best prices.

Since he had first visited the islands, Fortin had seen real "progress and improvement." The island fishermen now had more vessels, and had replaced those of thirty to forty tons by others of sixty to eighty tons. When on the North Shore, they also used equipment manufactured "on more recent and approved patterns" for seal, cod and herring. Some had bought large mackerel and herring seines. But they themselves should be able to cross the Atlantic to the best markets for selling their fish and buying the products they needed. In short, he saw the beginnings of a Quebec merchant marine.

"Consequently," he wrote, "I take the liberty of calling the attention of the Government to that most important subject." He suggested a special grant to the Îles-de-la-Madeleine. School commissioners could then hire a master capable of teaching navigation.[10]

In his report on his 1857 tour, Fortin proposed a "Plan for a School of Navigation on Board *La Canadienne*." Canada, he wrote, had very few sea-going captains. In all of Quebec, no more than eight or ten could navigate a vessel to Europe, the East Indies, Australia, or even the West Indies. Quebec shipbuilders had to send for British mariners to take their vessels overseas for sale, an expensive proceeding. "The captains of Canadian vessels are, with very few exceptions, merely coasting pilots." He again pointed out that Jersey companies dominated the transport of Gulf fish. In the summer, goods from the West Indies traveled to Canada principally in Nova Scotian vessels. In winter they went via American vessels to Portland, Maine, and other ports, and from there by rail. Meanwhile, Canadian vessels lay idle.

As he often does, Fortin now became visionary. This time he lauded the benefits of teaching navigation. Canada, he said, built vessels cheaper than anywhere else. However, hundreds of unemployed men hired on to American vessels fishing in the Gulf. "Why should we not send vessels into all parts of the world?" They could go to the whale fishery; they could take to the market some of our forestry produce; but especially, they could carry our fish overseas. He valued Canadian fish products at more than $600,000 annually. This would require one hundred of our own vessels. These could bring back produce from the West Indies in exchange for Canadian salted and dried fish, salt provisions, wood, and other goods.

To achieve this, he suggested making *La Canadienne* a floating navigational school. A war schooner of that size would carry forty to fifty hands. *La Canadienne*, with a twenty-five man crew, could take at least another twenty students. They would receive less than the regular crewmen, and would lose part of their wages should they not complete a three-year course. A master would teach them the theory and practice of marine navigation, and a boatswain would show them the work and manoeuvres needed on board. His duties in the Gulf, Fortin said, always left him some hours to spare every day. He himself might translate into English or French the lessons in navigation, and might also teach the students arithmetic, trigonometry, astronomy and geography.[11]

The government ignored the suggestions of Fortin, civil servant; but Fortin, member of the Commons, tried again. In 1868, as chairman of a select committee on the fisheries, he recommended establishing schools to teach navigation to Canadian mariners. "Canadian" now, of course, included those from Nova Scotia and New Brunswick. The government apparently took no action.

In 1869 he again chaired the fisheries committee, and moved that its second report be adopted. The report pointed out the difficulty of getting certificates of competency recognized throughout the British dominions. This problem placed shipmasters and officers of the merchant marine of Canada at a disadvantage, which was detrimental to the country's maritime interests.[12]

The disadvantages for Canadians arose from the British Mercantile Marine Act of 1850. After that date, new officers and masters in British foreign-going ships had to pass an examination for a certificate of competency. The problem for Canadians lay in the fact that masters of colonial vessels entering British ports also had to have certificates. Then, in 1869, another British act enabled colonial legislatures to provide their own methods of certification.[13] This led Fortin's committee to make two key recommendations, supported by nineteen petitions from Canadian port authorities. The committee first recommended setting up boards of examiners, similar to those in Britain, in the major ports. They would examine shipmasters and mates, and grant certificates. Second, to help "promote and encourage nautical instruction, Schools of Navigation should also be established in the large Ports, under the supervision of the Boards of Examiners."

In debate, Fortin emphasized that the boards of examiners would lead nowhere unless the government also provided the navigational skills. However, the opposition objected that the motion was not in

Fishermen at Longue-Pointe. From here, Fortin reported in 1859, a storm carried away twenty boats anchored for shelter. (William G.R. Hind/National Archives of Canada/C118617)

order—it involved spending money. The minister of Public Works, Hector Langevin, agreed. But he assured Fortin that "the matter would engage the attention of the government during recess."[14]

Success came in 1870, when the Canadian parliament passed the Masters and Mates Act. Candidates could take their exams in Québec, Halifax and Saint John under the supervision of the Department of Marine and Fisheries. The act also gave the government power to set up schools teaching the theory of navigation.[15]

In 1872 James Ferrier asked in the Senate if arrangements had been made for opening the navigation schools. A government spokesman, Peter Mitchell, replied. Schools were now in operation in Québec and Saint John, with another to be opened in Halifax. Of 109 candidates since last July, eighty-nine had passed as masters and twenty as mates. Anyone who had been a master or mate prior to passage of the act received a competency certificate. Those who had taken the training and passed their exams received a certificate of service. The certificate of service, he said, was equal to the highest British certificate.[16]

When the federal government subsidized the three schools in 1882, it placed them under the direction of William Seaton. Three years later, the two schools of the Maritime provinces showed they could maintain themselves without the federal subsidy. According to Mr. Seaton, they trained enough mariners to command all Canadian ships. The federal government therefore withdrew its subsidy, and the Québec school closed.

This move upset mariners, shipowners and merchants alike. The absence of a Québec school meant that the shipowners had to send to the Maritimes for their officers. "Towards the end of 1877," wrote Seaton, "a large deputation of influential merchants and other interested people went to see the [Quebec] prime minister [Charles-Eugène Boucher de Boucherville. He] at their representations, reestablished the school in 1878."[17]

By 1879 Fortin wanted more. He said in the Commons that while Canada had good schools, the government should introduce the British system of extra masters' certificates. This would show that a master "was a superior man. He was not a mere tradesman, he was a professional man." As such "he ranked among the professions in England." Canadian officers should not occupy a lower level than British.

Fortin insisted on professionalism in all matters concerning the merchant marine. In the same speech, he criticized the harbour commissioners in Québec and Montréal. They were, "in their proper trades and professions, good and clever men." But how could a drygoods merchant, a manufacturer, and a tanner "sit as a Court to judge knowingly, masters, mates or second mates" whose vessels had met with accidents? The commissions should include extra-masters.[18]

The Québec school of navigation remained open, under the auspices of the provincial government, until in July 1883 the province withdrew its $1,000 funding.[19] A request for money then went to the federal government. In the Commons' debate, Fortin received a compliment. Guillaume Amyot said the Québec school of navigation had been established twelve years earlier, "thanks to the intelligent efforts of the gentleman who now represents the county of Gaspé (Mr. Fortin)." A federal grant of $1,000 annually would "pay the salary of a professor, chosen by one of the most competent men, the hon member for Gaspé (Mr Fortin). [He] has always taken such a deep interest in Maritime questions."

In reply, Fortin described how the Québec navigational school had started and how he had urged the government to establish schools at the principal ports of the dominion.[20] By now, however, Fortin's career was nearing its end, his influence fading. The federal government turned down the request for funding.*

---

* Records are not clear, but at some point long after Fortin's death in 1888, the province again changed its mind. Records starting in 1897-98 show a grant of $1,000 a year to the Québec Navigation School. They finish in 1907-08. Quebec, Provincial Secretary's Department, Bureau of Statistics: *Statistical Year Book*, Vol. 1 (1914): 120

Fortin had dreamed of Gulf fishermen importing equipment and supplies and exporting their fish, all in their own vessels. The dream would not come true in his lifetime. Instead, the Company continued to dominate the fishermen of the Gulf until well after his death.

NOTES

1. Ferland, 186.
2. Fortin, *Report*, 1861.
3. Nelson, Wendy. "The 'Guerre des éteignoirs': School Reform and Popular Resistance in Lower Canada, 1841-50." MA thesis, Simon Fraser University, Vancouver, 1989: 70.
4. Fortin, *Report*, 1860: 129.
5. Béchard, 113-19.
6. Fortin, *Report*, 1860: 129.
7. Fortin, *Report*, 1864.
8. Fortin, *Report*, 1860: 128.
9. Fortin, *Report*, 1861.
10. Fortin, *Report*, 1860: 128.
11. Fortin, *Report*, 1858.
12. HOCJ, 15 May 1868, 378; 20, 21 May 1869, 108.
13. Sager, Eric W. *Seafaring Labour: The Merchant Marine of Atlantic Canada*. Montréal and Kingston: McGill-Queen's University Press, 1989: 95.
14. HOCJ, 20, 21 May 1869; 1870, Index: xxxv.
15. Canada, *Acts*, 33 Vic. c.17 (1870), Section 13.
16. Senate, *Debates*, 28 May 1872, 832.
17. QLAD, 1884, 710.
18. HOCD, 31 March 1879, 842.
19. QLAD, 1884, 710.
20. HOCD, 11 February 1884, 200-02.

IX

NATURALIST AND CONSERVATIONIST

Several themes, some contradictory, make up Fortin's attitudes to nature. First is the amateur scientist who catalogued many species of fish found in Gulf waters. As early as 1866, F.W.G. Austen praised Commander Fortin: he "has largely contributed to the cause of science by describing and classifying over sixty species of the fish of the Gulf."[1] Théodore Gill, a contemporary naturalist, credited the work of Fortin, among others, in developing his own taxonomy of Gulf fishes.[2] A later scientist, A.G. Huntsman, said that Canada owed a debt to Fortin's annual statistics on the fish.[3] And as recently as 1987, Aliette Geistdoerfer refers to Fortin throughout her work on the fisheries and fishermen of the Îles-de-la-Madeleine.[4]

Six important publications cataloguing Canadian fishes preceded Fortin's, but only four of them directly overlapped his work in the Gulf.[5] The first was J.R. Forster's *Catalogue of the Animals of North America*, published in 1771. Then came J. Richardson's *Fauna Boreali-Americana, Part 3–Fishes* (1836), Moses Henry Perley's *Reports of the sea and river fisheries of New Brunswick* (1852), and T.N. Gill's *Catalogue of the fishes of the eastern coast of North America from Greenland to Georgia* (1862). The last was published the year that Fortin began his catalogue. Fortin's *Reports* for the 1862-64 cruises were the first to concentrate on the Gulf.

For the non-specialist reader, the English version of Fortin's work uses colourful but sometimes ponderous prose. "The Angler has a still more repulsive aspect than the Bull-Head and is easily known by its enormously wide and depressed head, [and] by its mouth, armed with very large and sharp teeth.... The stomach of this fish is very large and its appetite is most voracious. It is generally crouched close to the bottom, buried in the sand.... [It] draws towards itself with [an appendage on its head] the fish which it does not fail to catch with its mouth. It generally feeds on fish, mollusca and crustacea.... The ordinary size of the Angler is from three to four feet."[6]

Dr. E.J. Crossman of the University of Toronto and the Royal Ontario Museum reviewed a number of Fortin's papers. He found some errors or obscurities. He writes:

There are the usual problems with the accounts, reading them today. For example, the blackspotted stickleback, *Gasterosteus wheatlandi* (Putnam 1866) was described only two years after Fortin's 1864 paper. As a consequence, we cannot be certain if Fortin's *Gasterotus biaculeatus* is that species or the common three spine stickleback, *Gasterosteus aculeatus*. Both species occur at the Magdalen Islands and his description is not adequate to determine definitely which species he had in hand, or had heard about.

Of the muskellunge, Fortin said fishermen on the Labrador coast sometimes caught them in their nets. Dr. Crossman says that the species has never occurred much further northeast than Trois-Rivières.* After pointing out confusion in the work between chain pickerel and pike or northern pike, he adds:

As was common at that time, he [Fortin] published information given him by others without the level of concern for accuracy that would be exerted today. He suggests that the pike sometimes appear in the sea. That occurs only in the Baltic Sea, and only when fresh water is layered over the lower salt water. Pike have a very low tolerance for salinity. None of this is intended as criticism of his work. Little enough was available at that time on Canadian fishes and he was a leader in making available information derived from what must have been not only his official function but also an interest of his.[7]

In his days on *La Canadienne*, Fortin also collected and mounted many birds of the Gulf. He willed the collection to Laval University.[8]

---

* Fortin sometimes seems to use the term "Labrador coast" to describe what is now often called the Lower North Shore. But it is very unlikely this usage could be stretched to include Trois-Rivières.

On 15 December 1877 a number of leading Quebecers, meeting in the library of the Quebec Assembly, decided to found the Geographical Society of Quebec. Fortin had called the meeting. "There you are gentleman," he told those present, "the aims of the geographical society: to understand, to study, to protect our natural riches and to encourage their exploration for ... colonization and commerce."[9] The members elected him president. This was a conspicuous honour, because members included many of the best minds in Quebec. Later, in the House of Commons, he spoke to his bill to incorporate the society. Some members objected that the matter properly belonged in the Quebec Assembly. The society's interest, Fortin replied, "did not confine itself exclusively to the geography of the Province," but "embraced the whole country and the whole world."[10] The bill passed and the Society functioned until 1939. In its first year, Fortin chaired an ambitious conference with the title, "The progress of geography and of geographical science since the earliest times until the discovery of America."[11]

When he was speaker of the Quebec Assembly, Fortin much expanded the parliamentary library. He secured many maps from the United States, France, Belgium, Norway, and several British colonies; the British Admiralty contributed more, and the French government donated some 500 books.[12] Unfortunately, the Quebec fire of 1883 destroyed the parliament building including the library.[13]

Fortin's love for the Gulf animals went much further than cataloguing and collecting them. He well knew the devastation man caused. Greenland whales, "so gentle by nature," were timid and slow. Whalers had pursued them so successfully that they no longer saw them in the Gulf or even on the Atlantic coasts. While on the North Shore, he wrote, "In accordance with a general law of nature, all animals, both great and small, which man has not succeeded in domesticating ... invariably fly at his approach." They flee to distant regions, hoping to find "an impenetrable asylum" from man's attacks. The walrus* was a good example. Although the first European visitors had found the animal "in vast numbers in many parts of the Gulf," it completely disappeared within less than 250 years. "It has taken refuge in the polar seas and the unfrequented coast of Hudson Bay."

Seals too, he went on, had abandoned much of the Gulf shores. When Europeans first arrived, seals ascended the St. Lawrence as far as Québec. Archeologists had in many places found remains of the fur-

---

* The report says "porpoise" but the text shows Fortin means "walrus."

naces used to boil down their fat for oil. Fortin felt that the seals would not leave the Gulf altogether, but their periodic migrations would take them far from the coast. This would rob some Canadian fishermen of part of their livelihood.[14]

The salmon was king of all fish according to Fortin, and his own primary duty lay in preserving Gulf stocks. While in Chaleur Bay in mid-October 1860, he wrote, "The taking of salmon on the spawning ground is an act more to be condemned and punished than all others." The fish was destroyed when its flesh was unwholesome. Worse, "thousands and hundreds of thousands of young fish are also destroyed." They would have hatched the following spring. Destroy the spawning grounds, and the salmon would speedily disappear.[15]

Fortin's report for 1859 shows him translating beliefs into action.

11-15 June: *La Canadienne* visits salmon and trout fishing posts on the Gaspésie rivers. Fortin checks that nets are set at not less than the regulation 200-yard intervals. He issues licences to each station, charging the highest prices at river mouths, lower prices upstream. He fixes the upper and lower limits of each station to avoid disputes.

25 June: "Anchored at the Moisie River" on the North Shore. He makes fourteen fishermen remove their illegal salmon nets.

13 July: "Anchored at Coacoacho Bay." He warns Joseph Aubé not to fish with an illegal weir.

October: At Port Daniel he visits a milldam on the South-West River. It is not more than four or five feet high, so that the salmon can ascend it but only with difficulty. He warns Mr. Bréaux that he is breaking the law and Bréaux promises to build a fishway. A dam on the North-West River is only eighteen inches high, and the salmon can easily ascend it.[16]

In his desire to protect this magnificent fish, Fortin stood in a long tradition. In 1215 Magna Carta gave a public right to fish for salmon in some areas belonging to the king. The Statute of Westminster of 1285, which codified much English law, established salmon-fishing seasons and listed punishments for poaching. The Scots in 1318 required operators of milldams to leave openings for smolts to pass.

Before the Europeans came, native people of the Gulf coasts caught salmon with nets in weirs. At night they used spears by the light of torches. Historians agree they did not catch enough fish to threaten the stocks. They may even have helped conserve the stock by reducing overcrowding on the spawning beds.[17] But by 1800 Micmac and Innu, early Europeans and Loyalists were all heavily fishing the Gulf rivers, and they had heavily depleted the stocks.

An 1807 Lower Canadian act made it illegal to drift net or to set nets for salmon above the first rapids on both the Ristigouche and Grand Cascapédia rivers. From August to November only Micmac could fish, and only to feed their families. The act also had an early environmental clause. "No ballast or anything else injurious to the rivers harbours or roads within the district of Gaspé shall be thrown out of any vessels."[18] Most ships ignored the prohibitions. In 1822 a legislative committee recommended that the Gaspé regulations be amended "to prevent the wasteful and unncessary destruction of fish, particularly of salmon."[19] The next major act, in 1824, tried to implement that policy. It allowed Micmac to spear salmon in daytime for their own use, but outlawed torchlight fishing and the diversion of salmon into nets.[20]

The problem for salmon lay not just in overfishing. They also suffered from river pollution and destruction of their spawning beds. In 1842 a Lower Canadian act forbade obstructing rivers with slabs, bark, wastes and other refuse from sawmills. However, it excluded sawdust, one of the worst offending substances.[21]

By 1850 overfishing was reaching crisis levels. Despite the law, nets stretched across rivers, milldams cut fish off from spawning grounds, and sawmills clogged rivers with lumber and sawdust. On the Ristigouche and its tributaries, clear cutting by foresters damaged the watersheds, and horse drawn scows destroyed spawning beds.[22] The battle over sawdust would continue until the early 1900s.[23]

Fortin helped draft the first general fisheries act for Lower Canada. Because of present practices, said the 1855 act, "It is expedient to provide against the destruction of Salmon, Maskinonge, and Trout fisheries in Lower Canada." Clauses outlawed killing fish during the spawning season, and taking them with stake or barrier nets, or by the aid of artificial lights at night. It set the minimum salmon net mesh size at two inches in diameter. The season would run from 1 February to 30 September. Although spearing as such remained legal, the act again outlawed torchlight fishing. The fine for each contravention was £2.10s.[24]

Sweeping new fisheries acts in 1857 and 1858 appointed a superintendent of fisheries for each of Upper and Lower Canada, with two overseers reporting to each superintendent. In Lower Canada, one overseer was responsible for freshwater fishing, the other for saltwater. A new system of leases and licences required permits for salmon fishing. The season ran from 1 March to 31 July for netting salmon, with an extension to 31 August for fly fishing. The act banned fishing by torchlight and fishing at salmon leaps or spawning pools. Salmon net meshes had to be no less than five inches. The act also outlawed nets that blocked salmon on their way to the spawning grounds. Dam owners had to provide fishways for salmon to swim through. Magistrates could "convict upon view" for offences.[25]

Before 1857 justices of the peace and local authorities had done little to enforce weak regulations despite warning signs.[26] Even after the stronger Canadian laws, competing jurisdictions were a problem. One bank of the Ristigouche, for example, fell under Canada, the other under New Brunswick. In 1859 on the Ristigouche, Fortin found Micmac illegally selling salmon speared by torchlight. Increasing settlement also threatened the fish. He wrote that the governments of Canada and New Brunswick should appoint a mixed commission with authority over all of the Ristigouche River. Until they did, "I fear much that it will be impossible to prevent the total extinction of the Salmon in those rivers formerly so full of fish."[27]

Two years later he found no offences on the Canadian side of the river, but on the New Brunswick side, white men and Micmac often violated fishery regulations. There, the legislature had enacted more stringent laws. Owing to some defect in drafting, however, the lieutenant-governor did not sanction them, so they could not be enforced. Magistrates in Dalhousie and Campbellton had appointed overseers, but not enough. Fortin hoped that proposed new clauses would soon complete the "assimilation" of the New Brunswick regulations with those of Canada.[28]

Fortin loved the salmon above all other fish, but he did not panic in taking measures to preserve them. In 1864 he reported seeing many beluga whales near the inner shore of Chaleur Bay. Because belugas fed on salmon, most fishermen believed they must badly injure the fisheries. They wanted the belugas killed, but could not pressure Fortin into hasty action. "I think we must await the experience of a few years more before committing ourselves to this opinion," he wrote. He wanted to verify the habits, especially the eating habits, of the belugas because the previous year he had seen just as many at the mouth of the Ristigouche River. Yet "It was not found that the salmon fishing was diminished in any remarkable degree."[29]

Fortin also warned about whales generally disappearing. Gulf species included beluga, minke whale, fin whale, blue whale and harbour porpoise. Occasionally, killer whales and humpback whales appeared. A contemporary of Fortin once reported seeing the lower St. Lawrence "white" with whales. They travelled in a school twelve miles broad,[30] but their numbers were now falling.

In July 1863 off Bonne-Esperance harbour, *La Canadienne* saw a boat under Captain Suddard chasing twenty whales. After a day's chase, they harpooned a middle-sized humpback. Captain Suddard then killed three more animals. They supplied only 1,440 gallons of oil. Six other whalers from Gaspé had been hardly more successful: one had 3,600 gallons of oil, another 2,400, and a third 2,100. The best time for whaling was finished and they did not expect to do much more till the season's end in early September.

To be productive, said Fortin, each boat should return with 5,000 to 6,000 gallons of oil. The hunt's failure was very important to the Gaspésie economy. He attributed it mainly to fewer whales frequenting the shoals in the Strait of Belle Isle. Whalemen seldom now met more than thirty or forty whales, and most of them were too lean to furnish much oil. Fortin concluded that the feeding grounds lacked prawns, usually very abundant. You can imagine, he said, "the enormous quantity of food required to satisfy their voracious appetites."[31]

Fortin protested American whale hunting with the Congreve rocket gun. This rocket killed the animal immediately by exploding inside it, but the body often sank before whalers could secure it. He claimed Americans slaughtered thirty to forty animals each year in this way, with only six to eight secured. Canadians, who used the older harpoon, secured most of the whales they hit.[32]

Pollution was growing in the Gulf, mainly through offal and ballast released by fishing vessels. A very limited 1841 act to regulate pollution had only prohibited the discharge of ballast or anything that would damage the rivers, harbours or roads of Gaspésie.[33] An 1857 act was more comprehensive. It too prohibited dumping ballast and fish offal in coastal waters and on fishing banks, but also provided that nets should neither impede navigation nor hinder fish on their way to the spawning beds.[34] Next year a strengthened act included minimum mesh sizes for cod nets.[35]

In his report for 1859, Fortin records how he enforced the regulations. The Innu names of the settlements he visits sweep like thunder around the Lower North Shore coast.

6 July: "Anchored at Natashquhan harbour." He issues salmon licences and settles a dispute between two schooner captains, one an American. He warns American schooners not to throw offal in the harbour, giving them copies of the fishing regulations.

9 July: "Anchored at Rekasca" again checking fishing nets.

10 July: "Anchored at Washeecootai Bay" visiting six American and five British schooners to check their nets and warn against pollution. Similarly at Coacoacho, Wapitigun, Etamamiou and Rivière du Gros Mécatina.[36]

Too often, however, he was unsuccessful in punishing the polluters. On 16 May 1859 he arrived at Amherst in the Îles-de-la-Madeleine. The harbour was narrow and shallow, its entrance only nine feet deep, and jammed with visiting schooners. Many vessels had jettisoned their ballast, but he could not find the culprits.

The 1840s saw several pieces of Canadian legislation that tried to conserve wildlife other than fish, but they usually applied only locally. One in 1843 forbade killing deer from 1 February to 31 July. It also regulated fishing for muskellunge in Memphrémagog and other lakes of the Eastern Townships.[37] Another in 1845 protected wild swans, geese, ducks, and other game birds during the breeding season, and outlawed snares or night hunting for quail and grouse.[38] An 1846 act made "stricter provision" for preventing the destruction of certain species of wild fowl in l'Îlet county.[39] In 1849 an act banned the use of strychnine and other poisons for destroying wild animals, since these poisons had been killing domestic animals "in great numbers."[40] An 1851 act set dates for spring and fall hunting seasons in Kamouraska county and forbade "destruction or carrying away of the eggs of any species of wild fowl" in Lower Canada.[41]

In a much stronger act in 1858, "two very important clauses ... were, at my suggestion, inserted," wrote Fortin. A stipendiary magistrate could now impose a fine of not less than $20 and not more than $100, plus costs, or imprisonment for two to four months. The vessel of someone convicted of robbing nests was forfeit. A magistrate could proceed summarily on the evidence of at least one credible witness, or by his own witness if he renounced all claim to a share in the penalty.[42]

As far back as Cartier, half-starved fishermen from Europe had used the eggs and flesh of seabirds for food and bait. By Fortin's time, the great auk, giant cousin of the razorbill, had long been extinct. Fishermen had decimated the terns, gannets, and even gulls. From six to eight schooners fitted out each season in Nova Scotia and came after the eggs in the Gulf. "Their great size, their excellent flavor and above all their peculiar color," made the eggs valuable. In the ports of Nova Scotia, and even in Boston, they brought "a very high price" of twenty to fifty cents a dozen. As well, the people of the North Shore used them for food.

The birders would land on the islands and smash all the eggs under their boots, then return when a second lot of eggs were laid. That ensured fresh eggs for them to collect, but it also ensured the birds would not produce a third batch of eggs that season. Originally, said Fortin, the huge flocks made the drop in numbers hardly perceptible.

However, these destructive proceedings were unceasingly and systematically carried on, and the birds pursued from island to island, and even to their most secret retreats which they had selected in order to save their precious brood from the covetous hand of man.... At length they disappeared from some of the islets from which the eggs were most easily removed, while on the others, their numbers had fallen off to an alarming degree. And thus the attention of the public was directed to the matter.

The measures he adopted, wrote Fortin, reduced the number of birding schooners to two or three. However, these "hid themselves so well amid the thousand islands, islets and rocks that stud the Labrador [North Shore] coast" that he could not easily find them. Or else they reached the coast in early spring and "hastened to depart so soon as they heard I was about to make my appearance." Still, each year he learned a little more about them. "Sooner or later, some of them were destined to fall into my hands."[43]

As early as 1852 Fortin had complained that foreigners were landing on small islands in the spring to raid the nests for the eggs of penguins and small divers. Two years later he left six men on the Îles aux Marmettes and at the Rivière du Gros-Mécatina to protect gull and gannet eggs. In 1859 at Wapitigun, Fortin visited the Rivière Étamamiou. He suspected six schooners of "purloining the puffins' eggs and gulls' eggs on Bird Island [Île aux Oiseaux] ... but one of my officers, Captain Bernier, whom I sent on board, found no signs of it." A schooner had earlier taken eggs for sale in Halifax.[44]

Often though, the commander had more success. In July 1865 *La Canadienne* visited the North Shore. Fortin heard that men on the Murre Islands [Îles aux Marmettes] were collecting the eggs of murres and penguins. Next day, sure enough, he found three men there gathering eggs. They were part of the crew of a schooner, the *Ocean Bride*, Alexander Myers master, of Halifax. The men were living in a hut on one of the rocks, and in three weeks had already collected 250 dozen eggs. "Their guilt was clear.... Nothing therefore remained for me to do but to inflict the punishment prescribed by law in such cases." He fined each $20 or, in default, two months imprisonment. Because they could not pay, he took them on board *La Canadienne* for transport to the jail at Amherst.

This action was but the start. That afternoon he hunted down the *Ocean Bride* itself, at anchor in Eggman Harbour. He found the hold half full of penguins' and murres' eggs, some 914 dozen. The captain and his two men pleaded guilty to violating the game laws. Fortin applied the law "in a summary manner," fining the three men $20 each, and confiscating the schooner with everything in it. As the men had no money to pay their fine, he took them on *La Canadienne.* They too were bound for two months in the Amherst jail. Fortin gave command of the *Ocean Bride* to the lieutenant of *La Canadienne*, Moise LeBlanc. With another man and a boy to help him, LeBlanc took the prize safely into Gaspé Basin.

Fortin also visited the Îles aux Oies and found a local man carrying off penguins' and murres' eggs. "I summarily condemned the individual to a fine of $20 and also confiscated his boat. The fine was paid the next day." Meanwhile, the *Ocean Bride* had left three more men on Boat Island [Île la Barque], and a few days later Fortin arrested them. They had collected 780 dozen eggs. On the 24th he found the last of the crew of the *Ocean Bride* at Studdard's Harbour [Havre Studdard] with 600 dozen eggs. None could pay the fine.

With eleven prisoners on board, Fortin now decided to leave the North Shore and take them to the jail at Amherst. Unfortunately, many eggs broke during the transshipments; "a far larger number" went bad in the hold of the *Ocean Bride*; while they left behind many eggs that had already turned. Out of the 2,000 and some hundreds of dozen eggs he had confiscated, only 1,650 were edible. At Gaspé in August Fortin sold the *Ocean Bride,* and also the eggs at fourpence a dozen. He adds, "A barrel or two, which were more or less good, remained over. I kept them on board." He does not say if they wound up on the crew's menu.[45]

After Fortin's election to the House of Commons and the Quebec Assembly, his bird-conservation work continued. He asked the Quebec government to print copies of an act protecting insect-eating birds helpful to agriculture, and proposed distributing the copies as an educational tool. The speaker ruled him out of order because it involved public expenditure. Again, in the Assembly he argued for stronger action to protect the eggs of nesting seabirds. Fishermen, he said, were still raiding the nests, and they seriously threatened the birds' future.[46] But for all his efforts, the slaughter continued.

NOTES

1. Austen, F.W.G. "Some of the Fishes of the St Lawrence," *Literary and Historical Society of Quebec: Transactions* (Québec). New series, parts 4 and 5 (1865-66): 103-20.
2. Gill, Théodore. "Synopsis of the Fishes of the the Gulf of St. Lawrence and the Bay of Fundy," *Canadian Naturalist and Quarterly Journal of Science* (Montréal). New series, vol. 2 (1865): 244-66.
3. Préfontaine, Georges. "Connaissance scientifique et pêcheries." *Actualité économique* (Montréal). Vol. 21, No. 2 (1945-46): 233-37.
4. Geistdoerfer, *passim*.
5. Scott, W.B. and Crossman, E.J. *Freshwater Fishes of Canada*. Bulletin 184. Ottawa: Fisheries Research Board of Canada, 1973: 11.
6. Fortin, *Report*, 1864.
7. Crossman, E.J., personal communication, 15 May 1996.
8. Potvin, *Le roi*, 110.
9. Morissonneau, Christian. *La Société de géographie de Québec*. Québec: Les Presses de l'université Laval, 1971: 26.
10. HOCD, 27 March 1878, 740-41.
11. Morissonneau, 40.
12. Hamelin, Marcel. *Les premières années du parliamentarisme québécois (1867-1878)*. Québec: Les Presses de l'université Laval, 1974: 334.
13. Potvin, *Le roi*, 118.
14. Fortin, *Report*, 1865: 51.
15. Fortin, *Report*, 1861.
16. Fortin, *Report*, 1860: 124.
17. Dunfield, 3, 15, 17.
18. Lower Canada, *Acts*, 47 Geo. III c.12 (1807).
19. "Special Committee ... (on) the Bill for the Better Regulation of Fisheries in the Inferior District of Gaspé," Lower Canada, House of Assembly, *Journals*, 1823.
20. Chambers, 138.
21. PCA, 6 Vic. c.17 (1842).
22. Dunfield, 125.
23. Gillis, Peter. "Pollution," *Journal of Canadian Studies* (Peterborough), Vol. 21 No. 1 (spring 1986): 84-103.
24. PCA, 18 Vic. c.114 (1855).
25. PCA, 20 Vic. c.21 (1857); 22 Vic. c.86 (1858); 21, 22 Vic. c.86 (1858).
26. Hodgetts, 143
27. Fortin, *Report*, 1860: 120.

28. Fortin, *Report*, 1862.
29. Fortin, *Report*, 1865: 7-8.
30. Hind, Henry. *Explorations in the Interior of the Labrador Peninsula.* 2 volumes. London: Longman, Green, Longman, Roberts and Green, 1863. Vol. 2: 91.
31. Fortin, *Report*, 1864.
32. Fortin, *Report*, 1857.
33. PCA, 4 and 5 Vic. c.36 (1841).
34. PCA, 20 Vic. c.21 (1857).
35. PCA, 21, 22 Vic. c.86 (1858).
36. Fortin, *Report*, 1860: 131, 114-16.
37. PCA, 7 Vic. c.12-13 (1843).
38. PCA, 8 Vic. c.46 (1844-45).
39. PCA, 9 Vic. c.76 (1846).
40. PCA, 12 Vic. c.60 (1849).
41. PCA, 14 and 15 Vic. c.107 (1851).
42. PCA, 21, 22 Vic. c.103 (1858).
43. Fortin, *Report*, 1866: 34.
44. Fortin, *Report*, 1860: 116.
45. Fortin, *Report*, 1866: 15-20.
46. QLAD, 1 April 1869, 232; 12 February 1868, 135.

X

CONSERVATION *VERSUS* JOBS

Fortin was a conservationist in that he tried to conserve the Gulf's wildlife, but his purpose involved little mysticism or animal-rights activism. Rather, he wished to conserve the God-given fish and animals for the welfare of future generations of fishermen and hunters. In today's terms, he believed in sustainable development, not in animal rights. Of the Gulf cod fisheries he wrote in 1862:

Must we not in viewing this abundant harvest, collected in so short a period and in so large a field of such fertility, and which is produced without any outlay, must we not, I say, thank Providence which provides with so generous a hand a supply for the numerous and continuous wants of man. What an immense quantity of alimentary substance is contained in these 408,000 codfish taken in thirty-four days by sixty-six men. And what a noble provision they form when dried in the sun by a process as simple as it is easy.... What wealth, and what a fine and unceasing resource for our Canada, which possesses this large extent of sea shores, abounding every year with innumerable shoals of such fine varieties of fish.[1]

Salmon were the aristocrats of Gulf fish, but cod provided the economic base for the Gulf people. Before 1500, Portuguese and Basques had crossed the Atlantic to the Grand Banks for cod. At times fish were so thick, feeding on plentiful stocks of mackerel, herring and caplin, that men could net them from the shore. Basques remained active in the Gulf till the late 1500s, but the English and French increasingly dominated thereafter.

Despite efforts from Champlain onwards to promote Gulf fishing, it remained a minor occupation in New France. The habitants preferred fur trading or farming. Jean Talon, the famous intendant, wrote, "Confronted with such riches [in fish], they behave as if they were paralytic."[2] The French set up a few small fishing stations on the North Shore in the 1600s. In the next century they were more active in Chaleur Bay and on the North Shore, including Baie de Brador, Rivière Étamamiou, and Rivière du Petit Mécatina. Soon after the Treaty of Paris gave New France to Britain, the Channel Islanders came to Chaleur Bay.

In Fortin's time, few saw any damage to what seemed inexhaustible Atlantic fish stocks. However, in 1864 George Perkins Marsh published his book *Man and Nature*. Using Newfoundland as an example, he wrote that man, unlike other predators, "angles today that he may dine tomorrow," and warned of potential devastation of fish stocks through waste. "Man's fisheries are so organised as to involve the destruction of many more fish than are secured for human use."[3]

Fortin expressed contradictory views on the possibility of exhausting Gulf fish stocks. In 1855 he complained that foreign fishermen were using seines up to 100 fathoms long and ten fathoms deep. One haul could catch enough fish to fill 2,000 barrels. In all, they filled some 50,000 barrels in a season.[4] Years later, in 1880, he argued in the Commons that Canada must protect its fisheries. American fishing methods would destroy the cod and other fish on the banks. He said he had demonstrated the previous year that many Canadian fishing banks were already half ruined. If Canada permitted Americans to use their present fishing techniques, half the current fish production would disappear in ten years. He hoped legislation would "protect our people against the greed of American fishermen and against their destructive fishery appliances." These had made fortunes for them while destroying Canadian fisheries.[5]

He held this view of foreigners. For his own Gulf fishermen, Fortin had very different ideas. The 1864 select committee on the fisheries heard some witnesses argue for regulations to stop fishermen taking cod, mackerel and herring when they came to the banks to spawn. This, they said, would conserve fish. Fortin opposed the view. Canadian fishermen should be allowed to catch saltwater fish whenever it was practical to do so. That was best done when they came onto the banks to spawn. "It is well known," he argued, "that a female herring contains within its ovaries several million (six million) of eggs. A female cod, almost as many, and even more, according to some naturalists." With so many eggs, "even though only one tenth, even one hundredth, even one thousandth part of them were to reach maturity, it is impossible that these highly valuable fish should become extinct." If ten female cod or herring in the Gulf had the usual number of eggs, he went on, if all the eggs hatched, and if all the fish reached adulthood, "then the ten female fish would alone suffice to restock the Gulf" even with full fishing.[6] Fortin himself must have realized the speciousness of this argument. Only a small minority of eggs hatch, and still fewer reach adulthood. Under the conditions he describes, the cod would be, in effect, extinct.

In these contradictory arguments Fortin set a pair of conflicting goals. Yes, he wanted to conserve the fish, but he also wanted to ensure the livelihood of the Gulf people. The best way to protect the fish stocks was to keep out the hundreds of foreign schooners, especially American, each of which had ten to thirty fishermen. The less destructive Canadians, fishing inshore, singly or in pairs, should be allowed to do so whenever the season was best for them.

As with cod, so with seals. Fortin saw "the generous hand of Providence" in the seal harvest on the North Shore and the Îles-de-la-Madeleine. In 1856, for example, five schooners from the North Shore, employing forty-nine men, took 3,330 seals on the icefields off Tête-à-la-Vâche.[7] The same year, twenty-one schooners from the islands took 4,923 seals on ice to the west of the Amherst harbour. The next year, nineteen schooners took nearly 6,000. This increase came when northerly winds on 24 March drove large icefields against the western coast of Amherst Island. Sealers killed about 4,000 young seals in three to four days. The winds drove more floating ice, covered with young seals, onto the north shore of Île-du-Cap-aux-Meules. In spite of the hunt's dangers, people of the area "hastened to profit of this splendid harvest Providence had given them." Fortin estimated that some 280 fishermen in the Îles-de-la-Madeleine killed the 6,000 animals worth more than $20,000. The rewards were rich, the dangers real. "A schooner belonging to that fleet, and quite new, was literally cut to pieces by the ice off Sydney."[8]

Fortin's desire to create jobs did not always imply an assault on existing species. He began one of the earliest Canadian attempts at fish, or more precisely oyster, farming. A clause in the 1858 fisheries act[9] flowed from recommendations Fortin had made in his report for that year.[10] It authorized £150 a year for three years to form oyster beds in suitable bays around the coast, and laid down penalties for anyone disturbing the beds. The practice of transplanting oysters to artificial ponds was not new. Fortin himself wrote in his report for 1858: "It is said that a Roman, named Sergius Orator, was the inventor of artificial oyster beds and Licinius Crassus was engaged in the cultivation of oyster beds, not only for his own use, but for the sake of the great profits they yielded." The conservationist writer, George P. Marsh, in 1864 described an oyster transplantation that had "recently succeeded well on a large scale in the open sea on the French coast."[11] Six years before Marsh's book appeared, Fortin became a pioneer in this new branch of the fisheries.

On 29 September 1859 *La Canadienne* entered Caraquet Harbour, N.B., opposite New Carlisle. Captain Bernier went to the banks and picked sixty barrels of oysters from the Caraquet beds. The boatswain went to the Bay of St. Simon, fifteen miles to the east, to buy more oysters. Fortin instructed both men to get only freshly picked shellfish. The oysters had to have "all their strength, and not been exposed to any accidents affecting their vitality." If the shell was injured, he explained, the oyster loses the liquor in its shell which it needs for respiration.

To preserve his stock, Fortin had to deliver them quickly to the new beds. Calms and contrary winds delayed the St. Simon oysters arriving. Only on 3 October, at 7:00P.M. did *La Canadienne* set out for New Richmond. A northwest gale delayed the vessel again and it did not anchor at New Richmond until 5:00P.M., two days later. After surveying the bay at Cascapédia, Fortin laid the oysters opposite the entrance of the Rivière Cascapédia. The beds had a muddy bottom, four to eight feet deep at low tide, and were well sheltered against the sea breeze. Despite a strong northwesterly, rain and hail, Fortin's crew deposited most of the oysters on the bank. The night of the 8th was calm and clear. In "splendid moonlight" that was almost "broad daylight," *La Canadienne*'s boats glided over a shoal "about four acres in length by three-fourths of an acre in width." The water was salt except during the spring and fall freshets, when it was brackish. There they laid the remaining oysters.

Fortin returned to Caraquet on 13 October and this time himself supervised the oyster collection. One hundred men in fifty barges worked in the beds. By 1P.M., the boats had a full cargo of 193 barrels. Again *La Canadienne* lay becalmed. The schooner reached Gaspé Basin on 16 October. Next day, after a careful survey of the basin, the crew began depositing the oysters. The bottoms chosen were "formed of mud of a certain consistency. [They] resemble very much the Caraquet oyster beds." The basin sheltered them well and water five to fifteen feet deep covered them. Fortin laid two beds. The first had eighty barrels of oysters, the second seventy. On 28 October at Basque Harbour, he laid the remaining forty barrels on the south side of the central channel.[12]

Two years later, he returned to take on 300 more barrels of Caraquet oysters, and he laid these at Gaspé. He also dredged up eighty oysters from the beds laid in 1859. Of these, one-quarter were living and in the best possible condition. They were fat, white and very fresh, he said, and lacked nothing of the delicate taste of the Caraquet oysters. "Far from it. We who tasted them (some of the principal people of Gaspé Basin and myself) found that they were, if not superior, at least equal to any other oysters. They seemed to have increased in size." On a second visit, out of forty oysters fished up, eighteen were living. "We fancied we saw small oysters on many." That meant the oysters had reproduced, even if on a small scale.

Fortin used ingenious experiments to help reproduction. Since currents carried off much of the spat (free-swimming larval oysters), he covered some beds with small branches of birch, held to the bottom with small stones. The spat would attach itself to the birch by the "viscid matter which encloses it at this period of its existence."[13]

For all Fortin's care, his oysters did not take permanently. Dr. René Lavoie, of the Department of Fisheries and Oceans, is a specialist on the Caraquet oyster. Of the Cascapédia transplants, Dr. Lavoie writes that, based on Fortin's notes, he had "laid his oysters on good bottom, under water depths sufficient to avoid ice damage. He moved enough oysters to create a critical mass sufficient to start a new oyster population, assuming suitable ecological conditions in the receiving areas." However, the oysters did not spawn, probably because water temperatures did not reach the critical threshold of 20°C.

The outcome of the transplants off Gaspé pose a greater problem. By Fortin's account, he had surveyed the bottom and carefully selected two beds similar to those at Caraquet. If the bottom and other conditions were as described by Fortin, then according to Dr. Lavoie, a loss of around 80 percent of the oysters after two years could well have been be due to predators, possibly starfish.[14] However, again in Dr. Lavoie's words, suitable ecological conditions in the receiving areas must be assumed. The puzzle arises here. Théophile Têtu, who succeeded Fortin as fisheries officer, searched the Gaspé beds in 1867. He wrote that the oysters had been "planted with all possible care, and according to the latest and most generally adopted European method." Fortin and "some of the principal people of Gaspé Basin" in 1861 had found the Gaspé oysters to be excellent. But Têtu found only some shells filled with mud and "covered with black mussels (*Mytilus aedulis*) ... but not a single live oyster." At the Caraquet beds, he went on, he had never seen so much mud on the fishermen's rakes as he saw on the rakes at Gaspé. "And this mud was black and stinking and seemed to me to be different from that at Caraquet. But after all, it may well be that the death of the oysters at Gaspé is due to other causes."[15]

Fortin was a careful, methodical man. He wrote that he had made "a careful survey of the whole basin." Then he deposited the oysters on the best beds "formed of a mud of a certain consistency, resembl(ing) very much the Caraquet oyster beds." We can be sure he did not mean "black and stinking mud." Nor did he find such mud in 1861. There are two possible explanations. Between 1859 and 1867, the bottom may have changed. Or perhaps Têtu searched in the wrong place. Either explanation is feasible. Dr. Lavoie says that in tidal bays such as this, the bottom often grades from sand into a more fluffy sand and then into thicker and thicker mud. The borders of these gradations follow the shoreline and can change over time. It would, therefore, be easy for Têtu to have searched in the wrong place, below the beds. Or he may have searched in the right place, but after the banks had shifted.

Regardless of the outcome of Fortin's experiments, Dr. Lavoie feels that transplanting the oysters was a feasible project then; it possibly remains so today, with potential economic benefits to Gaspésie. He writes that an astute grower in Cascapédia could turn the "cold water" disadvantage into an advantage. "Oysters grown in these conditions in clean waters would be in prime condition for market at the height of the tourism season when New Brunswick, Nova Scotia and P.E.I. oysters are not fit to eat due to the depleted body condition consecutive to reproduction." He adds, "New Brunswick growers would have an assured market for their seed oysters. Quebec growers would have a new opportunity to add a tourist attraction to the Gaspé coast, and a source of income through exports to well established markets in Quebec and Ontario."[16] In short, Fortin was once again ahead of his time.

In the Quebec Assembly, Fortin showed that his interest in the Gulf went beyond its waters, to the surrounding forests. Again he faced the tension of environment versus jobs. In March 1869 he called for government correspondence on bush fires that had swept the coastal forests in 1867 and 1868. They had consumed a North Shore forest he described as some thirty to forty miles long and fifteen to twenty miles wide, and had also destroyed several fishing posts. Fortin blamed "the criminal negligence of people from these establishments." Another fire near Cap Chat had caused immense destruction to forests and crops. Fortin was glad the new municipal code gave municipalities the right to fix the times when colonists could burn.[17] A committee, set up on Fortin's motion to study the fires, made him chairman. On 16 March the Assembly adopted its report.[18]

The following year, Fortin protested a grant of 1.5 million acres of forest land to build the thirty-mile-long Piles railroad. Government policy, he said, should be to protect our forests, the major source of our revenue. Forests still covered about one hundred million acres. However, we were already consuming one million acres annually. Fires consumed another seven or eight million. We also had to deduct the immense areas held privately by land owners. Thinking of all this makes one "tremble for the future." To this argument, Joseph-Adolphe Chapleau (Terrebonne) replied:

The forests have made the deputy from Gaspé (Fortin) chronically ill. Each year, he never ceases to cry about the end of the forests lost to fire and other things. He has a quite paternal or natural tenderness for the forests. He wants never to touch them. Soon he'll be asking to wrap them in cotton wool and never look at them. Undoubtedly, he would prefer to see fire destroy them, than to cede a part to the railway companies.[19]

Fortin's committee sponsored a bill forbidding the setting of fires in or close to standing timber. Felled timber could be burned only between 1 September and 30 June, and then only for clearing farm lands. The bill also laid down regulations concerning the safe use of such fires. It later became law.[20]

In February 1873 Fortin joined the Conservative cabinet of Gédéon Ouimet as commissioner of Crown lands. For the first time he could initiate legislation. Immediately, he faced a new form of his old problem in the Gulf fisheries. He wanted to preserve for tomorrow the God-given natural resources, but he also had to exploit them today for the livelihood of thousands of people.

A strong attack on Fortin and his predecessor came from Opposition member, P.-A. Tremblay. He attacked not only the forestry policy, but also alleged corrupt practices in the department. Tremblay was a bitter enemy of the lumber merchants, particularly the Price family of the Chicoutimi-Saguenay region. They gave heavily to the Conservatives, said Tremblay, and benefited accordingly. The Conservative ministers, he said, favoured their friends by building useless railways. These simply enhanced the value of the property belonging to Bleus.

Fortin defended the policies of himself and his predecessor. Only the sale of Crown lands, he said, would support the lumber industry and give work to lumbermen, carters, carpenters and colonists. "If we did not sell the Crown Lands, where would these colonists ... get what they need? They would be in the United States." No wood remained in the Eastern Townships, and the Ottawa, Saint-Maurice and Saguenay valleys were being exploited. The government must sell the woodlands of Témiscouata and Rimouski, and bring in a lot of money. This was better than leaving the land to "people of bad faith" who pillaged and then abandoned it. One historian wrote, "Fortin defended himself vigorously, and Chapleau supported him. The government withstood this assault well enough, and [opposition leader Henri-Gustave] Joly stopped his claims for an enquiry."[21]

The "people of bad faith" were local entrepreneurs who cut lumber illegally on licensed timber lots. This practice deprived the licensee of his rights and the habitants of their employment. It also deprived the government of stumpage fees. To counter this, Fortin gave instructions to bush rangers and secret inspectors to catch illegal loggers. If necessary, they were to confiscate illegally cut wood.[22] The government also tried to prevent licensees from underestimating the amount cut, since this practice minimized their fees. Fortin confidentially instructed Crown timber agents to watch the woodcutting, and to produce affidavits identifying the lots where the wood was cut.[23]

Fortin's stand on forestry was similar to his stand on fish. Conserve, certainly, but do so for the well-being of colonists. He saw the interests of colonists interwoven with those of the timber licencees. That meant licensing lumber companies to cut, and allowing farmers to clear, necessary woodland. In this way, many colonists settling areas with poor soil could work part-time in the forest industry. Only then could they survive.[24] The problem was a very real and a very modern one: jobs versus the environment. When jobs were not forthcoming, Fortin showed he could act decisively against the companies.

At that time several colonization societies were trying to recruit settlers from France. In 1871, for instance, the government had granted a reserve of 320,000 acres to the *Société canadienne limitée*, part in the

Beauce, part in the Matapédia valley. In return, the company contracted to settle 200 families annually. Three years later, Fortin, as commissioner of Crown lands, declared that the company had not met the conditions of the licence. He annulled the reserve.[25]

Nevertheless, his defence of his own and his government's forestry policy has a sad ring. In 1869, with no ministerial responsibilities, he had seen the matter differently. At that time, Fortin may well have read Marsh's *Man and Nature*, published four years earlier. Before Marsh, the writings of Henry Thoreau and the paintings of John J. Audobon had awakened the public conscience over conservation. *Man and Nature*, however, used some 180 earlier works as references, from Pliny the Elder to Lyell. The book was perhaps the first systematic treatment of conservation.

Of forests, Marsh wrote that in the normal cycle of seasons, "destructive tendencies of all sorts are arrested or compensated.... tree, bird, beast and fish alike find a constant uniformity of condition most favorable to the regular and harmonious coexistence of them all." But when the forest disappears, the earth loses too much heat in winter and gains too much in summer. "Bleak winds sweep unresisted over its surface." The plough breaks the soil's covering of leaves. "The face of the earth is no longer a sponge but a dust heap ... rendered no longer fit for the habitation of man."[26]

In the Assembly, Fortin deplored the destruction of the forests in similar terms:

> As for knowing when one can clear the forests without damage to the soil and without altering the climate while ensuring our future needs, that answers itself. We have today in North Africa a sad example of excessively despoiling the forests of a country. Once, North Africa was the granary of Rome, because of her great fertility and the abundance of grains she produced. I believe we are going to suffer the fate of North Africa if we continue to waste our forests ... without thinking of our ability to renew them. In a couple of hundred years we will have lost three-quarters of our forest riches.... In the old parishes, one can hardly see a single tree, and to construct our ships we are obliged to go to Ontario for oak and elm.... Even our pine forests are no longer common.... It is an attested fact that our climate is changing, and I do not doubt but that is due to excessive despoilage of our forests. Our floods and our droughts can be attributed to this. Forests maintain the freshness necessary for the fertility of a country.[27]

That could be a rallying cry for conservationists today.

NOTES

1. Fortin, *Report*, 1862.
2. Quoted in Dunfield, 30.
3. Marsh, George P. *Man and Nature, or Physical Geography as Modified by Human Behaviour*. Cambridge, MA: Belknap Press, 1965: 105-06 (re-issued).
4. Fortin, *Report*, 1856.
5. HOCD, 7 April 1880, 1221.
6. "Report of the Select Committee on the Working of the Fisheries Act," PCLAJ, 1864: App. 5.
7. Fortin, *Report*, 1857.
8. Fortin, *Report*, 1858; 1860.
9. PCA, 21 and 22 Vic. c.86 (1858).
10. Fortin, *Report*, 1858.
11. Marsh, 104.
12. Fortin, *Report*, 1860: 124-26; 1862.
13. Fortin, *Report*, 1862.
14. Dr. René E. Lavoie, Department of Fisheries and Oceans, personal communication, 3 July 1992.
15. Tétu, T., *Report*, 1867-68, 29-30.
16. Lavoie, personal communication.
17. QLAD, 10 March 1869, 145.
18. QLAJ, 1869, App. 2.
19. QLAD, 29 January 1870, 196.
20. Quebec, *Acts*, 33 Vic. c.19 (1870).
21. Rumilly, Vol. 1: 295-96.
22. NA, MG 24, G45 Salaberry family papers, Vol. 12: 3023-24, Fortin to Charles de Salaberry, 17 October 1873.
23. Little, J.I. *Nationalism, Capitalism and Colonization in 19th-century Quebec: The Upper St. Francis District*. Montréal and Kingston: McGill-Queen's University Press, 1989: 117, 123-24.
24. Linteau, Paul-André et al. *Quebec: A History, 1867-1929*. Toronto: James Lorimer and Company, 1983: 106-07.
25. Quinn, Magella. "Les capitaux français et le Québec, 1855-1900," *Revue d'histoire de l'Amérique française*, Vol. 24, No. 4 (March 1971): 527-66, esp. 542-43.
26. Marsh, 186.
27. QLAD, 10 March 1869, 145.

XI

"OUR RIVERS TAKEN FROM US"

Fortin was at New Richmond on Chaleur Bay in 1859 when he received a letter from Mr. Manderson of nearby Maria. Manderson wrote that on 28 September "Our active and energetic Fisheries overseer, R.W.H. Dimock" had laid a complaint against two Micmac, both named Louis Michel alias Manageset. By killing salmon they had violated the 24th section of the 1858 fisheries act. The accused admitted taking the salmon. The father, in extenuation, said he was ignorant of that law. The son admitted he was aware of doing wrong, but "he had had nothing to eat for himself nor his family." He expressed "apparently, sincere regret" for not trying to get food in some other way.

The law, said Manderson, left no discretionary powers to the magistrate, "whether it be a first offence or not or ... committed wantonly or out of dire necessity." His duty was clear, but before executing judgment, he wanted to consult Fortin. This was the first complaint brought against native people in that area. "However well aware they may be that they are violating the law, [they] cannot be easily made to understand the heinous nature of the offence." If Fortin came and passed sentence, it "would do more in bringing the [Micmac] to submit willingly ... than twenty convictions from any local authority." He believed Fortin's presence would again yield a "vast advantage to the ... inland fisheries of the locality."

Fortin went immediately to Pointe de l'Indien. The two accused were hiding upriver, waiting for his departure. One of Fortin's men found them ten miles away, and brought them back to appear before

Manderson and Fortin. Again they pleaded guilty. Louis Michel senior had killed fourteen salmon while Louis Michel junior had speared three. The magistrates fined the first £2 and the other £5, each with 1s. 3d. costs. "They both paid the fine at once. Mr Dimock, taking their extreme poverty into consideration, very charitably returned to them his share of the fine, as informer." Dimock later wrote to Fortin, "I trust in future the appearance of *La Canadienne*, under her noble Commander, will be a terror to evildoers."[1]

The indigenous peoples gave Fortin a pathetic problem in his battle to conserve the salmon. The Algonquian-speaking Innu occupied the eastern and northern parts of the Quebec-Labrador peninsula; the Micmac lived in Gaspésie. Both groups had respected their environment and prospered in it. It was ironic that Fortin, as the representative of European law, should lecture and punish them for conservation offences.

Micmac from what are now New Brunswick and Nova Scotia had moved into the Gaspé peninsula in the sixteenth century, probably conquering it from Laurentian Iroquois.[2] When the Europeans arrived, the Micmac were a migratory people. In summer they lived in large groups at river mouths on the coasts, collecting shellfish, fishing, and sealing. In winter they split up into smaller family units and moved to the interior to hunt moose, caribou and porcupine.[3] Accounts by early Europeans suggest that, except for occasional bad years, they had a high standard of living.

The Micmac showed a deep respect for the animals and fish, the forests and rivers, that sustained them. Hunting carried an element of worship requiring "gratitude expressed to the spirits or supernatural forces involved."[4] This was the manitou. As one writer expresses it, "The emphasis is on harmonious community relations in a largely classless society. There is no distinction between morals and mores. So environmental concerns are not a separate preoccupation. Morality is not a matter of following external rules ... but rather in forging a relationship with people, with the earth, and with animals."[5]

With the coming of the Europeans, French trading and missionary posts undermined the ancient beliefs, but the Micmac still largely "owned" their land. The urgent demands of later British settlers for land further battered the traditional way of life. These were the people whom Fortin lectured on the need for conservation. But it was not the Micmac who had first stripped the rivers of their salmon. The Ristigouche River, where Fortin spent so much energy protecting salmon, was a good example.

After the American revolution, fleeing Loyalists poured into Gaspésie demanding large tracts of land as compensation for their loyalty. In 1787 Grand Chief Claude of the Micmac rented land on the Ristigouche to a European. Claude saw himself and his people as still owning the land through "my father who has always lived in this place." He was soon disillusioned. Edward Isaac Mann, a Loyalist, settled on the Ristigouche near the Micmac village. He demanded that the government legalize his position by conceding the land to him. Years of legal disputes followed. Then the Gaspé commissioners gave Mann the land he claimed, despite Micmac protests. In 1826 the government confirmed the decision.

The Micmac reserve continued to shrink. When the men were away in the lumber camp, agents persuaded the women to sell more land to the Mann estate. Then it passed to John Thrasher. The government gave him permission to build a road, which reduced the Micmac waterfront to less than two miles and made return of the lost land impossible. When the Micmac asked him, the local missionary refused to give them permission to kill the thief.[6]

By Fortin's time, the Micmac lands were meagre. Almost as bad was the fact that the newcomers had clogged the Ristigouche and its tributaries with lumber and sawdust, damaged its watersheds with clear cutting, and ruined its spawning beds with horse-drawn scows. So now Fortin lectured the Micmac on conservation and prosecuted them for taking salmon illegally in their own river.

To the north, the Innu people had inhabited the north shore of the St. Lawrence for thousands of years. Europeans called them Montagnais (mountainmen) and Naskapi (which came to mean "unchristianized"). The Montagnais roamed the forests on the west side of the Labrador peninsula, the Naskapi ranged over the interior barren lands to the east. The Montagnais mainly hunted moose, the Naskapi caribou. In the spring, the Montagnais and some groups of Naskapi moved to the coasts for fishing and seal hunting. They too, like the Micmac, had many taboos to avoid offending the animals vital to their survival.[7] By the mid 1800s, European diseases had decimated the Montagnais-Naskapi peoples. The whites had overtrapped vast areas of their hunting grounds, and commercial forestry was making matters worse. The indigenous peoples could not fish in many salmon rivers, now leased to wealthy white sportsmen.

The Proclamation of 1763 stated the British intent towards Indian lands. Though originally restricted to certain areas, the proclamation recognized that native peoples retained occupancy rights for land they had not explicitly given up. The Crown had to evict anyone illegally occupying those lands. Under this interpretation, only native bands could surrender their lands, and then only to the Crown.[8] The usual mix of settlers' greed and official chicanery, however, often made the proclamation a farce, as the story of the Ristigouche reserve illustrates. Still, British policies and actions gave some credence to the claim that the native peoples were, if not sovereign, then certainly not subject. The Indian Department at least negotiated treaties and other arrangements with them.[9] But in the 1850s, legislation in the Canadian Assembly soon made clear their subject status.

An act of 1850 was called "An Act for the better protection of the lands and property of the Indians in Lower Canada."[10] It intended to prevent "encroachments" upon lands "appropriated to the use of the several Tribes and Bodies of Indians." It would also defend Indian "rights and privileges." The language of the act implies that Indian lands were not the lands of a sovereign people, but that the European was appropriating the lands from himself for Indian use. Since a commissioner "shall have full power to concede or lease or charge any such land," Indians no longer had responsibility even for lands appropriated for them. Another act the following year authorized setting apart up to 230,000 acres "for certain Indian tribes" in Lower Canada, vested in the Commissioner, with an annual payment to Indians up to £1,000.[11] With that tidied up, Europeans could go on with their lives. For 250 years they had depended on, or struggled against, native peoples. Those peoples were now irrelevant.

The law did, however, exempt native peoples from some restrictions placed on hunting and fishing by Europeans. As far back as 1807 and 1824, regulations had permitted them to spear fish for their own use in the Ristigouche and Grande-Cascapédia rivers. An 1858 Canadian act redefined the hunting laws. One clause protected the eggs of wildfowl in Canada, with transgressors to be fined not less than $20 or more than $100 after summary conviction by a stipendiary magistrate. Another clause did allow Indians to kill or possess listed species of wild fowl and animals, provided they could prove "reasonable presumption" that the game was "for their own immediate personal use and consumption." It could not be "for sale, barter or gift."[12]

A limited exemption also applied to salmon fishing. A clause in the 1865 Fisheries Act prohibited the use of grapplehooks, spears and other instruments against salmon and trout. However, the commissioner of Crown lands could license Indians to catch fish in certain waters and at certain times, though it must be "for their own use as food." It also permitted spearing of some species in some places between 14 December and 1 March.[13] The Innu and Micmac peoples found this poor compensation for losing the lands they once roamed. And Fortin enforced the laws against them.

The Godbout river, Fortin said in 1861, was "known to be, after the Moisie and the Natashquan, one of the best rivers on the North Shore. It is full of the finest kind of salmon and trout." An overseer had to be stationed there to make fishermen and Indians obey the law. Two Innu, accused of fishing within the limits leased by a Mr. Holiday, had escaped. Fortin "received instructions from the Government to have them arrested." As in earlier years, they ran into the woods when they saw *La Canadienne* arrive. Fortin talked with the few Montagnais families then at Godbout, explaining the main clauses of the Fisheries Act. "I showed them that they ought to be more interested in the preservation of salmon and trout than anyone else," since these fish were one of their principal means of subsistence. He also made them understand that "though the guilty Indians had escaped once more, they would be arrested sooner or later." If they again broke the law, "they would be visited with the heaviest penalties provided by the regulations." All the Montagnais promised faithfully to abide by the fisheries regulations, and they kept their promise. Observers reported no more infractions of the law in Godbout in 1861.[14]

22 May 1859: *La Canadienne* visited a Micmac village at the mouth of the Rivière Cascapédia. Fortin explained the fisheries laws. The Micmac objected only to the regulation against selling salmon speared by torchlight, but promised to obey it. The local magistrate reported no salmon killed after last July. This meant the spring salmon were again running back to the sea in large numbers.

29 May: Micmac at Anse-aux-Cousins and Anse-aux-Morts also strongly opposed the prohibition on the sale of fish speared by torchlight. Fortin noted that it would be very difficult to enforce this law.[15]

While Fortin punished the native peoples for transgressing, he also punished any European who benefitted from those transgressions. In 1860 at New Richmond, he fined A. Corbin £3 10s. with costs of £3 4s. for buying illegally speared salmon from the Micmac. Fortin trusted that the conviction would convince merchants, traders and others that they could not break the law with impunity. The statute, he wrote, did not intend to "interfere with the legitimate taking of that delicious fish." On the contrary, it was meant to "preserve and increase the supply in our rivers."[16]

Native people could win cases in his court. One Sunday in 1859, some fifty cod-fishing schooners sailed into Mingan Harbour. Fifteen came from the United States and the rest from Nova Scotia. The Halifax schooner *Lucknow* ran afoul of a schooner belonging to a Montagnais named Philippe, and broke her mainmast and jib-boom. Philippe brought a complaint. "I settled the matter," Fortin reported. "The master of the Lucknow agreed to replace the mast and jib-boom of the Montagnais' schooner."[17]

At times the impersonal tone of Fortin's reports breaks, showing a sympathy for the Montagnais, Naskapi and Micmac. In 1863 at Baie-de-Mouton, cod fishing had entirely failed. He found resident fishermen in bad shape. The indigenous people were worse off:

Some Indian families whom I had met with at St. Paul's River [Rivière-Saint-Paul], two weeks before, were in a similar precarious position and were nearly starving. Many of them asked to be allowed to eat on board, after having been more than a day without being able to get any food. There is no use saying that I considered it my duty to help, as they deserved, these poor unfortunates who cannot expect much assistance from the white population settled on the shore.[18]

Other comments show Fortin's attitude to the native peoples to be typical of his age. Their future, it was thought, lay in "civilizing" them. To this end, an act of 1857 was designed "to encourage the gradual Civilisation of the Indian Tribes in this Province," which would be achieved by "the gradual removal of all legal distinctions between [Indians] and Her Majesty's other Canadian subjects."[19] If the authorities judged an adult male to be intelligent and of good character, preferably literate, he could apply to become enfranchised, with his wife and children. Once enfranchised, he would receive fifty acres of the lands reserved for his "tribe." He would also get some cash as his share of the monies given to his "tribe." By accepting this, he gave up all claims on the "tribe" and lost his voice in its proceedings. The Europeans had taken most of the "Indian" lands; now they were trying to take their culture and identity. Few applied for enfranchisement, however, and only one native ever obtained it over the act's nearly twenty years of life.

Fortin also saw hope for the Montagnais and Naskapi of the North Shore by breaking them, at least in part, from traditional ways. In 1863 he saw with pleasure "that thanks to the zealous care of Father Oblats, the Indian post at Bersimi was in a decided state of progress." Solid wooden houses were replacing the fragile birchbark huts. Some, while not giving up "their favorite labours of fishing and hunting," were starting to cultivate the land, growing potatoes and vegetables. They even had some cattle. For these, he said, hay grew in abundance on either side of the river. "The Indians of this place ought not to be in future so exposed to distress ... which follows the failure of the winter hunt and seal fishing of summer."[20]

Fortin often pushed this utopian concept of colonization based on agriculture. Unfortunately, neither soil nor climate on the North Shore made agriculture economically feasible for native people or Europeans. The spread of forestry through traditional hunting grounds of the Montagnais-Naskapi worsened their condition. And more and more, salmon rivers of the North Shore were locked up for the entertainment of wealthy sportsmen.

In 1868 Sydney Robert Bellingham introduced a bill into the Quebec Assembly that would further curtail hunting and fishing rights of the native peoples. He described the large decline in game in Quebec forests, and claimed it resulted in part from "the permission given to the Indians to hunt and fish in all seasons of the year. They do it not so much to get food as to obtain furs, and because of a penchant for destruction."

Fortin, as deputy for Gaspé, had on many occasions fought against the right of private clubs to control salmon fishing. Now he argued that Bellingham's bill should go to a committee for study. He too deplored the declining game population which, he said, concerned not only sportsmen, but also the many people, presumably including native peoples, who made their living by hunting and fishing.[21] The bill did not pass, but private interests increasingly took over the fine salmon rivers.

Fortin lacked understanding of the native peoples' dilemma, but he showed no rancour. Not so W.F. Whitcher, a clerk in the Department of Crown Lands. Reporting on a trip along the North Shore in 1859, Whitcher felt sure that humane motives led to the qualified exemption of Indians from the fisheries regulations. However, "Experience dissipates this cause of sympathy." The Indians seldom spear salmon for subsistence. The fish "go to the salting vats of the highest trader—pork, tea, sugar, tobacco, and sometimes spirits, principally returning to the wigwam in exchange." If not for their "habitual indolence" the

Montagnais and Naskapi could easily live on trout, cod and seal. And anyway, he says, they do not endure privations as bad as those afflicting western Indians.

Whitcher includes an extraordinary description of Indian salmon hunting. Its sexual overtones—foreplay, orgasm and tristesse—tell more about his attitudes than about the Naskapi. Of spearing salmon by torchlight, he says:

> [It] has peculiar fascinations and to many is strangely exciting. Nothing can exceed the wild excitement with which these men pursue it. The sombre night scene of the forest river seems to delight them.... The murmur of waterfalls and rapids drown those exclamatory 'Ughs!' and the frequent splash that would else disturb the pervading stillness.
>
> With steady, stealthy speed, the light birchen boat enters the rapid.... The blazing torch ... glares with dazzling lightness.... Like moths, [the salmon] sidle towards the fatal light; their silvery sides and amber colored eyeballs glisten through the rippled water. The dilated eyes, the expanding nostrils and compressed lips of the swarthy canoemen, fitly picture their eager and excited mood. A quick deadly aim, a sudden swirl, and those momentary convulsive wriggles tell the rest. The aquatic captive, with blood and spawn and slime and entrails, besmear the inside of the canoe.
>
> The bed of coarse bows—the chill and hungry awakening at sunrise—the mixture of peril and fagging which form the return down a swift stream broken by falls and rapids, with here and there a tedious portage over which several hundred pounds of fish, and bruised and blistered canoes, must be transported. All these exertions appear but natural to Indians.[22]

This diatribe against the Naskapi, based on their fishing techniques, contrasts with the gentlemanly sportsmanship of the Europeans, delicately playing the fish with rod and fly. During a visit to the "great Natashquhan River," Fortin reported that Mr. Powell, the lessee, had never seen so many salmon at the foot of the rapids, most of them very large. Powell and his two companions had already taken several hundred salmon on the fly—one of them took thirty-three fish in one day. Fortin later said that the three men had taken about 450 salmon.

Powell and his friends were probably among the sportsmen who came to the North Shore and Gaspésie every summer from Upper Canada, the United States and even from Britain. Years later, Fortin would deplore the presence of these "aristocrats," whose destruction of the salmon would not earn one dollar in exports. But in that same visit, as magistrate, he enforced the law regardless. Immediately after reporting Powell's success he added, "I learned that certain Montagnais Indians had, contrary to law, taken a quantity of salmon within Mr. Powell's limits. As they were absent, I put off the matter until my return visit." When *La Canadienne* returned a few days later, the accused were still absent. He could not wait, and "All I could do was to confiscate the produce of their unlawful fishing, upon the evidence of the fisheries overseer, and I did so."[23]

In rebuttal of clerk second-class Whitcher, but also in reproach to magistrate Fortin, the Montagnais at Moisie in 1861 wrote a petition to the government:

Can our words meet your views, we Indians? can our words enter into your hearts, you that govern, we who live here, we who are born here, and consider ourselves possessors of the soil, by the will of the Great Creator of the Universe? Our lands and country now ruined, we can no more find our living. Our rivers taken from us, and only used by strangers. Through your will, we can only now look on the waters of the rivers passing, without permission to catch a fish, we poor Indians. And now, what are your intentions towards us? You have no doubt, all the means to live, though not we. Would you consider our poverty and take compassion on us? We pray you to send us some help. Our poverty does not arise from laziness and want of energy, but from being unable any more to procure, for ourselves and families, food. And we are all of one mind, that since our lands and rivers afford us no more the means to live, you who govern should take our present distress into your consideration without loss of time, and for which we will most gratefully ever pray.—Signed: Domenique, chief; Bartholemy and Jerome.[24]

NOTES

1. Fortin, *Report,* 1860: 124.
2. Upton, Leslie F.S. *Micmacs and Colonists: Indian-White Relations in the Maritime Provinces.* Vancouver: University of British Columbia Press, 1979: 8.
3. Jenness, Diamond. *The Indians of Canada.* Ottawa: Queen's Printer, 1960: 267-68.
4. Collins, John James. "Native American Religions: A Geographical Survey." Lewiston: E. Mellen Press, 1991: 269.
5. Pomedli, Michael. "Native Approaches to Morality," *Actes du vingtième congrès des Algonquinistes.* Ottawa: Carleton University, 1988: 299.

6. Bock, Philip K. *The Micmac Indians of Restigouche, History and Contemporary Description.* Ottawa: National Museum of Canada, 1966: 14-21.
7. Montagnais-Naskapi, *The Canadian Encyclopedia,* Vol. 2: 1154.
8. Harper, A.G., in Bock, 12.
9. Milloy, John S. "The Early Indian Acts," Ian A.L. Getty and Antoine S. Lussier, eds. *As Long as the Sun Shines and Water Flows.* Vancouver, University of British Columbia Press, 1983: 56.
10. PCA, 13 and 14 Vic. c.42 (1850).
11. PCA, 14 and 15 Vic c.106 (1851).
12. PCA, 21 and 22 Vic. c.103 (1858).
13. PCA, 29 Vic. c.11, 17.8 (1865); Canada, Acts, 31 Vic. c.60, 13.8 (1868).
14. Fortin, *Report,* 1862.
15. Fortin, *Report,* 1860: 107-08.
16. Fortin, *Report,* 1861.
17. Fortin, *Report,* 1860: 127
18. Fortin, *Report,* 1864.
19. PCA, 20 Vic. c.26 (1857).
20. Fortin, *Report,* 1864.
21. QLAD, 12 February 1868, 135.
22. Province of Canada "Report of the Commissioner of Crown Lands," Sessional Papers, 1860: No. 12, App. 34, 160-62.
23. Fortin, *Report,* 1866: 15, 27.
24. Quoted in Hind, *Explorations,* Vol. 2: 115-16.

XII

FIGHTING WITH THE BUREAUCRATS

Fortin worked in a network of bureaucratic relationships. Until 1860 the provincial secretary had paid his expenses, while the Board of Public Works owned and maintained *La Canadienne*. After 1860 Fortin and his fisheries protection service fell under Crown Lands, but the care, fitting and control of expenses for the schooner remained with Public Works. And Fortin had "extra duties as stipendiary magistrate" under the provincial secretary.

Those duties as magistrate throughout the Gulf included aiding customs and local authorities, fighting the illicit traffic in liquor, and maintaining order among the Gulf population, especially among foreign fishing vessels frequenting the Gulf "since the adoption of the Reciprocity Treaty." As a fisheries officer, he had to enforce the fisheries acts. He also had to "issue Season Licences and Licences of Occupation, collect the fees, adjust differences, maintain regularity at the fishery stations, protect the Crown Lessees and Licensees, visit the Innu and Micmac settlements, procure statistics of fish and fish-oil trade and of the conditions of the settlers and fishermen in the various fishing districts, etc." There were also "many minor duties" following from specific departmental instructions.[1]

In bureaucratic jargon, Fortin was a line, not a staff man. One historian says that his reports must have been a "constant source of revelation to the 'landlubbers' whose knowledge of their country generally stopped at Kingston or, at the farthest, Québec."[2] Bureaucratic tensions usually exist between staff people at headquarters and line people in the field. The staff often see themselves as policy makers, controlling and guiding line workers. This approach might work in a bureaucracy where line work is routine and clerical, but it could not work in the Gulf, not when field personnel include people like Pierre Fortin. They often see "policy makers" at headquarters as ambitious deadweights, their chief function being to stifle field initiative in case it damages their own well-being. Evidence given in 1864 before a parliamentary committee on fisheries makes this tension very clear.

The assistant commissioner of Crown lands, Andrew Russell, was the senior civil servant in the department. Russell described for the committee the job of W.H. Whitcher, clerk second-class, at headquarters in Québec. Russell said it was Whitcher's duty "to receive instructions from the Commissioner of Crown Lands" about the management branch business "and to convey those instructions to the outdoors officers." He was "authorised to sign the ordinary routine correspondence, reserving letters of importance for the signature of the Commissioner. I call a letter of importance one involving a new principle." The field officers had to "follow the instructions transmitted to them by Mr Whitcher." Whitcher also "examines the accounts of the Branch and submits them for approval." By this description, Russell explicitly ruled himself out of the line between the commissioner and the field. He implied that Whitcher transmitted rather than originated orders. He also said that Whitcher "prepares" the fishery regulations before they were submitted to the Executive Council. However, they were "based on consultation with the chief officers, and on their reports and other information."

In his testimony before the committee, Whitcher had no doubt he was in direct authority over the field officers. He said he had been in the department since 1858, and was now "at the head of the Fisheries Branch of both provinces," responsible for "the general conduct of the fisheries business." He had one clerk at headquarters to help him.

Whitcher had been attacked for spending money on trips on the North Shore instead of staying in Québec. In reply, he referred the committee back to a memorandum of 17 May 1859 describing the reasons for his journies along the North Shore. He performed this service "to the best of my humble ability." It had cost him "no very considerable expense and fatigue." Whitcher did not lack courage in facing down a parliamentary committee. After that defence of his North Shore trips, he attacked. An annual salary of £250 after sixteen years' service was "manifestly too small," he claimed; he should have a salary of at least £400, the minimum for clerks in charge of branches. Then he "would diligently do any work required in this service without a solitary extra charge." This raise would also avoid suggestions that "occasional outdoor service" was simply "cutting out work and pay" for himself. He objected to posting these expenses in the public accounts; they "but eke out an insufficient salary," while exposing him "to this invidious publicity." Whitcher also objected to commissions and committees that made him "justify over and over again what has been paid to me, in a sort of post mortem."

The advantages of sending the clerk on field trips were, he felt, very clear. They gave the person in charge an opportunity to learn of the "localities, their resources, their inhabitants, their engagements, and the traffic carried on." He could learn "the natural history and physical features of the various fishings" in the waters of Canada. The department head had to know about the "fishing community, the drawbacks of their pursuit, their wants and prospects." He went on, "Without this knowledge, efficient management is altogether unattainable." This was true "however diligent and capable may be the subordinates engaged—however wise the regulations of the government—however well meant the suggestions offered from any quarters."

However diligent and capable Fortin and his fellow subordinates may be! The patronizing tone of a man who only occasionally sallied into the field must have irked Fortin. He had put his life on the line for a dozen years.

Whitcher added that efficiency, economy and despatch were advanced by his field training. What he learned led to economies. He could "advise with superiors, direct, consult or counsel the agents, and conduce to the harmonious and profitable working of affairs in and out of the department." Whitcher always selected his words reasonably. He avoided offence to commissioners above and superintendents below. Who could argue with a staff officer wanting to "consult or counsel the agents and conduce to harmonious and profitable" affairs in the department? Unfortunately, somebody was indeed prepared to argue, and Whitcher admitted to interdepartmental conflict. The new commissioner, he said, had redefined "the relative duties" of himself and the other officers. This was necessary because of "conflicting ideas" of whether control belonged to the superintendents in the field, or to the fisheries branch "as in any other branch in the Department." The conflict as Whitcher described it did not lie between the field men and himself, but between the field men and the fisheries branch.

A member asked what amendments he would suggest to the fisheries act to end this conflict. Whitcher replied that inspectors should be named by the commissioner of Crown lands, not appointed under letters patent. "The term 'superintendent' should be done away with and replaced by 'inspector.' This would remove misapprehensions about the powers which the term *superintendent* was supposed to convey. These inspectors should act under instructions from the Commissioner of Crown Lands through the Fisheries Branch. [This was] the practice in the other branches of the public departments." As Whitcher had it, he should have control of the department.

Then a committee member asked: Did he know anything of Commander Fortin's service? Was it properly done?

Whitcher replied, "The service performed by Captain Fortin is important and peculiar.... So far as I am aware, his duties are well and industriously performed."

A century and a quarter later, the atmosphere of the committee room in Québec, and the battle for power, show through that sceptical qualifier and lukewarm endorsement. Russell also distanced himself from Fortin:

Q: How does Mr Fortin perform his duties? Efficiently or not?
A: Efficiently, I am informed by Mr Whitcher.
Q: What is his salary? Should it be increased and to what extent?
A: His salary is $1200. As the business of the Fisheries Branch is conducted by the Commissioner ... I am not prepared to answer the latter part of this question.

The headquarters staff heard from, the committee now turned to David H. Têtu, a man who knew much about the Gulf fisheries. A member asked him his opinion of the efficiency of Nettle, Whitcher and Fortin. Têtu said he thought Nettle had insufficient knowledge for his position as superintendent of fisheries for Lower Canada. He was "capable of sacrificing all the other kinds of fisheries to protect that of salmon and trout." As for Whitcher, said Têtu, he "has little to do."

Têtu kept his praise for Fortin. "Commander Fortin has always shown that he takes an interest in the fishermen by making every effort to reconcile them, so that the difficulties which had arisen among them have disappeared." He does this "by charging a moderate price for the fishing stations, and by doing everything in the interests of the government and of the fishermen."

Another witness, Michel Lesperance, testified, "The service performed by Mr Fortin is most useful, both on the North and on the South Shores. I have observed great changes since he has been amongst us. The laws are more strictly observed, and his services are now indispensable." He recommended Fortin be given a steamer and that his powers to proceed summarily be expanded.

Finally, Fortin had his say. A member asked if he could protect Gulf salmon rivers without assistance from Whitcher and Nettle. He replied that yes, he could do so "with my officers, my men, and the fishery overseers stationed at various points of my Division." And he could do so "as I did before, alone, for several years."[3] Fortin, a man of the line, just wanted the staff to leave him alone to do his job.

The quarrel over who was top dog in the department returned next year. In debate on the new fisheries bill in 1865, Sir Narcisse-Fortunat Belleau spoke. He clearly felt that Whitcher was now, indeed, head of the department. Belleau objected. The previous year's committee, he said, had recommended that the head be a man of practical experience. Belleau had "confidence in the zeal, general intelligence and attention of the present superintendent [Whitcher]," although he lacked the "practical and intimate knowledge of fishing matters which was so desirable." Belleau considered Whitcher "not exactly" what the committee thought needed in the interests of the important fisheries. He also suggested giving Fortin judicial powers "similar to those exercised by a Judge of the Circuit Court." Alexander Campbell, the minister sponsoring the bill, said it intended just that.

The next day, Luc Letellier de Saint-Just continued the defence of Fortin. What was the use, he asked, of the commander visiting point after point around the Gulf when a subaltern in Crown lands could overrule him? "What necessity is there for giving such directions to a person so competent as Commodore Fortin?"

Campbell replied, "The authority of Captain Fortin has not been interfered with, nor is there the slightest desire to interfere with it. I have had a conversation with him recently and know his views."

At that, D.E. Price, chipped in ironically, "Make him Commissioner of Crown Lands."

When Campbell repeated that there was no interference with Fortin, Letellier replied, "Why should there be another officer, superior in position, in the department. What I say I say strongly, because I know injustice has been done by officers who do not know the habits of our population. I do not wish to raise the question of nationality, but there would have been less difficulty if the officer in question had known more of the language spoken by our people."

In this exchange, Fortin gets rapid promotion from commander to captain to commodore to commissioner. And "nationality" (that is, language) is raised for the first time, at Whitcher's expense.

Still, Whitcher had his friends. Price now attacked Fortin. The commander, he said, seemed to want to be commissioner of fisheries. He was "a very efficient officer," but his responsibilities had "been too great for him." Price then charged that Fortin had never done justice to the North Shore. It had "never seen anything of him.... *La Canadienne* is a great deal of time on the South Shore." There, courts are "established and suitors can have justice." However, "*La Canadienne* is only for a very short period on the North coast" where it was needed. Fortin was not a departmental officer. He "must receive his instructions from his official chief through someone charged with such duties in the department." Fortin wanted to be commissioner of Crown lands, but "the departmental officer who gives him his instructions ought to be if not his superior, at least his equal."

Fortin did become commissioner of Crown lands, but the charge of his neglecting the North Shore is not fair. True, his reports show little of the affection for the North Shore, with its cold and fog, that they show for Gaspésie and the Îles-de-la-Madeleines, but despite the smaller population, he spent much time there. In 1860 for instance, *La Canadienne* travelled for 139 days along the various coasts, excluding time crossing the Gulf or sailing to and from Québec. Of this, Fortin spent sixty-six days (47 percent) on the Gaspésie shores, fifty-two days (37 percent) on the North Shore, and twenty-one days (15 percent) in the Îles-de-la-Madeleines. A spot check of other reports shows this was not exceptional—usually, the Îles-de-la-Madeleine got the least.[4]

The minister now found himself attacked from both sides. Fortin's friends wanted him clearly in charge and felt that Campbell was not supporting him. Fortin's enemies wanted him under the clear leadership of Whitcher. Campbell tried to come down on both sides. He said that Fortin's "province, his peculiar duty, is to go down to see that the laws are observed.... And in doing that, there is no interference with him. His authority in this respect has been recognised to the full." Campbell assured Fortin's friends that the commander had the full support of the department. Indeed, he was sure Fortin "would be ready to declare he had received all due aid and countenance." He was an administrative officer who had discharged his duties with "the greatest energy and intelligence." His instructions were from the department, but of course, they had to pass through the head of the Fisheries Branch [Whitcher] who also discharged the duties of his office with rare ability. He felt sure that Fortin had always received the most cordial assistance of that officer. He would be extremely surprised if Captain Fortin had any knowledge of, or acquiesced in, the complaints here made apparently in his behalf.[5]

At the day's end, Whitcher had won the struggle. He became head of the Fisheries Department and remained so for some years after Confederation.[6]

One historian claims that the bureaucrats finally got to Fortin, and that his later reports show much less enthusiasm.[7] This is true, but perhaps fifteen years of patrolling the Gulf and writing annual reports was enough. Another career offered itself. On 1 September 1867, Fortin resigned from the service and he handed over *La Canadienne* to Théophile Têtu. "I am happy to be able to say [Têtu] possesses in the highest degree all the requisite qualities to fit him for the office." He had been Fortin's assistant for the last six years, and Fortin asked the provincial secretary to make the promotion permanent. "I conclude by recommending to your kind care and special attention, the officers and men of *La Canadienne*. [Their] services you have been pleased to tell me, on several occasions, you appreciated."[8]

With that last kindness to his crew, Commander Fortin became a politician.

NOTES

1. Province of Canada, "Report of the Commissioner of Crown Lands," Sessional Papers, 1863: App. 24.
2. Hodgetts, 147.
3. "Report of the Select Committee on the Working of the Fisheries Act," PCLAJ, 1864: App. 5.
4. Fortin, *Report*, 1861.
5. Province of Canada, *Legislative Council Debate on the Fisheries Bill of Hon. Alexander Campbell, 9-10 March 1865*. Quebec: Daily News Office (1865): 12-21.
6. Chambers, 166.
7. Hodgetts, 149.
8. Fortin, *Report*, 1867-68: 14.

XIII

FORTIN, THE CONSERVATIVES, AND CONFEDERATION

The summer of 1867 saw the first federal and provincial elections of the new Canadian confederation. John LeBoutillier had represented Gaspé in the Province of Canada Assembly. When he was appointed to the Quebec Legislative Council, constituents from all parties asked Fortin to stand for the Conservatives, or Bleus.[1] The Jersey commercial houses also supported Fortin. At that time a member could sit in both the Quebec Assembly and the House of Commons. Gaspé elected Fortin, with no opposition, to both houses.

In Montréal in 1849, Fortin had ridden to the rescue of the Reform (or Liberal) party against the Tories (or Conservatives). Now, in 1867, he fought for the Conservatives against the Liberals. Had Fortin changed as he aged? Or had he remained constant as the parties changed around him?

After the Reform Party achieved responsible government in 1848-49, rifts appeared within each wing. The Upper Canada Grits of George Brown grew more and more anti-French, whereas the Lower Canada Rouges were nationalistic and anticlerical, with republican, pro-American strains. In the 1850s the conservative elements among the Reformers joined with the more progressive Tories to form the Liberal-Conservative party of John A. Macdonald and Georges Cartier. The rump of the Reform Party then split into three factions: the moderate Reformers, the more extreme Anglophone Grits, and the equally radical Francophone Rouges. By the 1860s no party could command a clear majority in the Assembly. Then in 1864 Brown offered to join with the Conservatives in seeking a new federation. This initiative resulted in the 1867 confederation of the colonies of Canada (Quebec and Ontario), Nova Scotia and New Brunswick.

In the confederation debates in Canada, almost all Bleus supported the measure. The Rouges opposed it as too centralizing and as a threat to French-Canadian identity. One or two Bleus did dissent. Henri-Élzear Taschereau called it "a mortal blow to our nationality." Honoré Mercier, later a nationalist leader, in 1866 recognized "no influence strong enough to make [him] sacrifice ... the future of the French-Canadian race."[2]

Fortin had little choice about which party to support. The Rouges were mainly young radicals. They not only opposed confederation, they also wanted to repeal the Act of Union, once again separating Upper and Lower Canada. They advocated universal suffrage and the election of most government officials. They saw the future of Quebec as republican, and even wanted annexation to the United States. They were also anti-clerical, and opposed the ultramontane doctrines of church authorities in Canada, thereby earning themselves the moral condemnation of many clerics.

Fortin must have found all this foreign to his instincts and training. He had been taught from his childhood to respect authority, and trained by his adult career to exercise it. He once said in a speech to the House, "He did not want mob rule. He wanted the authority to come from above."[3] The Bleus supplied Fortin's natural home. His Catholic upbringing would strengthen that view. In 1867 several Quebec bishops issued pastoral letters supporting the Bleus and confederation. The archbishop of Quebec was typical. It was God's command, he wrote, to accept that which emanated from legitimate authority. Therefore, voters ought not to support anyone fighting confederation.[4]

The first election of the new Canada in 1867 revolved around attitudes to confederation. The Conservatives won easily. Nationally, they took 108 seats to their opponents' 72. In Quebec they took 47 to 17.[5]

Fortin clearly believed in the future of confederation. In 1867 he pressed in the House of Commons for the Intercolonial Railway. "Without it," he said, "Confederation cannot be considered an accomplished fact." As a means of communication between the different parts of our country, it would "unite the people and thus form a complete whole of these provinces."[6] Nevertheless, he saw the dangers of confederation for Quebec. "In promoting colonization with all our strength, we will re-establish the balance between the two rival provinces, and escape the threat of Upper Canada dwarfing us."7

Some members of a highly politicized House must have felt Fortin had a naive attitude to confederation. In 1868 he moved for a special committee to study the fisheries and to recommend "the best modes of fostering and developing them." Introducing the motion, he said:

We were a new nation, and the various members of the nationality should make themselves acquainted with each others' remarks. He would ask whether at present the gentlemen from New Brunswick and Nova Scotia were acquainted with the fisheries of the upper lakes.... And he would ask the gentlemen from Ontario, and even the Province of Quebec, whether they were well acquainted with the fisheries of Nova Scotia and New Brunswick, and even the fisheries of Quebec in the Gulf and the lower part of the St. Lawrence.8

In fact, politicians of Upper and Lower Canada showed little interest in learning about each other's fisheries: fish did not supply much in the way of votes. Potvin goes further. Public men from Ontario, he said, objected to Fortin's recommendations about the Gulf. These men were "opposed to the progress of Quebec."9

This may be true, but the one supporting example Potvin gives is false. He writes that when Fortin first boarded *La Canadienne* it was old and unfitted for the task. Ontario politicians, Potvin claims, opposed his getting a new vessel. Only when *La Canadienne* went aground years later did it get the refit Fortin wanted.10 In fact, the government had built *La Canadienne* in 1854 specially for the Fisheries Branch, and to Fortin's design.

In the Assembly of the Province of Canada, some Upper Canadians had opposed the Fisheries Protection Branch having an armed vessel. In 1855 Brown moved to amend a resolution of supply. The amendment stated, "the Naval protection of the Province is a duty devolving on the Imperial government.... It is inexpedient to maintain a Provincial Naval Establishment." However, the House voted down the amendment and then passed the government motion that provided expenses for *La Canadienne*. The Upper Canadian Conservatives voted with the Bleus "for Fortin." But the Francophone Rouges joined Brown, Mackenzie, and the Upper Canadian Liberals "against Fortin." That is, the vote opposed Conservatives/Bleus to Liberals/Rouges, rather than Upper versus Lower Canadians.11

With his election, Fortin must have thought that the move from bureaucrat to legislator would enhance his influence. Surely he would be able to do more to improve life in the Gulf. Now, however, he had to cope with party discipline. True, the art of keeping members in line by a system of rewards and punishments had not reached present-day levels, but it was not easy for a man such as Fortin to be a "loose fish." He could not lightly go against the authority of his party.

Indeed, in the five sessions of the first parliament, the member for Gaspé proved himself a good but not a slavish party man. Fortin participated in ninety divisions, and missed only three* despite his obligations in the Quebec Assembly. Of those ninety divisions, Fortin voted with his front bench on all but three. By far the majority of these concerned matters affecting most of Fortin's constituents only marginally or not at all. With technical votes on supply, and ways and means, and with questions such as superannuation for the civil service, organization of the Department of Agriculture, trademarks, insurance, the militia, banking and currency, the Pacific railway, etc., Fortin consistently voted with the government. Most of his constituents were probably indifferent.

In another group of divisions, Fortin's pro-government votes probably reflected the views of most of his constituents. He supported action on the Intercolonial Railway, which would help open up Gaspésie; on tariffs rather than free trade as urged by the Opposition; on the settlement of the Quebec/Ontario debt on terms favourable to Quebec; and on the settlement, at least temporarily, of the problem of Louis Riel and the Métis by the creation of the province of Manitoba.

On the three occasions when Fortin voted contrary to his front bench, one was a private member's bill concerning expansion of the Central Canada Railway north from Ottawa and involving land grants.[12] The second, more important, came on 4 May 1868. The government had proposed that the governor general be paid $35,000 annually. An Opposition amendment would have lowered that to $30,000. The government argued that the British North America Act called for the higher salary. Without it, the best people would not accept the posi-

---

* Unfortunately, newspapers sometimes confused the Rouge Moise Fortier, MP for Yamaska, with Conservative Pierre Fortin. On several occasions, "Mr. Fortier" voted both against and for the government. I have assumed the government supporter was Fortin, the Opposition supporter, Fortier. In the listing of members of the Commons for 1872, the error was reversed and the member for Yakamaska is given as Moise Fortin instead of Moise Fortier.

tion. Francis Jones expressed an opposing view. The "specimens" of aristocracy "in England or this country were not such as to induce the people to regard them with much favour. He would far rather see nature's noblemen, and would expect far better service from them. He did not want to encourage the English aristocracy to come here and take root."[13] Fortin did not give reasons for his vote reducing the governor general's proposed salary, but years later he also stated his views on aristocracies. "We are a people of liberty and quality, we have no aristocracy and no landlords and we do not want landlords in this country."[14]

Fortin's most important break with his government came in 1872 over the Treaty of Washington. He said the treaty "would injure in a very material way" the interests of the Maritime population, including Gaspé's 2,500 fishermen. Fortin first voted against two Opposition amendments. On the crucial reading on the bill itself, however, he voted against the government.[15] The following year the Opposition tried to reopen the debate on the treaty. Now Fortin voted with the government to defeat the attempt, though he did not take part in the debate.[16]

Two other votes were interesting in suggesting Fortin's views. On several occasions he voted against granting divorce bills.[17] This was consistent with his church's position on divorce. And, in defence of his own interests, he voted against abolishing dual representation (the right of members of the Commons to sit simultaneously in a provincial assembly).[18]

If Fortin seldom voted against his government in the early sessions, he sometimes made embarrassing speeches or asked embarrassing questions. Once he asked for correspondence complaining of the absence of senior Quebec judges. The request touched a sore spot and the Liberals attacked the government. Mr. Masson, for instance, said that two senior Canadian judges "were men out of their heads," two were of "bad moral character," and another was very deaf. When a man sued for $10, the deaf judge gave judgment for $100. Antoine-Aimé Dorion claimed that of twenty-three Quebec judges, thirteen were unfit from one cause or another. Cartier, the minister responsible, admitted that four Quebec judges should be pensioned off. Unfortunately, ten years ago, the government had offered a pension to the 85-year-old judge Fortin mentioned. The pension was two-thirds his salary. The judge had refused.[19]

As chairman of the committee on fisheries and navigation, Fortin often spoke on these and other topics affecting the Gulf and its people.

He seldom spoke on the national issues of the day, doing so only when questions such as the Conservatives' National Policy or the Treaty of Washington directly affected his constituents. His votes on contentious national matters, however, usually went to the government, as in the first Riel affair.

In 1870 Louis Riel had established his provisional government on the prairies. A Métis court martial found a young roughneck from Ontario, Thomas Scott, guilty of treason. Riel allowed Scott's execution to proceed on 4 March. To Quebec, Riel was the defender of French and Catholic rights in the West, a national hero. Ontario wanted him caught and hanged as a traitor and murderer. Instead, the Conservative government reached an agreement with the Métis. An act of parliament on 12 May 1870 created the province of Manitoba. It granted 1.4 million acres to the Métis, along with the right to bilingual services. However, Riel and other Métis leaders fled the country.

The next year an opposition member alleged that Conservative Louis Delorme had been a member of Riel's government. If so, he was guilty of high treason. Delorme denied it. In a procedural wrangle, Fortin briefly defended Delorme. More significantly, he voted with the government. The Commons decided there was no case to bring before a committee of the House.[20] Later, the Opposition moved, "This House regrets that the government of the day have done nothing towards procuring the punishment of the murderers of Thomas Scott." Fortin again voted with the majority to support his government.[21] Most Quebecers condemned the Bleus as traitors to French-Canadian rights in the West. The Riel question would return to haunt Fortin.

Next month, another crisis turned out worse for Fortin, at least in the short run. On 17 May 1871 the New Brunswick government passed a schools act abolishing provincial separate schools. Roman Catholics protested strongly, and Quebec backed them. The next year a Commons member moved to disallow the New Brunswick act. Cartier, Langevin and Macdonald argued that this was a provincial matter. For the federal government to overrule the legislation would be unconstitutional and a dangerous precedent, especially for Quebec.[22] The matter went to the courts, but this simply postponed the dilemma for Fortin and his Bleu colleagues.

The Red River rebellion, the New Brunswick school law, and the Treaty of Washington cast a shadow over the Conservative election campaign in Quebec in 1872. The Liberals in Québec improved their position to twenty-seven seats, though the Conservatives still won thirty-eight.[23] The people of Gaspé again elected Fortin unopposed.

In February 1873 Fortin joined the Quebec cabinet as Commissioner of Crown lands, but retained his seat in the Commons. Later that year, the New Brunswick Supreme Court ruled that the act abolishing separate schools was constitutional. Bitter debates recurred in the Commons. Honoré Mercier led the Opposition. He demanded that Quebec members be French-Canadian and Catholic before being Bleu and Rouge, and persuaded many Quebec members to his side. He did not win over Langevin and Robitaille, federal ministers, nor Archambeault and Fortin, provincial ministers also serving in the Commons.[24]

In a letter, Quebec politician C. Beausoleil lamented the position taken by the Bleus. Archbishop John Sweeney, a New Brunswick cleric, had visited the caucus seeking support. "I wish to stress to you that I am profoundly indignant and discouraged" by the Conservative and Catholic deputies, said Beausoleil. Sweeney, he explained, had asked the Bleus to sign a memorandum to the government: it must disavow the law, or the caucus would vote with the Opposition. This caused a storm in caucus. "O'Reilly, Ryan and Fortin also opposed any initiative that would endanger the government." Sweeney, said Beausoleil, had left very disappointed—he had looked to Quebec as the only hope for his cause.[25]

Quebecers lamented the failure of the Bleus to uphold New Brunswick separate schools, which they saw as the first of a series of great betrayals. These would occur periodically through the next eighty years, to the Conscription Crisis of World War II, and beyond to the 1980s. One historian said that in the New Brunswick schools question, Fortin and Archambeault showed "more submission than their colleagues to the directions of the Federal ministers ... a sign of the dependence of the provincial cabinet." As a result, "the names of Langevin, Robitaille, Archambeault and Fortin were pilloried" throughout Quebec.[26] Fortin found himself included among the first *vendus* (sell-outs).

Fortin, however, soon discovered a cause on which he could defend himself against Quebec nationalists. With confederation, the debt of the old Province of Canada posed a problem. How should Quebec and Ontario divide it? By the British North America Act, the new dominion government had assumed most debts of the provinces. A formula based on population gave each province a debit or a credit. Quebec and Ontario inherited from the Province of Canada a shared debt of $10,400,000.[27]

The two new provinces immediately started arguing over how to split the common debt. Quebec based its argument on the 1840 Act of Union. At that time, Lower Canada had objected to sharing the $5,900,000 debt of the spendthrift Upper Canadians, while the Upper Canadians had been delighted to share the $190,000 credit of the parsimonious Lower Canadians. At Confederation, Quebec claimed, Ontario should take $6,090,000 of the debt, based on the 1840 position, and Quebec and Ontario should split about equally the balance of $4,310,000 incurred since then. That left Quebec to pay a little more than $2,000,000, Ontario about $8,000,000.

Both the Ontario and federal representatives rejected this solution. The Quebecer, outnumbered, resigned in protest. The two remaining arbiters estimated that in the Province of Canada, Upper Canada had incurred about 53 percent of the provincial debt, Lower Canada 47 percent. The commissioners therefore split the $10.4 million in the same ratio: $5.5 million for Ontario and $4.9 million for Quebec.[28]

The Quebec government, most unhappy with the awards, went to the courts and lost. Politically, however, Quebec had more success. After some pressure, the federal government changed the formula so Ontario and Quebec had no payments to make. This meant the other provinces saw their payments from the dominion increased.[29] Everyone was happy.

In the Quebec Assembly, Fortin used the victory to deny Rouge charges. His provincial government was not, as alleged, just a branch of the federal one. True, he said, both worked in the interests of the country. Local and federal Conservatives did form an alliance. This, however, had a happy result. Look how the Quebec government had defended Quebec's position in the dispute between Ontario and Quebec over the public debt![30] The defence helped restore Fortin's standing in the province, and the Assembly would later unanimously elect him speaker.

Back in Ottawa, the Conservative government had problems. In November 1873 the Canadian Pacific Railway scandal became acute. Accusations that Macdonald had taken election funds from Sir Hugh Allan and other businessman threatened defeat. To avoid it, the government resigned. The Liberals under Mackenzie took power and Fortin found himself in opposition.

The right of members to sit in both the federal and provincial legislatures had always been controversial. In 1872 a private Commons' bill had tried to abolish dual representation. Opposing it, one member said constituents should decide if they wanted the same representative in both houses. The bill was defeated.[31]

Fortin voted against abolishing dual representation. Still, when legislation finally abolished it in 1873, he might well have been happy to leave federal politics. While scandal marred his federal party, he now held the ministry of Crown lands in the Quebec government. Provincial politics looked the place to be. For the next five years, Fortin represented Gaspé in the Quebec legislature only. However, with the 1878 federal election, Fortin quit Quebec politics. His constituents returned him to the Commons.

The Liberal government enacted some worthwhile but dull reforms. Then dissension in the cabinet and an economic depression cost the Liberals votes. Meanwhile, Macdonald's Conservatives promoted the National Policy of nation building: protection and immigration would bring prosperity. In Quebec, the Ultramontanes were strong. These right-wing clerics and laymen demanded that the church take precedence over any political party in defining government policy on education and other social matters. They backed the Bleus, headed by J.-Israël Tarte. The Conservatives were victorious nationally and in Quebec. There, the Bleus, including Fortin, outnumbered the Liberals 47 to 18.[32]

As a good Conservative, Fortin supported his government's National Policy. "England did not build up her power and wealth by Free Trade," he said, but adopted it only "after she had become supreme as a manufacturing and naval power." Fortin "would never be hostile to the interests of Great Britain. [She] was the Mother Country, and from her we received the blessing of Constitutional Government. But we must look to ourselves and protect our interests and find employment for our starving people."[33]

However, he wanted changes in the National Policy. He argued that it should correct an injustice to Canadian shipbuilders. They had to pay duty on material they imported, whereas Americans, under the British shipping act, could bring ships to Canada and sell them without paying duties. Shipowners might benefit by buying foreign ships for less than they could buy Canadian. The government, however, should also look after Canadian shipbuilders by removing duties on shipbuilding materials. In short, Fortin wanted a little bit of free trade.

By the 1882 election, prosperity was quickly returning to Canada. Macdonald could claim that his National Policy, his all-Canada transport policy and the settlement of the West were all building a greater

Canada. In case policy were not enough, he enthusiastically gerrymandered Ontario constituencies. The Ontario Liberals argued without much effect that Quebec dominated Macdonald and his Conservatives.[34] In Quebec, the church again condemned the Rouges:

[At Trois-Rivières], the archbishop sounded aloud his most eloquent maledictions [against the Rouges]. The Rouge candidate finally understood his sinfulness and withdrew, on the eve of the vote. The [Rouge] adversary of Pierre Fortin made the same gesture, the same day, at Gaspé. Even before the vote, the Conservatives had elected twenty-one deputies, the Liberals only one.[35]

The election swept the Conservatives back into power nationally. In Quebec the Bleus won fifty-one seats, among them Fortin's, the Liberals thirteen.[36]

In the 1883 session Fortin returned to the National Policy. As an exercise in logic, his position on protection versus free trade was hardly consistent. His problem lay in reconciling his government's policies with the interests of his constituency:

I did not support Protection alone. But I went for the National Policy which is more than Protection. The National Policy means protection for the manufacturers of this country by means of fiscal duties. But when our market is abroad you have to adopt Free Trade. You have to allow all the utensils and tools used in any particular industry to come in as cheap as possible. [Then] our people, being able to work as cheap as in other countries, we have the same chance as in other countries.

Fortin insisted he was no free trader, repeating that Britain had favoured free trade only "when she had nothing more to protect." Canada had much to protect in the fishing industry. However, he believed "the government should find some way of protecting the rope manufacture, and still allow the cordage used by fishermen to be free as previously." Again, Fortin wanted it both ways.

Sir Leonard Tilley, minister of finance, replied that Fortin "may be considered as the representative of the fishermen of the Dominion in this House." He had listened to him carefully, and reminded Fortin that because of his advocacy, fishermen had won many advantages. They had got cable and telegraph in the Bay of Fundy. The duty on sail duck had been lowered to 5 percent. Nearly every other article used by the fishermen—lines, twines, etc.—was admitted free or at 5 percent. Only cordage was 10 percent and would have to remain so.[37]

In 1884 Fortin again returned to the National Policy. He argued that in matters of trade Newfoundlanders must be considered foreigners. He asked if they were going "to get special privileges over our own people." The Newfoundlanders, as "sharp and shrewd as they are" were not under the National Policy. "It is we who have been outraged."[38] Two years earlier Fortin had explained the problem posed by Newfoundland. Canadian fishermen had to pay a large fee for compulsory government inspection of their fish and fish oils. In contrast, Newfoundlanders exported pickled herrings to Canada, and had to pay only a nominal fee for inspection by their own inspectors. This let the ingenious Newfoundlanders play a fast one on the Canadians.

"I have a list of all the fishery inspectors of Newfoundland for the year 1880. [From this] it appears there are no less than 127. This confirms ... that every [Newfoundland] fisherman who wants to be a fishery inspector has only to apply to the merchant who supplies him, and he becomes inspector of his own fish." So Newfoundlanders paid themselves only two cents a barrel inspection fee. A Canadian fisherman had to pay from twenty to twenty-five cents a barrel or have his fish seized. "I say it is not fair play."[39]

Then his position against the National Policy hardened. Preferential treatment for Newfoundlanders, he said, had excluded Îles-de-la-Madeleine fishermen from the Quebec market. He might expect that under Liberal free-traders, but a protectionist policy should apply to herrings as well as cottons. If not, then "I cannot support it [the government] any more. I do not believe in two weights and two measures—one weight and measure for the cotton manufacturers of Montréal.... Another weight and measure for the fishermen and the fishing merchants of the Gulf of St. Lawrence." As a result of the National Policy, many fishermen on the North Shore were in bad shape. They would starve if the federal and provincial governments did not send provisions. They "have been reduced consequently to a destitute condition.... I appeal to the people of Nova Scotia and to New Brunswick to endorse the stand I take."[40] The speech took more than three columns of densely packed statistics. Nevertheless, the National Policy remained unaffected by Fortin's figures or his pleas.

Fortin, then, was generally silent in the great national debates of the Commons. Only when they directly touched his constituents did he speak out. When it came to local affairs, he never stopped working.

NOTES

1. Bélanger, Jules, et al. *Histoire de la Gaspésie*. Montréal: Boréal Express, 1981: 502.
2. Quoted in Beck, 5.
3. HOCD, 19 March 1879, 561.
4. Rumilly, Vol. 1: 118.
5. Beck, 12.
6. HOCD, 19 December 1867, 317.
7. QLAD, 16 November 1870, 33.
8. HOCD, 26 March 1868, 407.
9. *l'Opinion Publique*, 23 December 1875, 601-02.
10. Potvin, *Le roi*, 82.
11. Province of Canada, Legislative Assembly, *Debates*, 1855 (V, VII, P VIII), 3624.
12. HOCD, 20 April 1870, 1097.
13. HOCD, 4 May 1868, 627.
14. HOCD, 15 May 1883, 1203.
15. HOCD, 4 May 1872, 579, 16 May 1872, 646-47.
16. HOCD, 5 May 1873, 144.
17. See for instance HOCD, 26 May 1869, 459, 30 April 1872, 127.
18. See for instance HOCD, 23 May 1872, 798.
19. HOCD, 30 March 1868, 420-23.
20. HOCD, 10 April 1871, 999.
21. HOCD, 11 April 1871, 1050.
22. HOCD, 20 May 1872, 705.
23. Beck, 21.
24. Rumilly, Vol. 1: 261.
25. Beausoleil, C. "Correspondence autour de la question scolaire du Nouveau-Brunswick, 1873," *Revue d'histoire de l'Amérique française*, Vol. 4, No. 4 (March 1951): 568-72.
26. Rumilly, Vol. 1: 264.
27. Dawson, R. MacGregor. *The Government of Canada*. 4th edition. Toronto: University of Toronto Press, 1964: 106.
28. Maxwell, J.A. *Federal Subsidies to the Provincial Governments in Canada*. Cambridge, MA: Harvard University Press, 1937: 51-53.
29. Dawson, 106.
30. QLAD, 9 December 1873, 29.
31. HOCD, 23 May 1872, 798.
32. Beck, 37.
33. HOCD, 6 March 1879, 183.
34. Beck, 38.
35. Rumilly, Vol. 3: 197.

36. Beck, 45.
37. HOCD, 17 April 1883, 670-71.
38. HOCD, 7 April 1884, 1395.
39. HOCD, 15 March 1882, 369.
40. HOCD, 7 April 1884, 1395.

XIV

A CONSTITUENCY MAN

In the first session of the Quebec Assembly, Fortin pursued the causes he had pursued as commander on *La Canadienne*.

13 January 1868: Fortin asked if the government intended to set up schools of navigation. The Conservative prime minister, P.-J.-O. Chauveau, hedged. The federal government was responsible for navigation, the provincial for education. The government would consider the question.

21 January: He asked if the government intended to prevent Crown lands along the Intercolonial Railway from falling into the hands of speculators. Those lands should go to worthy colonists. Chauveau said existing laws were sufficient but the government would look at the matter.

6 February: Fortin and M.C. Hamilton (Bonaventure) moved for a committee to investigate the Fisheries and Coal Mining Company of Gaspé. In 1843 the government had sold the company 130,000 acres of "the best" Crown land in Gaspé and Bonaventure for $200,000. The company undertook to improve the land but was now selling it at inflated prices with no improvements. Poor colonists could not afford it, claimed Fortin. The legislature formed a committee to see if the company was fulfilling its obligations.

11 February: Fortin moved for and got another committee to investigate land ownership on the Îles-de-la-Madeleine.

12 February: He argued that a bill amending the law protecting game and fish required further study. He also wanted action to stop fishermen raiding the nests of seabirds for their eggs.[1]

Fortin continued along the same lines in the second session. He supported colonization (26 February), seconded a bill encouraging repatriation of Canadians living in the United States (1 March), called for papers on the fires that swept the North Shore in 1867 and 1868 (10 March), and he successfully moved that a Committee be set up to study the problem (12 March). He introduced a bill on the hiring of fishermen and the payment of their wages (15 March) and saw it pass third reading (22 March). He introduced another to incorporate the Saint-Michel Société ecclesiastique (20 March) and moved third reading of a bill incorporating the Quebec Association of Dentists (31 March). He proposed printing and distributing copies of an "Act for the protection of insect-eating birds and others useful for agriculture," but the speaker ruled him out of order since this involved public expenditures (1 April).[2]

Fortin's activities and interventions in his first two sessions are striking in their practicality. They ranged from major themes of colonization and immigration down to methods of hitching horses: he seconded a bill that would change the method of attaching shafts to sleighs, with the shaft so placed that the runners followed the tracks of the horse.[3]

In the provincial election of 1871 the Conservatives returned to power. Fortin was unopposed. Over the next two sessions, he was much less vocal. In 1871 he became chairman of the committee on elections. On 5 December he supported subsidies for repatriating Canadians from the United States. He felt they should have priority over immigrants from Europe; expatriates, he said, knew better what to expect. And on 21 December he wanted to withhold judgement on the Treaty of Washington until all the papers were available and had been studied.[4]

In 1872 Fortin chaired yet another special committee studying land ownership in the Îles-de-la-Madeleine. On 6 December he denied charges the government favoured its own constituencies when distributing road subsidies. And on the 18th he urged the government to move against land speculation on former Crown lands and by the seigneurs.[5]

Fortin for long made colonization his crusade. From the 1830s, overpopulation along the arable St. Lawrence valley lands had forced thousands of young habitants to migrate to Ontario and the West or, worst of all, to the United States. The church increasingly deplored this drift. For the church, rural life in the St. Lawrence valley embodied all the virtues of French and Catholic culture. The cities, now a powerful magnet for the young habitants, were sinful; they were also English-speaking. Migration to Ontario and the United States would undoubtedly mean loss of language and of faith. To counter this movement, the church promoted the idea of colonization. Young habitants should be encouraged to take up lands in remote areas of Quebec and to follow a traditional agricultural life. So they settled in Gaspésie and the Eastern Townships, and in the Saguenay/Lac Saint-Jean and Ottawa Valley regions. They even went to the small, infertile valleys of the Shield itself.[6]

In Gaspésie colonization meant both bringing in new settlers and encouraging fishermen to turn more to agriculture. In the mid-1800s, Abbé Gingras had promoted *agriculturalisme* among the fishermen.[7] Fortin had taken the same view in his days on *La Canadienne*. In 1861 *La Canadienne* anchored off Rustico, P.E.I., where Fortin planned to take on board Acadian families waiting to emigrate to Gaspésie as farmers. The local priest told him that many families were preparing to leave Rustico later that year for Matapédia. Unfortunately, none were yet ready to embark. They were harvesting and could not go before November. Someone had made a bureaucratic blunder, so *La Canadienne* returned with no passengers.[8]

Politics, especially the Quebec Assembly, gave Fortin a wider platform. He supported an 1869 bill to encourage societies for the colonization of Quebec Crown lands, and he urged the government to open more roads for settlers. Otherwise colonization would not work. "The life of a colonist is a difficult life. [It is] a life of self-abnegation and often of misery." One summer too dry or too wet, and the colonist faced a long, hard winter. He had little food for his family and no seed grain for the spring. "It is then that the Colonization Societies can come to his aid" and enable him to survive. Canada needed farmers and skilled workmen wherever they came from, Fortin continued, but especially those from Great Britain. The presence of farmers and artisans "would add to the wealth, the prosperity and the stability of the country." He also hoped the government would do all in its power to encourage Canadian emigrants to the United States to return. They could then take part in colonization.

Fortin's appeals for funds for colonization, and especially for roads, continued. On 1 March 1869 he wanted Assembly committees to study how colonization could help achieve this reverse labour drain. On the 12th he wanted free land concessions to colonists, with adequate roads.

If you really want a successful country, he said, "you have to spend money, and lots of money. Money is the nervous system of colonization."[9]

In a speech the next year, Fortin thought the colonization societies had been successful so far. However, they could not do the job if the government refused to open colonization roads. Some members claimed the colonists should pay for the roads. That would be a serious mistake. "Amongst us," he said, "the taste for rural life is so little developed that rarely do rich people or middle class farmers become colonisers. This difficult but nation-building work is left to the poor. And what are their resources? An axe, a strong arm, a good will, and much resignation. Yes, we need to give them help."

Colonization, continued Fortin, was a social project as well as one of high politics. It was social because it permitted a large segment of the Canadian family—English, Scots, Irish, and French—to enjoy their part of the public lands. He spoke of the thousands of French-Canadian expatriates in the United States. Colonisation meant they could return to their native land rather than remaining refugees in a foreign land. It was also a political project because it promised the only way to correct the population imbalance between Quebec and Ontario. Until now this had favored Ontario politically. "In promoting colonization with all our strength, we will reestablish the balance between the two rival provinces and escape the threat of Upper Canada dwarfing us."

In November, Fortin questioned the Department of Crown Lands about the sale of public lands. The law required buyers to make improvements, but were they holding land for speculation? This violated the conditions of sale. "The government has reduced the price of land, but that has produced abuses by greedy men, hungry for gain" through land speculation.[10]

In a bitter debate with P.-A. Tremblay, Fortin showed he could hold his own in a partisan squabble. Tremblay had criticized the rules governing the sale of crown lands. Fortin countered that the rules operated fairly and to the rightful advantage of the colonists. True, some lots had been reconfiscated, but only if settlers had contravened regulations. He said Tremblay was unhappy with the rules because his friends, his relatives, and perhaps he himself had had lots confiscated.

Tremblay denied Fortin's allegations. On 9 December Fortin returned to the attack: "I have accused [Tremblay]," he said, "for holding four lots without conforming to the regulations. I have made this accusation directly, without insinuation. I have accused him of wishing to speculate. I have accused him directly of having blamed the government because he owns the lots. And I persist in my accusations. Let him prove the contrary."

Tremblay replied, "I had the lots but the Commissioner confiscated them because I had not made the impossible improvements. I say it was impossible to improve the lots that I had taken for my impoverished relatives."[11] He claimed he had no personal motives. He was just pleading the cause of the colonists who, it appears, included his impoverished relatives.

Another problem for colonists lay in hunting and fishing rights. Early in the century, Lower Canada had started leasing the North Shore salmon rivers to private interests. Throughout his career, Fortin opposed leasing. He did so even when, as magistrate, he upheld the law on which it was based. Many private clubs leased rivers for sports purposes. Some of the clubs practised conservation and saved their salmon rivers. The Quebec Fish and Game Club had taken over on the Rivière Jacques-Cartier in the 1860s. It was then near death, but they had brought the salmon back.[12] For Fortin, this was the wrong way to do it; the answer to overfishing lay in public regulation. Such regulation must conserve the fish stocks for those who lived by them. Private regulation by sportsmen for their own enjoyment aggravated the problem.

Fortin fought his strongest battles for the fisheries in the House of Commons rather than in the Quebec Assembly. On 7 December 1870 he argued that old land and water rights would have to change to make colonization work. Sportsmen should lose their privileges. Thirteen years later, he fought the same fight. Debating a fisheries bill, he said that wealthy sportsmen from England, America and Canada went to the salmon rivers to fly fish. If allowed at all, they should pay a hefty licence fee. "They do not catch them for the purpose of food. And when caught they do not make an article which is worth one dollar for exportation." These fishermen would deplete the salmon in their breeding grounds and destroy an industry employing many commercial fishermen. Fortin had seen poor fishermen turned away from a river where they had made their living for years.

Canadians did not want landlords. Talk to coastal fishermen, he suggested. You would hear them speaking against the government for giving the rivers to gentlemen for a few hundred dollars. "Not the present Government," Fortin added, "but past Governments." One Gaspé river went to a gentleman for $200 or $300, and he managed to make about $1,000 a year by subletting.[13] The same speech showed that Fortin did not fully trust the provincial government. He was sure the province would try to get maximum revenues from the salmon fisheries by giving as many permits as possible for fly fishing. The province had no interest in commercial net fishing because it involved leasing, and lease revenues went to the federal Treasury.

In 1868 Fortin urged appointment of a committee on fisheries. Two opposition members wanted the question postponed. Then Sir John A. intervened. He thought a committee could be helpful. The motion carried, and Fortin became chairman of the Committee on Fisheries and Navigation. He presented four committee reports in 1868. The first was procedural. The second recommended a fee of $4 a ton on American vessels fishing in Canadian waters, the fees to be used "for the benefit of the fishing industry." As well, Canada and Prince Edward Island should discuss common action against foreign intrusion. The third recommended, among other things, a drawback of duty on cordage, canvas and chains used for fishing. The last recommended that inspection of inland water fisheries should continue. River spawning, said the report, affected all Canadian fishing.[14]

The fisheries committee (and for "committee" we can probably read "Fortin") composed a questionnaire with forty-six questions, twenty-one on the sea fisheries, thirteen on inland fisheries, and twelve on navigation. Some thirty-two individuals or groups from Ontario, seventy-six from Quebec, seventeen from New Brunswick, and fifty-five from Nova Scotia answered the questionnaire. A synopsis of replies occupies 178 pages. The questions ranged from the best methods of taking various fish to whether the Americans were destroying the cod fishing (they were, said most) to the need for teaching navigation.[15] The questionnaire makes one description of Fortin at work very believable. He was "from morning to evening shut up with one or two secretaries in a room specially provided by the government."[16]

On 18 May 1868 Macdonald moved third reading of the new fisheries bill. Under it, the government would increase the fee for foreign fishermen from $1 to $2 a ton, less than the $4 Fortin's committee had recommended. In addition, a foreign captain found fishing without a licence within three miles of the Canadian coast could forfeit his vessel and cargo.[17] The member for Gaspé spoke to the bill. Earlier, Fortin said, he had approved it. Now he objected to the omission of a bounty for Canadian fishing vessels. This again was a constant Fortin theme. As fisheries officer, he had helped draft the 1858 act, which provided bounties for fishing vessels.[18] Bounty, Fortin said in 1868, had had "good results during the few years that it had lasted." An American bounty levied over sixty years had enabled them to build a fishing fleet of 1,000 vessels, the best equipped in the world.

While the prime minister assured Fortin he was "alive to the importance" of the fisheries, he was adamant in denying bounties to Canadian fishermen. "For good or for evil, that question had been settled for the present session."[19]

The government later reinstituted bounties, but Fortin kept pressing for higher subsidies. Unfortunately, he was absent from the House in 1883 when his campaign finally won through. During the 7 May debate, M.H. Richey, "in the absence of Mr. Fortin," enquired if the government had considered augmenting the fishing bounty on fishing boats? Had it come to a decision?

"Mr [Mackenzie] Bowell: The government has decided to double the bounty to fishing boats and to fishermen."[20]

Bounties, Fortin maintained, were necessary for the economic health of his fishermen, but their lives depended on efficient navigational aids around the dangerous coasts of the St. Lawrence. During his years on *La Canadienne*, Fortin had often made safety recommendations. In 1856 he had urged the government to build a crescent-shaped jetty at Percé, where any wind off the sea made it impossible for ships to anchor. A jetty would provide shelter for fifty to sixty vessels. The next year he wanted a lighthouse at Paspébiac: wooden, twenty feet high, with a red light to distinguish it from house and ship lights. He also recommended coloured lights at dangerous points along the coast.[21]

The matter of navigational aids also came under federal jurisdiction. In 1867-68, as chairman of the Commons special committee on fisheries and navigation, his recommendations carried more weight than they had when he was a fisheries officer. The committee report recommended fifteen new lighthouses in the lower ports of the St. Lawrence, and "insisted on such lights" at the Îles aux Oiseaux and the reef at Île Vert. It also recommended a new warning system of foghorns, bells, guns and other aids to navigation.[22]

Fortin kept up the pressure throughout his years in both the legislatures. In 1883 he gave a long speech in the Commons on the need for hydrographical surveys on the Great Lakes, the St. Lawrence River and Gulf, and off Canada's other coasts. His statistics included the tonnage at the ports of Quebec and Montréal, showing a decline over ten years. He attributed this to the dangers of navigation on the St. Lawrence.

Such dangers also caused the high insurance rates that he quoted. He remembered discovering how much better the Americans charted their coasts.

The Minister, Archibald W. McLelan, was gracious. He said Fortin had made many valuable suggestions about navigation on the Gulf. "In fact all the hon. gentleman's suggestions have been of great value to the country." Fortin would admit that the government had always shown its willingness to follow his suggestions. "Many lights have been added. Fog alarms and whistles have been placed at different points. And telegraphic communications [have been] furnished nearly throughout the length of the Gulf."[23]

In an appendix to his 1858 report, Fortin had included a letter from an agent of Lloyds of London. He asked Fortin to report to the government on the need for navigational aids on the coast, including "an electric telegraph from the lighthouse at Cap des Rosiers to the head of the Bay."[24] Ten years later, Fortin again pushed for extension of the telegraph on the peninsula. Government purchase of all the Canadian lines would, he said, unite telegraphic and postal services. That would make the former "more complete, more efficacious, and especially more economical." He wanted the telegraph extended to all the shores of the Gulf, and to the Great Lakes. The prime minister replied that the British government was considering this. He would await results of the actions.[25] Two years passed. Fortin asked again if the government intended to buy up the existing telegraph lines in the Dominion. Macdonald replied that as yet it did not.[26]

In the Quebec Assembly, Fortin often pushed for extension of the telegraph system around the Gulf. As well, in 1875 he wrote letters to *Le Canadien*. Newspapers had given much publicity to six ships overdue at the beginning of the navigable season. "Had they foundered on the high seas?" Fortin asked in one letter. "Had they been driven ashore by ice? Or were they simply detained by an impassable ice barrier at the entrance of the Gulf? No one knew, no one could know." There were no means of communication.[27]

Such urgent questions about the fate of supply ships went back to the earliest days of New France. For Fortin, the solution lay with the lighthouse, manned by three keepers, on the Bird Rocks [Rochers aux Oiseaux], which sat in the middle of the Gulf opposite its main entrance. They formed "a sentry box, [with] vigilant sentinels in it." The lighthouse keepers, he said, were "perched" 140 feet above the water, and had no doubt seen the lost steamers. They knew the state of the ice and whether the steamers could be freed. They knew when the ice began to disappear. All this and more information would be useful here and in Europe, but the lighthouse people "cannot communicate it to us." It needed only a telegraph line between the Îles-de-la-Madeleine and the Rochers aux Oiseaux to supply this urgent information.[28]

The Quebec *Morning Chronicle* strongly supported Fortin's idea. The government should use "the sentinels, as Mr. Fortin expressively calls them" on Bird Rock. The editor of *Le Canadien* said that the boards of trade of Montréal, Québec, Halifax, and several other cities, as well as the Dominion Board of Trade, also supported Fortin's attempt to extend the telegraph system around the Gulf.

Shipowners and seamen, and then an 1876 Commons committee, pushed the idea. In 1879 the government voted $35,000 to start a system between Halifax and Canso, and one between the Îles-de-la-Madeleine and Anticosti. The first attempt did not succeed. By 1881, Fortin said, the Îles-de-la-Madeleine had eighty-three miles of telegraph line. They joined with Cape Breton's 126 miles of line via fifty-five miles of undersea cable. Similarly, lines linked Anticosti to Gaspé, Malbaie to Mille Vaches on the North Shore, Halifax to Canso, and Grand Manan to the mainland.

Fortin now proposed extending the line along the North Shore to Forteau Bay, Labrador. The bay was always open during the navigation season, and a terminal there "will then be in constant connection with Canada, the United States, and in fact the whole world." A ship stopping there could send "dispatches, lists of passengers, private messages, etc., etc., after a run of five days only from Moville, Ireland.... It would be in a sense a realization of the greatly desired five day journey between Europe and America."

Fortin quoted the current commander in charge of fisheries protection, Dr. Wakeham. The North Shore fisheries, said Wakeham, had been overabundant that year. With telegraph available, men on the poor South Shore could have come north to take advantage of it. Fortin developed this theme. He suggested posting bulletins every day at noon at all telegraph stations to give details of where the fish were, the state of bait supply, weather reports, and other information. A three-page form he designed gave a comprehensive code displaying the information fishermen would want. In his letters, Fortin included copies of many letters of support, "from scientists, fishery outfitters, leading fishermen and others engaged in the fishing industry."[29]

The telegraph finally did link the Îles-de-la-Madeleine with the mainland, and Fortin tried to use it whenever possible. His private member's bill, introduced on 6 March 1882, would have allowed transmission of island election results to the mainland when ice prevented communications by ship, but the bill died on the paper. At this time, Macdonald called Fortin, "The great telegraphic authority in our country."[30] A map (dated 1876, with additions in 1881) is held in the National Archives. It shows the existing and proposed telegraph routes throughout the Gulf. The map, inscribed as "Delineated under the Direction of Hon. P. Fortin," must have been started during his period as commissioner of Crown lands.[31]

As well as roads and telegraph, Fortin also pushed for Gaspésie rail links. The 1867 Intercolonial Railway bill gave the cabinet the right to choose the route from Rivière-de-Loup to a Maritime port. This line would give Ontario and Quebec ice-free access to the Atlantic without crossing American territory. The question had bedevilled provincial relations long before Confederation. Quebec, Nova Scotia and New Brunswick, or factions within each region, all demanded that the new line run through their territory.

The member for Gaspé spoke first after the prime minister had introduced the bill. He started this, his first major speech in the newly created House of Commons, on high ground. The subject, he said, was more important to the Dominion than just the cost of $20 million. Militarily, the railroad would closely affect "even our national existence.... [It] will, during the winter months, unite together the remotest parts of our country, and will for months of the year be the only means of communication with the Mother Country."

Of the three suggested routes, Fortin favoured the so-called Major Robinson route running across the base of the Gaspésie Peninsula from Mont Joli on the St. Lawrence, to Campbelltown, N.B. Using statistics, he argued that this route was the most economical and the best protected against American invasion. He added almost as an aside that it would also benefit his constituency. "The Peninsula of Gaspé is larger than several European Kingdoms, and could keep and maintain half a million souls." But lack of communications made it almost a desert. More than 1,200 miles of coast, from Sainte-Anne-des-Monts to Fox River [Rivière-au-Renard], had no highways nor even footpaths. Travellers were confined to the beaches.

Moreover, the Robinson route would aid the fishing industries of Quebec, New Brunswick and Nova Scotia. In 1866 in Bonaventure alone, fishermen caught 4.8 million pounds of fish, but 2.4 million had to be used for manure because it could not be shipped to Quebec, Ontario and American markets. Instead of 40,000 fishermen, the area could easily support 80,000 if this Intercolonial route were to open new markets. "I see as a reality my most ardent wishes," Fortin said, "and I see with eyes of hope this Intercolonial route bringing activity, progress, wealth" to many localities that "have not attained the hundredth part" of their potential.[32]

In 1875, the cabinet finally accepted the Major Robinson route Fortin wanted. Almost immediately, Fortin began fighting for a Chaleur Bay railway to link the Intercolonial with communities along the south coast of the peninsula. In one speech, Fortin cited a recent case. Ice had trapped a dozen schooners carrying provisions for Gaspé and Bonaventure. Many families suffered near-starvation through that winter. Some winters, large quantities of fish remained in the hangars of Gaspé, with no means of transport to the large cities. This deprived hundreds of families of their earnings. A railway would ameliorate this.[33]

Ten years later Fortin was still fighting for the Chaleur Bay railway. On 16 April 1884 he told the House he supported government railway policy, including the Chaleur Bay railway. He again used statistics to show that the railway would open up the counties of Bonaventure and Gaspé, which comprised more than 5,000,000 acres of land and a fast-increasing population of 40,000.[34] However, the first train, from Matapédia to New Carlisle, did not run till 1 June 1893, six years after Fortin's death.

In 1868 Fortin had criticized the maladministration of justice on the peninsula. In 1878 in the Quebec Assembly, he again attacked by opposing a bill that would amend the constitution of the Quebec Superior Court. The bill, he said, was unjust. Those living in isolated areas, where communications were difficult, had as much right to legal services as city dwellers. It was a retrograde measure because it attacked the system of decentralization set up twenty years earlier. The old system gave two judges to the Gaspé district (Gaspé and Bonaventure counties plus the Îles-de-la-Madeleine); the new bill reduced that to one judge. Too often, said Fortin, the assembly refused to acknowledge the rights of Gaspésie. Loss of fishing bounties in 1867 was bad enough, but a poor system of justice was still worse.

"A government," he said, "cannot distribute wealth everywhere. It cannot give prosperity to all parts of the country.... But there is one thing that a wise and well intentioned government can give to everyone, without parsimony, without reserve: and that is justice." His constituents suffered with two judges over such a huge area. How much worse with only one![35]

Fortin was still complaining about justice in Gaspésie in 1882. The judge in Gaspé was "itinerant," he said in the Commons. They saw him twice a year and he stayed only two or three days. Neither Conservative nor Liberal governments had insisted on Gaspé judges residing there, and justice suffered. One judge refused to hear cases involving $20 to $30, despite witnesses coming long distances. He said they were not important enough. Another judge sat at Gaspé for two days and then closed the session, without accomplishing anything. "Mr St. Croix, from Jersey, Channel Islands ... had to remain in the county all winter to follow his case for this term, but his case has again been deferred."

The situation, said Fortin, was even worse for people from the Îles-de-la-Madeleine. If an islander had a case at Percé, he first got the dates from the court calendar. He took the steamer for Pictou, 120 miles away, then travelled from Pictou to Percé, another 370 miles. At Percé he was likely to find the judge absent, so he made the 490-mile journey home. In all, he had travelled 980 miles at a cost of from $50 to $60. Add to that "his disappointment at finding no Court, and damage to his case and his business." This process might be repeated many times over.

Fortin could plead eloquently for the people of the Gulf, and his pleas read much more effectively than the long tables of statistics he often inflicted on the House. "In short, all the Governments have shown, for the judiciary interests of that county, a heedlessness, a carelessness and disdain, which I am utterly at a loss to explain." The governments showed "No solicitude, no benevolence and no pity, I may say, for the population who are colonizing those distant regions." The colonists suffered "all kinds of difficulties and hardships." They also helped make "this country rich by their being great consumers of the products of the manufacturers." Fortin could explain this heedlessness in only one of two ways:

Either we are thought by the Government to be an inferior people inhabiting an inferior country, and that anything is good enough for us. Or else the government is returning to the old ideas of centralization. [These ideas] if carried out, will be fatal to this country. [Canada] increases its population only in the vast regions which lie at its extremities on the north, south, east and west. No pity for them! They must be worked and have nothing. No railways, no general improvements, not even a good administration of justice. But Sir, the measure is full and it overflows.

Fortin's complaint roused some big guns, including Prime Minister Macdonald himself, who admitted that Gaspé needed a resident judge. Mackenzie said that his government had tried to appoint such a judge, but the man had decided to live elsewhere. Wilfred Laurier, obviously hoping to embarrass the government, claimed that Gaspésie was certainly not the only area with judicial problems.[36] Despite all the sympathy, Fortin would not yet get equality for the people of the Gulf.

When discussing poverty on the peninsula, Fortin did not exaggerate. Just before he first took *La Canadienne* to the Gulf in 1852, the Montreal *Gazette* had reported on the disastrous conditions prevalent in Gaspésie. "With regret, we find that the most painful accounts of scarcity of food for cattle, and even for human subsistence" continue to come from Gaspésie. At Matane, winter dragged on into March. Most animals died of hunger, "both forage and grain had become exhausted." Use of seed grain for fodder had put in jeopardy next year's crops. The *Gazette* quoted a letter saying that famine threatened Carleton. The stock of fodder was gone and farmers had had to feed grain to the cattle. Worse, "an epidemic has carried off numbers of animals after the painful sacrifice made by their owners to preserve them from dying from natural starvation."[37]

Fortin knew such conditions were simply the extreme of the everpresent hardship for the Gulf peoples. In his last expedition in 1867, he wrote from Gaspé of the scarcity of seed grain and potatoes. "I regret very much having to have to record in this Report" that land had to be left unsown. The people feared "sufferings from want in the ensuing winter, even greater than in the winter which has just ended. (And that is what, unfortunately, did happen.)"[38]

All his life, Fortin pushed for the colonization of Gaspésie, for financial help for its fishermen and farmers, for safety in the Gulf, for better communications. He saw the future of Gaspésie in rosy terms, but the peninsula never got the financial help he hoped for, nor attained the standard of living he described. In Gaspésie at least, the great colonization dream of a prosperous farming community proved utopian, because the land and climate simply could not support it.

Nor did Fortin solve the problem of land ownership for the people of the Îles-de-la-Madeleine. His 1875 Commons committee on that question found only two habitants on the islands who owned their land. The rest leased their properties, for varying periods but always at a high rent, from the legatees of Sir Isaac Coffin. The people saw "no possibility of recovering the fruits of their labour." They could not better themselves "by energetic and perservering work." Nor could they dream of ever gaining title to their land. As a result, many were emigrating elsewhere. The committee asked that the government act to allow the habitants to own their lands. Fortin's report was ignored, then forgotten.[39]

In February 1873 Fortin reached the peak of his parliamentary career when Quebec Premier Gédéon Ouimet gave him a seat in cabinet as commissioner of Crown lands. The bureaucrats in his old department were now his direct responsibility, and he soon had to defend the record of himself and his predecessor against attacks by the Opposition.

The first attack came from Fortin's old opponent, P.-A. Tremblay, who charged that corruption existed in the Department of Crown Lands. Fortin admitted errors by an old employee, but claimed the man had done nothing criminal, and should not be fired. He had no pension and had served the department faithfully up to now. Two days later a member again attacked Fortin's competence. Fortin again admitted his agent had been "negligent" but denied fraud.[40] In short, Fortin showed the same loyalty to his "crew" that he expected from them. He stuck by the old retainer and the affair fizzled out. But a much more serious scandal replaced it.

In July 1874 Fortin was touring the province when he received word that Premier Ouimet wanted him back in Ottawa. He replied in a telegram, dated 1 August 1874, and sent from Pointe-Saint-Pierre to Ouimet. "I am visiting electors all over county. Important for me to stay at least one week."[41] But he had to hurry home. The Tanneries affair had reached a crisis.

Louis Archambeault was commissioner of public works when land speculation in Montréal was rife. Under Archambeault's auspices, the government exchanged one section of land for another. The land acquired was much the less valuable of the two, but its price had been artificially inflated, and speculators had shared part of the profits with their political associates. Archambeault had some $50,000 deposited in a bank account in his name, though this was probably for party rather than personal use.[42] In September 1874, Fortin, with no personal blame, resigned with the whole Cabinet.

The 1874-75 session saw Ouimet replaced by another Conservative, Charles-Eugène Boucher de Boucherville. Ouimet gave his explanation of the Tanneries affair to the Assembly. Fortin followed with his own account. Fortin had thought the two pieces of land were roughly equal in value.[43] In fact the Crown land was valued at $160,000, the land exchanged at $38,000.

John Rollo Middlemiss was a beneficiary of the land exchange and probably instigated the affair. When the next government began procedures to annul the deal, Middlemiss launched a suit against the lieutenant-governor and his ministers. In the fall of 1875 Judge Johnson found for the provincial government. He found no proof of conspiracy or of fraud by any ministers. Since the ministerial decision did not exceed the powers of the government, it was valid. Ouimet and his cabinet, including Fortin, "were once again, morally, potential ministers."[44]

As a private member again, Fortin appears much less active, except when dealing with some of his old themes. He moved amendments to the electoral land qualifications that would enfranchise more colonists. He argued for forest protection. He defended his government against other charges of impropriety. This time the charges involved an advance of $80,000 to the North Shore Railway the day before the Ouimet cabinet resigned.[45]

The Tanneries affair was not enough to defeat the Conservatives in the next 1875 provincial election. Gaspé too returned Fortin, with help from the church. In earlier years, the Opposition had not stood a candidate against Fortin but this time, the Liberals put up Edmund James Flynn, professor of Roman law at Laval University. Flynn was not a radical Rouge and later would join the Conservatives. However, the bishop of Rimouski wrote a warning to the priest of Sainte-Anne-des-Monts. The priest must remind his flock of all the good works Fortin had done for Gaspésie: "the railway, telegraph, light houses, colonization roads." He called the possible election of Flynn "deplorable." The people seemed to be under the mistaken impression they could vote Rouge "without offending God." The letter was widely circulated. According to one historian, in Sainte-Anne-des-Monts sixty-six voters risked offending God by voting for Flynn, while sixty-nine voted for Fortin.[46]

Unfortunately for Fortin, another scandal, much more personal than the Tanneries affair, now emerged. Three Percé men contested his election under the Controverted Elections Act of 1875. Despite this and the Tanneries affair, the Assembly unanimously elected Fortin speaker for its next session. The charges, however, continued, and Fortin resigned as speaker on 10 November 1876. On 24 March 1877 the Quebec Superior Court gave its decision, finding that the election was null and void. Fortin had to pay the petitioners' costs, but the court also reported, "No corrupt practice was proved to have been committed at the said Election by or with the knowledge of any candidate at the said Election." According to the evidence, "one of the agents of the Defendant was guilty of corrupt practices."[47] This agent had, apparently without Fortin's knowledge, given away liquor at the polls. Gaspé immediately re-elected Fortin (again over Flynn) in a by-election on 2 July 1877.[48]

In the provincial election of 1878, the returning officer reported that ice prevented navigation to the Îles-de-la-Madeleine. He could not therefore post the election proclamation, and that cost the islanders their vote. Fortin had always received a large majority from the Îles-de-la-Madeleine. He protested the returning officer's decision by refusing to stand,[49] and Flynn replaced him by acclamation. For the first time since 1867, the Liberals won Gaspé and took power in Quebec. Fortin quit Quebec provincial politics for good, and returned to Ottawa.

NOTES

1. QLAD, 1867-68, 31, 55, 114, 131, 135.
2. QLAD, 1869, 91, 99, 145, 153, 159, 196, 188, 226, 232.
3. QLAD, 31 March 1869, 123.
4. QLAD, 1871, 145, 194, 228.
5. QLAD, 1872, 70, 150, 231.
6. Linteau, 104-05.
7. Gingras, 492.
8. Fortin, *Report*, 1862.
9. QLAD, 26 February 1869, 90-91; 1 March, 97; 12 March, 155.
10. QLAD, 16 November 1870, 33; 30 November, 78.
11. QLAD, 2 December 1870, 90; 9 December, 110.
12. Dunfield, 141.
13. HOCD, 15 May 1883, 1202-23.
14. HOCD, 1 April 1868, 441-42; 21 April, 523; 4 May, 617; 7 May, 645.
15. "5th Report of the Select Committee, on Fisheries, Navigation ..." HOCJ, 1869.
16. "L'honorable Pierre Fortin."
17. Canada, *Acts*, 31 Vic. c.61 (1868).
18. Canada, *Acts*, 21 and 22 Vic. c.86 (1858).
19. HOCD, 18 May 1868, 729.

20. HOCD, 17 May 1883, 1025.
21. Fortin, *Report*, 1856.
22. HOCD, 4 May 1868, 617.
23. HOCD, 27 February 1883, 82-83.
24. Fortin, *Report*, 1859: Appendix. Letter from Philip Vibert.
25. HOCD, 21 November 1867, 109.
26. HOCD, 10 May 1869, 226.
27. Fortin, Pierre. *Letters from the Hon. P. Fortin, MP, on the Telegraph and Signal Service in the Gulf of St. Lawrence; on the United States' Signal Service; and on the Norwegian Telegraph System*. Ottawa: MacLean, Roger and Company, 1879: 3.
28. Quebec *Morning Chronicle*, 7 May 1875, quoted in Fortin, Pierre, *Letters*, 20.
29. Fortin, Pierre, *Letters*, 5-15.
30. HOCD, 6 March 1882, 220-21.
31. NA National Map Collection, Coast Telegraph Chart of the Gulf and Lower St. Lawrence, no. 0025306.
32. HOCD, 19 December 1867, 317-19.
33. QLAD, 5 February 1875, 251.
34. HOCD, 16 April 1884, 1626.
35. QLAD, 23 February 1878, 235.
36. HOCD, 27 February 1882, 110.
37. *Gazette*, 15 May 1847.
38. Fortin, *Report*, 1867-68.
39. "Report of the Select Committee on ... the Magdalen Islands," QLAJ, 1874-75.
40. QLAD, 17 and 19 January 1874, 173, 190.
41. NA, MG 27, F8, Gédéon Ouimet papers, Fortin to Ouimet, 1 August 1874.
42. Trépanier, Pierre and Trépanier, Lise. "Archambault, Louis," *Dictionary of Canadian Biography*, Vol. 11 (1982): 25-27.
43. QLAD, 3 December 1874, 13.
44. Rumilly, Vol. 2: 22, 43, 76.
45. QLAD, 20 February 1875, 344.
46. Hamelin, 216.
47. QLAJ, 1877-78, Appendix 1.
48. Bélanger, 503.
49. *Canadian Parliamentary Guide*. Ottawa: Citizen Printing and Publishing, 1879: 169.

XV

FINAL DAYS

Fortin remained physically strong all his life. As late as 1882, Mackenzie said of him, "I am sorry that, after the hon. gentleman has shown what the products of Gaspé are, there should be any desire manifested to live out of a district where men grow so stout and strong as its representative in this House." [1]

Nevertheless, he was aging. As early as 1871, his contemporaries noticed that even his first years in the two legislatures had changed him. "The representative of Gaspé," wrote Achintre, "has now become serious, even a little sad; his political work and his studies absorb him, only rarely relaxing with the laughter and gaiety of other times." [2]

During his first period in the Commons (1867-73), Fortin's speeches were often long and crammed with statistics, but they were readable and cogently argued. On his return to the Commons, he still gave long speeches and many statistics. At fifty-five, however, he began to lose some of the vigorous, clear thinking of the young commander. His speeches too often meandered as memories replaced hopes. They became personal and anecdotal, often about his old friend *La Canadienne*, lost in 1875 while supplying lighthouses off the Nova Scotia coast.

In 1879 members of the House were telling "war stories" of corruption at the polls and civil-service interference. Fortin made a rambling speech. He told his colleagues that he had been a civil servant for sixteen years in the Gulf. During that time, he had not meddled in politics. His masters, the Conservative government, would never have allowed it. Having left the service in 1867, he went on, "A most inveterate Reformer" passed himself off as a Conservative and got himself appointed to Fortin's old job. Then, as soon as the Liberals gained power, he "turned his coat back again and became a most violent partisan." The people were not going to contest Fortin's election, but this man, "in violation of his duty, left the North Shore and came hurriedly into Gaspé Bay," where he went to his Liberal friends. They collected money for a petition to unseat Fortin, and arrived back in Percé just in time to get the petition registered. Only a government vessel, burning government coal, made it physically possible to get the petition drawn in time, Fortin claimed. The House, he said, was aware how unfortunate he had been. His first lawyer had taken sick and died in a couple of days; the second had met with an accident. Since Fortin was not a lawyer, he had had to give up the case.

Fortin: The steamer this official used was the celebrated *Glendon*. She did not go fast but she went fast enough at that time.
    Sir John A Macdonald: Slow but sure.[3]

The fisheries officer reproached by Fortin was Napoléon Lavoie. Fortin's immediate successor, Théophile Têtu, had died soon after his appointment.

In 1880, Fortin described himself as "tormented" by the so-called Middlemiss affair. This matter arose from the aftermath of the Tanneries' scandal, when a Quebec court cleared the Ouimet cabinet of wrongdoing. In handwriting that is strong but sprawling and hard to read, Fortin wrote from Ottawa to Ouimet in Québec. He said that M. Saint-Pierre had "once again begun tormenting me on ... the costs of the Middlemiss lawsuit." He thought the question was settled—Saint-Pierre had no claim against him. A month later, an anxious second letter asked if Ouimet had received the first, as Fortin had had no response.[4]

On the back of Fortin's second letter, Ouimet wrote two draft replies, both dated 13 March. One, to Fortin, expressed "my surprise that M. Saint-Pierre persists in making his demands on you." The other, to Saint-Pierre in Montréal, said that Fortin had not authorized anyone to act in the Middlemiss affair, and he was not responsible. Ouimet thought that St. Pierre had given up on this matter. In reply, Saint-Pierre wrote in French, "I received your letter concerning the Middlemiss matter." He added the comment, in English, "Everything is *all right*" (his emphasis). The correspondence finished with Ouimet assuring Fortin that the Middlemiss affair was dead.[5]

The possibility of owing money in this matter clearly distressed Fortin. We know very little about his financial affairs. As member of the Commons about this time, his salary would have been £1,000 (about $2,400) a year, plus mileage. He also had some business interests and in 1876 was a director of the Isolated Risk Insurance Company.[6] On his death, he left his daughter a $10,000 insurance policy.

If Fortin sometimes grew anecdotal in the House, he still loved statistics. In 1883 he asked for all letters and papers about reciprocal trade agreements between Canada, Brazil, the West Indies and Mexico. He also wanted a statement of customs duties imposed by these countries on their imports and exports, a statement of the qualities of different articles (manufactured or unmanufactured), imported from these countries into Canada, and a statement of the commercial treaties (if such existed) between any of these countries and Great Britain.

Fortin later addressed the House. He craved the indulgence of the House, "if I should be somewhat lengthy and perhaps tedious." His comments and trade statistics include five large tables supplemented with various pieces of correspondence, and occupy more than ten densely packed columns, making for a very long and almost incomprehensible speech. However, he said, he wanted to make his statement complete. That way, "the House, and the Government, and the country might know what course to take." He concluded that Canada should abolish the $2,000,000 annual duty on sugar and molasses from Caribbean countries. In exchange, he wanted them to give freer entry to Canadian goods. He finished by apologizing "for any imperfections of expression." He would have liked to have spoken his own language, "but out of deference to the majority of the hon. members of this House, and in order that my remarks might be understood by all, I have spoken in the English language."[7]

Too often now, some colleagues saw little importance in the matters Fortin raised. This was obvious on 23 January 1884, when he again discussed pickled herrings from Newfoundland. He told a rambling story of "the famous Dutch Admiral, Van Tromp, [who] swept the British channel and dictated peace to the English." Ruyter and other Dutch admirals had command of the sea because they had herring fishermen, "recognised to be the best seamen in the world" on board. Indeed, Holland had possessed mastery of the sea for centuries because the famous Dutchman, Beukels, had discovered a means of preserving herring by pickling them. At first sight, that invention would seem of little account, but it had created a revolution in the herring trade. "The great Charles V ... when he visited Holland, expressed his opinion that Beukels ... was one of the greatest benefactors of humanity." Now, "these poor humble herring fishermen on our coasts and bays are well worthy of our attention."

Fortin ended on a sad note of disillusionment. He knew that for many, herring fishing was a very small affair. "I dare say if I had spoken of salmon, trout or of fly fishing, or of something relating to sport, many people perhaps would have been pleased." But commercially and economically, if not politically, the herring fishery was of very great importance for his people of the Gulf. Again, Fortin found the House more interested in sports fishing than in the well-being of the Gulf fisherman.

In 1884 Fortin received one of those small compliments that had been common in his early parliamentary days. The minister of fisheries, Mr. McLelan, promised him a report on the London International Fisheries Exhibition. Canada "had presented a collection of food fishes which has not been excelled in the world. [It received] the highest prizes given." He thanked the member for Gaspé who had helped in the collection of fish that won the gold medal.

But a few weeks later in debate on a militia bill, Mr. Haggart (South Lanark) compared the "efficiency of the Militia of this country, and that of our Navy. A few moments ago I observed Commander Fortin in his seat. Let us see how men in the navy have learnt that the first duty is obedience." According to Haggart, "On one of the little excursions down the St. Lawrence River," Fortin was on board. Crewmen, while fishing, hauled a porpoise on to "the steamer." Haggart went on, "Commander Fortin said it was a shark. The men all thought it was a porpoise. But the Commander said it was a shark, and ever from that day to this, wherever the broad pennant of the Canadian navy floats, a porpoise is known as a shark." Now that, he said, showed real discipline.

Fortin, always protective of his honour, took this mildly malicious anecdote to heart. The next Wednesday he rose to make a personal statement. He said that *La Canadienne* had not been a steamer but a sailing vessel and a faithful friend. The "tallness of her masts, the great spread of her wide sails, and her fine lines" made her eminently fit to "protect the fisheries, and to prevent evil doers from doing evil." It was the officers and crew he wished to defend from this attack "on our honour." The crew "understood what honour was, what duty was, what truth was ... and [they] obeyed without reluctance in any way." But it was he, Fortin, who had been personally attacked:

The people of this country, and perhaps the people of other countries where the speech ... may be read, will suppose that I do not know the difference between a porpoise and a shark. Sir, I hold in my hand printed reports for thirteen years. In [these] reports I have described minutely eighty-three species of marine animals and fishes. I think that hon. gentlemen, and the public generally who know how long and hard I worked in describing these fishes, will believe that I can make a distinction between a porpoise and a shark.

Certainly "there was rigid discipline on board, and the men had great regard for truth and honour." They would not have followed such an order. If anybody "in this House or in the country wish to sneer at the old Commander of *La Canadienne* and her officers and sailors, let them first go round the St. Lawrence Gulf. [They should] question the mariners who have seen us, and the fishermen who received help from us, as to the manner in which we performed our duty."

At that, Mr. Haggart apologized. He had had "not the slightest intention in the world of saying anything uncomplimentary" about Fortin. He had heard the story from another member but had no intention of insulting the commander or the crew.

The Minister, Peter Mitchell, clearly shared Fortin's sense of injury. He said he had been minister of marine and fisheries when Fortin was serving. He praised Fortin "for efficiency, for discipline, for cleanliness and order, for the manner in which he fulfilled the duties of the very important office he held as Chief Magistrate or Judge." His responsibilities "extended along a thousand miles of coast. His conduct ... reflected the greatest honour alike upon himself and upon the government he served." The country "owes to my old friend the Commodore a debt of gratitude for his practical services, and for the manner in which he performed important and delicate duties along that coast where now his present constituency lies." He had earned the respect and confidence of its inhabitants. "In the Department over which I presided, we all liked him, we all loved him.... I can only say that I regret that he has had to come before this House and make the personal explanation he did." This sad little incident closed when Fortin, now a commodore, accepted with pleasure the explanation and apology of the member for South Lanark.

Fortin's career was nearly ended. In the 1884 session he was a bit player in another curious incident. He had left his seat in the Commons chamber to go to the gallery. While he was there, a motion was read to the House. He listened, returned to his seat, and voted. The Opposition challenged this, since the rules said a member could not vote on a motion unless he had heard it read in the House. Yes, Fortin had heard the motion. But was the gallery part of the House? If not, then the member for Gaspé could not properly vote since he had not heard the motion in the House. After a long argument, the speaker ruled that in future the gallery would be "part of the House except for speaking and voting." Oddly, this left open the crucial question: Was the gallery "part of the House" for "hearing?"[8] This metaphysical problem was not settled until two cases in 1891 and 1924 raised the same issue. Now, according to Beauchesne, "A member must be within the House ... it is not sufficient to hear [the motion] while in the Gallery or behind the curtains."[9]

Next session, the House heard the member for Gaspé only once. On 9 February 1885 he asked for the number and amounts of all claims for fishing bounties. He also wanted the names of fishermen receiving the bounties and many other details. In earlier days, the House had seldom refused his requests for papers. Today Mr. McLelan said this would require examining some 40,000 papers, an enormous task. He asked the member for Gaspé to withdraw his motion until the annual report of the Department of Fisheries came down next month. Fortin acquiesced.[10] The House never again recorded his voice.

Though February 1885 saw Fortin's last speech in the Commons, he later participated silently in a most controversial and tragic event in Canadian history, and was vilified in Quebec because of it.*

On 19 March 1885, Louis Riel, "Prophet of the New World," once again moved onto the national scene. Canadian expansionism, riding the new railway, had pushed from Manitoba to Saskatchewan. In the parish church at Batoche, Saskatchewan, Riel declared himself head of a provisional government. In Ontario, memories of the "murder" of Thomas Scott flooded back. The church also condemned Riel's religious pretensions. For two months Métis and Indians fought 7,000 troops rushed there on the new railway before Riel surrendered. A jury found him guilty of treason, but recommended mercy. Appeals as high as the Privy Council in London failed. Bitterness welled up again between English and French Canada. The one saw Riel as a twofold traitor and

---

* This widespread reaction should not be confused with the savaging of Louis-Napoléon Fortin, Liberal MLA for Montmagny who, with Pierre's old opponent Flynn, switched to the Conservatives in 1879. See, Frechette, Louis. *Les Renégats du 29 Octobre: Paquet, Chauveau, Flynn, Racicot et Fortin:* LES TRAITRES! LES VENDUS!

murderer who had already escaped justice once, the other as perhaps misguided, but still a patriot who deserved mercy. He had served, as well as he knew how, the maltreated, French-speaking, Catholic Métis. Even the diplomacy of Macdonald could not reconcile the two views.

By late 1885 most of Macdonald's Bleus had joined the Quebec-wide protest against the planned hanging of Riel. One group of back-benchers telegraphed Macdonald, warning him that to hang Riel would bitterly divide both his party and Canada. Fortin told the group he would not cosign the telegram. *La Presse* reacted savagely. "Thirty years of servility," it said of Fortin, "have atrophied whatever patriotic sentiments he had."[11]

Macdonald, hammered on either side by Ontario and Quebec, finally refused to stop the execution. In March 1886 the Commons debated the resolution, "This House feels it its duty to express its deep regret that the sentence of death, passed on Louis Riel, convicted of high treason, was allowed to be carried into execution." Fortin was silent. But on the 24th he concurred in the decision to hang Riel by helping vote down the resolution. Once again, much of Quebec condemned him as a traitor, along with twenty-two other Francophone members who had voted with him. *L'Électeur* published their names. "Compatriots," the paper exhorted, "engrave in your memory the name of the traitors who have just soaked their hands in the blood of the unfortunate Riel, assassinated 16 November 1885."[12]

By 1887 the Conservatives looked bad federally. The National Policy could not cure a world depression. Immigration and western settlement were slowing down. Nova Scotia threatened to pull out of Confederation. Manitoba fought the CPR monopoly. Above all, Quebec Bleus were squabbling with one another, especially after Macdonald's Quebec lieutenants had accepted his decision to allow Riel to hang. After the election, the Conservatives still formed the government (126 to 89 seats), but they had only a one-seat margin in Quebec.[13] Fortin was not on the government benches, since illness had prevented him from standing. Shortly after, he became a Senator. There is no record of him speaking in the upper house.

•

Two traits were fundamental to Fortin's character: total honesty and respect for authority. Israël Tarte said of him, "I am sure M. Fortin has never told a lie in his life. He is above all a man of honour. [He is] honest in his motives, in his acts, in his correspondence. [He is] honest to the point that he is alone in the world of politics that lives only for intrigue and trickery."[14] An 1875 article in *l'Opinion publique* said that Fortin had been offered "several honorable and lucrative posts." One was as commissioner of the Québec police, but "because of his commitment to his constituents," he refused.[15]

The scandals in his career do not disprove his honesty, for they hardly touched him personally. Indeed, as Tarte hints, the scandals demonstrate an innocence in Fortin going beyond the technical innocence of the legal system. That innocence at times bordered on naiveté.

Second, Fortin always insisted on his authority. At one level, this seems to be just personal pride. He was not a certified ship's master or mate, yet he gave himself the rank of "commander." Others often inadvertently "promoted" him to captain and beyond, and he made no attempt to correct such errors. Indeed, the census of 1861 lists him as "Capt. Fortin."[16] His attraction to titles is in line with his youthful practice at McGill of calling himself Petrus rather than Pierre. At another and more important level, he used rank and status, along with letters of praise from people around the Gulf, as a sword against Whitcher and his like at headquarters. Any good bureaucrat of the line knows the value of a title as he knows the value of a skilfully written memo and report. If Commander Fortin's memos boosted himself, they also made it more difficult to refuse him the budgets and staff he needed.

Most important of all, he knew that *La Canadienne* and her commander could not maintain law and order in the Gulf without the respect of both resident and visiting fisherman. In 1879 the Commons discussed the grounding of the *Lady Head*, a government steamer. The incident had led to the dismissal of its master, Captain Purdye. The Opposition attacked the government but Fortin strongly supported the dismissal. Purdye, said Fortin, was incompetent and lacked even paper qualifications. The chief mate, who had once sailed under Fortin, was illiterate. For the second time in a few months, they had run the *Lady Head* ashore. A government vessel had to work with foreign men-of-war, call at many ports and meet many vessels. Fortin always "felt humiliated" because the *Lady Head* "carried two officers entirely incompetent."[17]

He was a churchgoer, but we have no documentation on the depth of his religious beliefs. A free vote in the House on a divorce bill showed Fortin following church teachings and voting against it.[18] He strongly pushed colonization, a favoured church policy. With the church, he disapproved of the Rouges' fascination with the United States and its republican institutions, and opposed "the introduction of the American system."[19] The Church repaid him, for at least two elections, the support of clerics for Fortin was clear, vocal and decisive.

Fortin clearly believed in the future of the new Canada. As a Bleu, he had helped create it. But within confederation, he wanted a strong Quebec to offset the strength of Ontario. By nurture, by education and every other influence, he was a Canadien with a strong loyalty to his language and culture. Potvin goes further. In 1858 Fortin visited Saint-Pierre and Miquelon to report on fishing methods there for the Canadian government. Potvin says that Fortin "had a profound love for France," and after an especially pleasant visit to the islands, "One could say that though he sailed under the British flag, he carried in his heart the flag of France."

Potvin also quotes the New York French newspaper, the *Courrier des États-Unis*, unfortunately not dated. Describing Fortin's visit to France, the paper said his trip took in Normandy, which all Canadiens "burned to see." He returned "regretting more than ever being obliged to fly the Union Jack rather than the tricolour of France at the masthead of *La Canadienne*."[20] Not surprisingly, Fortin, always respectful of Britain in his speeches, reports no such feelings in his official journals, and Potvin offers no confirming evidence.

Despite Fortin's commitment to Quebec and to things French, many factors alienated him from the nationalist Rouges. They saw him as a Bleu, supporting and supported by clerics. They saw him as one who refused to protest in Parliament the treatment of Riel in 1871 and the New Brunswick Common Schools Act. For this, they denounced him as a *vendu*, with bloody hands. He and his fellow ministers, the Rouges claimed, had made the Quebec government a mere branch of the federal Conservatives.

Was Fortin more or less consciously a member of the political and economic elites, imposing harsh laws on the peoples of the Gulf? Was he a true representative of the people, attempting to present their case to, and modify the policies of, the elites? Or was he simply a cypher, a blind instrument of a state itself shaped by blind economic forces?

In his role as politician, before even his commitment to the Bleus, Fortin saw himself as representing his constituents. Certainly, he saw the great fishing companies as constituents, but he also represented the people. "All the governments," he said, had "shown a heedlessness, a carelessness, and disdain" for his people: "no solicitude, no pity, no benevolence."[21] In the Commons he was a good party man and on general questions voted with the government. But when party policy came into conflict with the interests of his constituents, he quickly criticized his leaders. With the Treaty of Washington, the National Policy as it affected fishermen, fishing bounties and other local matters, he even took on the "Old Chieftain," Sir John A. himself.

As a magistrate, however, Fortin's position brought tensions. There is no evidence he misused his position to gain the support of the Channel Islands companies, but his strong sense of legitimate authority created contradictions. His reports from the Gulf often show a magistrate coldly and rationally applying the law. In his court he met starving Indians who had illegally speared salmon by torchlight, or fishermen who had deserted hard taskmasters. He coolly stated their crimes and the strict punishments he imposed. He hobnobbed with representatives of the influential Gaspé commercial companies and sat with them in harsh judgment on their employees and contractors. For Fortin, the law was the law—authority must be upheld.

In contrast, his reports did publicize the poverty of these people, and he described their problems in detail. He pleaded for and often succeeded in getting better education, more navigational aids, higher fishing bounties, better transportation, a fairer system of justice, and improved living conditions. Granted, many of these things would help the fishing companies as well as the fishermen and their families. But he also promoted schools of navigation and the free port of Gaspé as improving the condition of the fishermen against the interests of the fishing companies.

An 1862 quotation suggests something more behind his court judgments than a bleak interpretation of the law. Speaking of the North and South Shores, Fortin wrote, "The right of possession in seal and salmon fisheries used to give rise to so many difficulties (especially between neighbours), to trespass and often make encroachments, committed by the strongest to the prejudice of the weakest." He was pleased that only four such cases had occurred that year.[22] Three years later he wrote, "The weakest as well as the strongest, the poorest as well as the richest fishermen, whether engaged in the seal or the salmon fishery, has no longer anything to fear with respect to the possession of his fishing grounds."[23]

This softer, more humane Fortin, trying to protect the weakest from the strongest, appears in a tribute from a judge at New Carlisle.

Peter Winter wrote of him that many "poor sick people" of the Gulf owed him their gratitude. As doctor and surgeon, he had given "generous assistance ... quickly and freely."[24] His constituents clearly showed respect by repeatedly electing him to both legislatures.

The most poignant question, however, remains. Despite his rhetoric, did his life and work make any real difference, one way or another, to the economic and social structure of the Gulf?

Some of his most important causes clearly did not succeed, certainly not in his lifetime. The slaughter of Gulf birds and belugas continued into the twentieth century. Gaspésie never became the great agricultural/fishing region he prophesized. He could not turn aside the political and economic forces that forced the sellout (as he saw it) of the Gulf fisheries in the Treaty of Washington. Equally clearly, railways, telegraph and navigational aids would have come to the Gulf even without Fortin's advocacy. We could argue that as an early voice in environmental protection he shares some credit for today's environmental movement; that he helped modify the effects of the Treaty of Washington by his contribution to Canada's claims for compensation; and that although modern communications would inevitably have arrived in the Gulf, without him they may have come at a different pace and in a different way.

All this is true, but at this level of analysis our anecdotal evidence cannot prove whether or how the history of the Gulf might have been different without Fortin. We can only judge him at the level of its individual citizens. Many thousands of them felt the effects, good or ill, of the actions and words of Pierre Fortin, commander and magistrate on *La Canadienne*, and member for Gaspé of two legislatures. Perhaps Captain Philéas Sirois best summed up Fortin's contribution to the people of the Gulf in a letter to *Le Canadien* in 1865. The previous fall, Sirois and his schooner, *Marguerite*, had left Pointe-Saint-Pierre. Night brought a violent northeaster, and the schooner would not obey the helm. A squall hit the vessel, breaking a mast and carrying away the mainsail. Sirois decided to make land, if possible, through the heavy seas, and tried steering towards Malbaie. Ten minutes later, he saw a longboat coming from a vessel he recognized as *La Canadienne*. Fortin came on board to see for himself how severe the damage was. Then he left sailors under the command of Bernier to help. Sirois wrote:

If the noble and dignified conduct that [Fortin] showed to me and my men had been an isolated fact, I would be content to thank him in a private way.

But his constant good actions, his irreproachable conduct as a public employee, compels me to join that concert of praise on his account that one hears everywhere, and to publicly thank him, both in my name and in the name of all the inhabitants of the North Shore.[25]

At least at the level of individuals, the lives of many fishermen and their families would have been quite different without Fortin.

The Riel affair adds another dimension to our picture of the man. Fortin was only a minor player, and our attitudes to Macdonald and to Riel will probably determine our judgment of him. However, his actions in this last tragic affair were quite consistent with his life's principles. Rightly or wrongly, Fortin remained loyal to his party leader and to his church, just as he had expected loyalty from the crew of *La Canadienne*. Rightly or wrongly, he saw Riel's execution as the culmination of the due legal process.

More than that, Fortin stands in a long tradition of Canadiens and Canadiennes who saw themselves as carrying civilization into the wilderness. Adventurous, ambitious, intellectually curious, sometimes compassionate, often ruthless, always courageous, they founded a French civilization in North America. Over nearly 400 years it first endured, and now prospers.

We see Fortin, dressed in his commander's uniform, standing on the deck of *La Canadienne* as it crossed the line into the Gulf. And we can sense the pride he must have felt in sailing the course that Champlain once sailed. He had spent his life bringing to the wilderness not just law and order but education, science and technology; in a word, civilization. Grosse-Île in 1847, Montréal in 1849, and the Gulf, had each in its own way been a sort of wilderness. He had helped to "civilize" them. There lay the recurring patterns of his life. Crushing the Northwest rebellion, with its defiance towards legally constituted authority, secular and clerical, must have seemed to him a clear extension of that work. The commander was following the traditions of the heroes of New France. They too had brought law and order and the knowledge of God to the wilderness.

There are more subtle moral questions, however. What gave the heroes of New France or the heroes of Confederation the right to define what was wilderness? What justified them imposing their own system of law and order upon it? This question would have occurred to Pierre Fortin no more than it would have occurred to his ancestor, Christophe Crevier, as he escorted three captured Iroquois from Trois-

Rivières to Québec. Crevier and Fortin were each men of their times. Their moral judgements sprang from the clear belief that their god and their laws were superior to those found in the wilderness surrounding them. And their actions could not escape those ethnocentric judgements.

In the last two years of his life, the proud, aging commander had protested a mild joke at his expense in the Commons. He must have suffered cruelly from the abuse following the Riel affair. He would have suffered even more had he lived to see the results of his actions. They helped destroy his party in Quebec, and inflict on his country a wound that would never heal. Civilizing the wilderness brought a heavy price.

When Fortin was appointed to the senate in March 1887, he must already have been a sick man. After suffering a long and painful illness "with the resignation of a true Christian,"[26] he died at his home in Laprairie on 14 June 1888. *La Patrie* said that many friends and admirers had attended the funeral in his home town on the 19th.[27] The newspaper tributes flowed.

La Minerve quoted Israël Tarte. The Treaty of Washington, said Tarte, had set up a tribunal to look into the fisheries. Fortin travelled 500 miles in the Maritimes collecting affidavits, and had made a very strong witness. "We won our case," said Tarte. He stressed that Fortin had refused payment for his services, he had not even accepted expenses.[28] *L'Événement* praised Fortin for getting "the magnificent" underwater telegraphic cable system around Gaspésie. It called Fortin "one of the great figures of our political world.... A hardworking man devoted to the interests of his constituency."[29]

Three years before, *La Presse* had called Fortin servile, lacking patriotic sentiment. The paper now described him as "one of the most justly popular names in Canada for the past forty years."[30] The Montreal *Gazette* had, in 1849, ridiculed "Fortin's dragoons." Nearly forty years later, a *Gazette* editorial of 16 June said, "A stalwart figure is removed from parliamentary life." The newspaper's assessment of Fortin's achievements was reserved. His was "a useful rather than a brilliant career," the *Gazette* said. "A Canadian in the fullest sense of the word, he did more real service than many of more brilliant parts." But the Commander, whose honour had meant so much to him, would have taken pride in the final tribute by his old enemy. "In his death it can be truly said, his country has lost an honorable man."[31]

NOTES

1. HOCD, 27 February 1882, 113.
2. Achintre, M.A. *Manuel electoral. Portraits et dossiers parlementaires du premier parlement de Québec.* Montréal: Des Ateliers typographique de Duvernay, frères, 1871: 63-64.
3. HOCD, 19 March 1879, 560-61.
4. NA MG 27 F8 Ouimet papers, Fortin to Ouimet, 27 January, 2 March 1880.
5. Ouimet papers, Ouimet to Fortin and Ouimet to St. Pierre, [probably 14 March 1880]; St. Pierre to Ouimet, 27 March 1880; Ouimet to Fortin, 5 April 1880.
6. *Canadian Parliamentary Guide.* Ottawa: J. Durie and Son. 1885: 82; 1878, 261.
7. HOCD, 23 April 1883, 767-72.
8. HOCD, 23 January 1884, 32-33; 31 January, 80; 10 March, 745; 12 March, 808-10; 13 March, 821-22.
9. Fraser, Alister et al. *Beauchesne's Parliamentary Rules and Forms*, 6th edition. Toronto: The Carswell Company, 1989: 94.
10. HOCD, 6 February 1885, 56.
11. *La Presse* (Montréal), 14 November 1885.
12. Rumilly, Vol. 5: 164.
13. Beck, 46.
14. *Le Cultivateur*, 10 June 1882, cited in Potvin, *Le roi*, 136.
15. *L'Opinion publique* (Montréal), 23 December 1875.
16. NA RG 31 A1 (mfm C-1289), 1861 Census, Village of Laprairie.
17. HOCD, 5 March 1879.
18. HOCD, 6 May 1868, 641.
19. HOCD, 19 March 1879, 561.
20. Potvin, *Le roi*, 130.
21. HOCD, 27 February 1882, 110.
22. Fortin, *Report*, 1862.
23. Fortin, *Report*, 1865: 23.
24. Potvin, *Le roi*, 103.
25. *Le Canadien*, 17 November 1865.
26. *La Presse*, 16 June 1888.
27. *La Patrie* (Montréal), 20 June 1888.
28. *La Minerve* (Montréal), 16 June 1888.
29. *L'Evénement* (Montréal), 16 June 1888.
30. *La Presse*, 16 June 1888.
31. *Gazette*, 16 June 1888.

SOURCES

The major sources of information in this book are the annual reports of Pierre Fortin, magistrate commanding the expedition for the protection of the fisheries in the Gulf of the St. Lawrence. They were printed as appendices to the *Journals* (1852-53 to 1859), or in the *Sessional Papers* of the Legislative Assembly of the Province of Canada (1860-66), or in the *Sessional Papers* of the House of Commons (1867-68). They are cited in the endnotes in this form: "Fortin, *Report*, [year of publication]."

	PATROL	PUBLICATION Date (Number)	
Journals	1852	1852-53 (11)	App. I.I.I.I.
	1853/54		
	1855	1856 (14)	App. 25
	1856	1857 (15)	App. 23
	1857	1858 (16)	App. 31
	1858	1859 (17)	App. 20

	PATROL	PUBLICATION Date (Number)	
Sessional Papers	1859	1860 (18)	Crown Lands 12, App. 33
	1860	1861 (19)	Crown Lands 15, App. 33
	1861	1862 (20)	Crown Lands 11
	1862	1863 (21)	Crown Lands 5, App. 42(d)
	*#1863	1864 (23)	Crown Lands 5, App. 40
	#1864	1865 (25)	Separate paper 25
	#1865	1866 (26)	Separate paper 36
	+1866	1867-68	Separate paper 43

\# Half year
* Summary only
\+ Includes reports by Fortin (p. 2) and by Théophile Têtu, Fortin's successor (p. 15).

NB: Page numbers are cited when given in the original appendices.

OTHER GOVERNMENT PUBLICATIONS

Canada. *Acts*.
———. Department of the Secretary of State. *The Canadian Style: A Guide to Writing and Editing*. Toronto and London: Dundurn Press, 1985.
———. Department of the Environment, Canadian Hydrographic Service. *Sailing Directions for Gulf and River St. Lawrence*. Ottawa, 1975.
———. House of Commons *Debates* (HOCD).
———. House of Commons *Journals* (HOCJ).
———. Senate *Debates*.
Great Britain. *Acts*.
Lower Canada. *Acts*.
———. House of Assembly *Journals*.
Province of Canada, *Acts* (PCA).
———, *Consolidated Statutes*.
———, Legislative Assembly *Debates*.
———, Legislative Assembly *Journals* (PCLAJ).
———, *Legislative Council Debate on the Fisheries Bill of Hon. Alexander Campbell, 9-10 March 1865*. Québec: Daily News Office (1865).
Québec, Legislative Assembly *Journals* (QLAJ).
———, Legislative Assembly *Debates* (QLAD).
———, Bibliothèque de la législature, service de documentation politique. *Répertoire des parlementaires Québecois, 1867-1978*.
———, Coast Telegraph Chart of the Gulf and Lower St Lawrence and Maritime Provinces; 1876 with additions, May 1881. NA National Map Collection, No. 0025306.
———, Commission de Toponymie du Québec. *Répertoire toponymique du Québec, 1987*. Québec: Éditeur officiel du Québec, 1987.
———, Ministère des Terres et Forêts du Québec. *Répertoire géographique du Québec*. Québec: Commission de Géographie, 1969.

GOVERNMENT SOURCES HELD BY NATIONAL ARCHIVES OF CANADA

NA MG 24 G45, Salaberry Family Papers.
NA MG 27 F8, Gédéon Ouimet Papers.
NA MG 28 III 18, Robin's Correspondence.
NA MG 29 D61, Henry James Morgan Papers.
NA MG 40 J4, National Maritime Museum, Lloyd's Register of British and Foreign Shipping.
NA National Map Collection.
NA RG 1 E1, State Minute Books.
NA RG 4 CI, Canada East Provincial Secretary's Office Correspondence.

NA RG 8 I, British Military and Naval Records.
NA RG 31 A1, Census, Village of Laprairie, 1851, 1861, 1871.

GOVERNMENT SOURCES HELD BY ARCHIVES NATIONALES
DU QUÉBEC

Québec. Registry of Births, Deaths and Marriages 1849 and 1877, Parish of La-Prairie-de-la-Magdalen. mfm No. B-140 and Index.

OTHER PUBLICATIONS

Achintre, M.A. *Manuel électoral. Portraits et dossiers parlementaires du premier parlement de Québec.* Montréal: Des Ateliers typographiques de Duvernay, frères, 1871.
Armstrong, Robert. *Structure and Change: An Economic History of Quebec.* Toronto: Gage, 1984.
Austen, F.W.G. "Some of the Fishes of the St. Lawrence," Literary and Historical Society of Quebec, *Transactions.* New series, parts 4 and 5 (Québec) 1865-66: 103-20.
Beausoleil, C. "Correspondence autour de la question scolaire du Nouveau-Brunswick, 1873," *Revue d'histoire de l'Amérique française* (Montréal), Vol. 4, No. 4 (March 1951): 568-72.
Beck, J.M. *Pendulum of Power: Canada's Federal Elections.* Scarborough, Ont.: Prentice Hall, 1968.
Béchard, August. *La Gaspésie en 1888.* Québec: L'Imprimerie Nationale, 1918.
Bélanger, Jules et al. *Histoire de la Gaspésie.* Montréal: Boréal Express, Institut Québecois de la Recherche sur la Culture, 1981.
Bernier, Jacques. *La médecine au Québec.* Québec: Les Presses de l'université Laval, 1989.
Bock, Philip K. *The Micmac Indians of Restigouche: A History and Contemporary Description.* Ottawa: National Museum of Canada, 1966.
Bosse, Eveline. *La Capricieuse à Québec en 1855.* Montréal: Les Éditions la Presse, 1984.
Brown, Desmond H. *The Genesis of the Canadian Criminal Code of 1892.* Toronto: University of Toronto Press, 1989.
Cadieux, Lorenzo. *Lettres des nouvelles missions du Canada, 1843-1852.* Montréal: Bellarmin et Maisonneuve et Larose, 1973.
Canadian Parliamentary Guide. Ottawa: Citizen Printing and Publishing, 1878, 1879; J. Durie and Son, 1883.
Le Canadien (Québec).
Chambers, E.T.D. *Les Pêcheries de la province de Québec: 1ère partie, Introduction Historique.* Québec: Département de Colonisation, 1912.

Charland, Thomas. *Histoire de Saint-François-du-Lac*. Ottawa: Collège Dominicain, 1942.

———. "Crevier de Saint-François, Jean," *Dictionary of Canadian Biography*. 13 volumes and 2 indices to date. Toronto: University of Toronto Press. Vol. 1 (1966): 238-39.

Chartrand, Phebe. Archivist, McGill University. Personal communication, 30 January, 1990.

Chevalier, Joseph. *Laprairie: notes historique*. Laprairie [?], 1941 [?].

Collins, John James. *Native American Religions: A Geographical Survey*. Lewiston: E. Mellen Press, 1991: 269.

Crossman, E.J. Curator Emeritus (Ichthyology), Centre for Biodiversity and Conservation Biology, Royal Ontario Museum, and Professor Emeritus (Zoology), University of Toronto. Personal communication, 15 May 1996.

Cunningham, R.J. and Mabee, K.R. *Tall Ships and Master Mariners*. St. John's: Breakwater Books, 1985.

The Daily News (Québec).

Damphouse, Patricia. *The Legislative Assembly of the Province of Canada: An Index to Journal Appendices and Sessional Papers, 1841-66*. London: E. Phelps, 1974.

Daveluy, Marie-Claire. "Chomedy de Maisonneuve, Paul de," *Dictionary of Canadian Biography*, Vol. 1 (1966): 212-21.

Dawson, R. MacGregor. *The Government of Canada*, 4th edition. Toronto: University of Toronto Press, 1964.

Dear, Ian and Kemp, Peter. *The Pocket Oxford Guide to Sailing Terms*. Oxford: Oxford University Press, 1976.

De Celles, Alfred D. *The 'Patriotes' of '37*. Glasgow: Brook and Company, 1920.

Desjardins, Joseph. *Guide parlementaire historique de la province de Québec, 1792-1902*. Québec: 1902.

Douville, Raymond. "Boucher, Pierre," *Dictionary of Canadian Biography*. Toronto: University of Toronto Press, 1966–. Vol 2: 82-83.

Drapeau, Stanislas. *Études sur les développements de la colonisation du Bas-Canada depuis dix ans (1851-1861)*. Québec: Léger Brousseau, 1863.

Dunfield, R.W. *The Atlantic Salmon in the History of North America*. Ottawa: Department of Fisheries and Oceans, 1985.

Elgin, Lord. *Elgin-Grey Papers*. Ottawa: King's Printer, 1937.

Elliott, Charles Burke. *The United States and the Northeastern Fisheries*. Minneapolis: University of Minnesota, 1887.

L'Événement (Montréal).

Faucher de Saint-Maurice, Narcisse-Henri-Edouard. *Promenades dans le Golfe Saint-Laurent*. Montréal: Librarie Saint-Joseph, s.d.

Ferland, Abbé J.B.A. *La Gaspésie*. Québec: Nouvelle édition, 1877.

Fingard, Judith, *Jack in Port: Sailortowns of Eastern Canada.* Toronto: University of Toronto Press, 1982.
Forsey, Eugene. *Trade Unions in Canada: 1812-1902.* Toronto: University of Toronto Press, 1982.
Fortin, Cora. *Premier Fortin d'Amérique: Julien Fortin.* Québec: Société de généalogie de Québec, 1974.
Fortin, Pierre. *Letters from the Hon. P. Fortin, M.P., on the Telegraph and Signal Service in the Gulf of St. Lawrence; on the United States Signal Service; and on the Norwegian Telegraph System.* Reprinted from *Le Canadien.* Ottawa: MacLean, Roger and Company, 1879.
Fraser, Alistair et al. *Beauchesne's Rules and Forms of the House of Commons of Canada.* 6th edition. Toronto: The Carswell Company, 1989.
Frechette, Louis. *Les renégats du 29 Octobre: Paquet, Chauveau, Flynn, Racicot et Fortin:* LES TRAÎTRES! LES VENDUS! Montréal: [s.n.] 1879.
Frosh, S.B. *McGill University for the Advancement of Learning.* 2 volumes. Montréal: McGill-Queen's University Press, 1980: Vol. 1 (1801-1895).
Fyson, Donald. "Criminal Justice, Civil Society, and the Local State: The Justices of the Peace in the District of Montreal,1764-1830." PhD thesis, Université de Montréal, Québec, 1995.
Gagnon, Serge. *Plaisir d'amour et crainte de Dieu: sexualité et confession au Bas-Canada.* Sainte-Foy, Québec: Les Presses de l'université Laval, 1990.
The Gazette (Montréal).
Geistdoerfer, Aliette. *Pêcheurs acadiennes: Pêcheurs madelinots.* Québec: Les Presses de l'université Laval, 1987.
Gill, Théodore. "Synopsis of the Fishes of the the Gulf of St. Lawrence and the Bay of Fundy," *Canadian Naturalist and Quarterly Journal of Science* (Montréal), new series, Vol. 2 (1865): 244-66.
Gillis, Peter. "Pollution." *Journal of Canadian Studies* (Peterborough), Vol. 21, No. 1 (spring 1986): 84-103.
Gingras, Nerée. "Impressions de Gaspésie en 1857." *Le Canada français* (Québec), Vol. 26, No. 5 (January 1939): 483-97.
Gossage, Patrick. "Les enfants abandonnés à Montréal au 19ième siècle: la crêche d'Youville des Sœurs Grises, 1820-1871," *Revue d'histoire de l'Amérique française*, Vol. 40, No. 4 (spring, 1987), 537ff.
Grandbois, Maryse. "Le developpement des disparités régionales en Gaspésie 1760-1960." *Revue d'histoire de l'Amérique française*, Vol. 36, No. 4 (March 1983): 483.
Grant, W.L. ed. *Voyages of Samuel de Champlain.* New York: Barnes and Noble, 1907.
Greer, Allan. *Peasant, Lord and Merchant: Rural Society in Three Quebec Parishes: 1740-1840.* Toronto: University of Toronto Press, 1985.
———. "The Pattern of Literacy in Quebec, 1745-1899." *Social History* (Ottawa), Vol. II, No. 22 (November-December 1978): 293-335.

Greer, Allan. "Birth of the Police in Canada," Allan Greer and Ian Radforth, eds. *Colonial Leviathan: State Formation in Mid 19th-Century Canada.* Toronto: University of Toronto Pess, 1992: 17-49.

Groulx, Lionel. *L'enseignement français au Canada, 1 - dans le Québec.* Montréal: Librairie d'action canadienne-française, 1931.

Hamelin, Marcel. *Les premières années du parlementarisme Québecois (1867-1878).* Québec: Les Presses de l'université Laval, 1974.

Hind, Henry. *Explorations in the Interior of the Labrador Peninsula.* 2 volumes. London: Longman, Green, Longman, Roberts and Green, 1863.

Hodgetts, J.E. *Pioneer Public Service: An Administrative History of the United Canadas, 1841-67.* Toronto: University of Toronto Press, 1965.

Innis, Harold A. *The Cod Fisheries: The History of an International Economy.* Toronto: University of Toronto Press, 1954.

Isham, Charles. *The Fisheries Question: Its Origin, History and Present Situation.* New York: Putnam, 1887.

Jenness, Diamond. *The Indians of Canada.* Ottawa: Queen's Printer, 1960 .

Jetté, Ireneé. *Mariages du comté de Laprairie, 1751-1972.* Sillery, Que.: Pontbriand, 1974.

Jordan, John. *The Grosse Isle Tragedy and the Monument to the Irish Fever Victims, 1847.* Québec: The Telegraph Printing Company, 1909.

Le Journal de Québec (Québec).

Kerr, William Hastings. *The Fisheries Question: Or American Rights in Canadian Waters.* Montréal: Daniel Rose, 1868.

Labarrère-Paule, André. *Les Instituteurs laïques au Canada français, 1836-1900.* Québec: Les Presses de l'université Laval, 1965.

Landry, Frédéric. *Laboureurs du Golfe.* Québec: Le Marteloire, 1985.

Lavoie, René. Assistant Director, Biological Sciences Branch, Department of Fisheries and Oceans. Personal communication, 3 July 1992.

Leavitt, Robert M. *The Micmacs.* Markham, Ont.: Fitzhenry and Whiteside, 1985.

Lebel, Jean-Marie. "Duvernay, Ludger," *Dictionary of Canadian Biography.* Vol. 8 (1985): 258-63.

Leclerc, Paul-André. "Le marriage sous le régime français." *Revue d'histoire de l'Amérique française.* Vol. 13, No. 3 (December, 1959): 374-401.

Lee, David. *The Robins in Gaspé, 1766 to 1825.* Markham, Ont.: Fitzhenry and Whiteside, 1984.

Lepage, André. "Le capitalisme marchand et la pêche à la morue en Gaspésie: La Charles Robin and Company dans la Baie des Chaleurs, 1820-1870." PhD thesis, université Laval, Québec, 1983.

Linteau, Paul-André, et al. *Quebec: A History, 1867-1929.* Toronto: James Lorimer, 1983.

Little J.I. *Crofters and Habitants: Settler Society, Economy, and Culture in a Quebec Township 1848-1881.* Montréal and Kingston: McGill-Queen's University Press, 1991.

Little J.I. *Nationalism, Capitalism and Colonization in 19th Century Quebec: The Upper St. Francis District.* Montréal and Kingston: McGill-Queen's University Press, 1989.
McCullough, A.B. *Money and Exchange in Canada to 1900.* Toronto and Charlottetown: Dundurn Press, 1984.
MacDermott, H.E. *History of the Montreal General Hospital.* Montréal: Montreal General Hospital, 1950.
McNicholl, Martin K. "Fortin, Pierre-Etienne" in *The Canadian Encyclopedia.* 3 volumes. Edmonton: Hurtig, 1985.
Magnuson, Roger. *A Brief History of Quebec Education: From New France to the Parti Québecois.* Montréal: Harvest House, 1980.
Marsh, George P. *Man and Nature, or Physical Geography as Modified by Human Behavior.* Cambridge, MA: Belknap Press, 1965 (re-issue).
Maurault, O. *Le Petit séminaire de Montréal.* Montréal: Derome, 1918.
Maxwell. J.A. *Federal Subsidies to the Provincial Governments in Canada.* Cambridge, MA: Harvard University Press, 1937.
Milloy, John S. "The Early Indian Acts," Ian A.L. Getty and Antoince S. Lussier, eds. *As Long as the Sun Shines and Water Flows.* Vancouver: University of British Columbia Press, 1983: 56.
La Minerve (Montréal).
Monière, Denis. *Ludger Duvernay et la révolution intellectuel au Bas-Canada.* Montréal: Québec-Amérique, 1987.
The Morning Chronicle (Québec).
Morissonneau, Christian. *La Société de géographie de Québec.* Québec: Les Presses de l'université Laval, 1971.
Nelson, Wendy. "The 'Guerre des Eteignoirs': School Reform and Popular Resistance in Lower Canada, 1841-50." MA thesis, Simon Fraser University, B.C., 1989.
Occhiette, Serge. "Grosse Île," *The Canadian Encyclopedia,* vol. 2: 776-77.
O'Gallagher, Marianna. *Grosse Île: Gateway to Canada, 1832-1937.* Sainte-Foy, Québec: Carraig Books, 1984.
Ommer, Rosemary E. "The Truck System in Gaspé 1822-27." *Acadiensis* (Fredericton), Vol. 19, No. 1 (fall 1989): 91-104.
———. "Nouvelles de mer: The Rise of Jersey Shipping 1830-1840," Eric Sager, ed. *The Enterprising Canadians.* St. John's: Memorial University of Newfoundland, 1979: 147-82.
L'Opinion publique (Montréal).
Ouellet, Fernand. *Lower Canada, 1791-1840: Social Change and Nationalism.* Toronto: McClelland and Stewart, 1980.
———. *Economic and Social History of Quebec, 1760-1850.* Toronto: Carleton Library Series, No. 120. Ottawa: Carleton University Press, 1980.
Parent, Roger D. *Duvernay le magnifique.* Montréal: Montréal institut de la Nouvelle-France, 1943.
La Patrie (Montréal).

The Pilot (Montréal).
Pomedli, Michael. "Native Approaches to Morality," *Actes du vingtième congrès des Algonquinistes*. Ottawa: Carleton University, 1988.
Potvin, Damase. *Le roi du Golfe: Le Dr. P.-E. Fortin, ancien commandant de la "Canadienne."* Québec: Éditions Quartier Latin, c. 1952.
———. *Les oubliés*. Québec: Roch Poulin, n.d.
Préfontaine, Georges. "Connaissance scientifique et pêcheries." *Actualité économique* (Montréal). Vol. 21, No. 2 (1945-46): 233-37.
La Presse (Montréal).
Punch in Canada (Montréal).
Pye, Thomas. *Canadian Scenery, District of Gaspé*. Montréal: Lovell, 1866.
Quinn, Magella. "Les capitaux français et le Québec, 1855-1900," *Revue d'histoire de l'Amérique française*, Vol. 24, No. 4 (March 1971): 527-66.
Roy, Charles Eugène. *Gaspé depuis Cartier*. Québec: Moulin des lettres, 1934.
Roy, Joseph-Edmond. *Histoire du notariat au Canada*. 2 volumes. Outremont: La Revue du notariat, Vol. 1, 1899: 214-15.
Rumilly, Robert. *Histoire de la province de Québec*. 35 volumes. Montréal: Éditions Bernard Valiquette, Vol. 1 to 16; Montréal-éditions, 17 to 23; Chantecler, 24 to 26; Fides, 27 to 35; 1940[?] to 1966.
Sager, Eric W. *Seafaring Labour: The Merchant Marine of Atlantic Canada*. Montréal and Kingston: McGill-Queen's University Press, 1989.
Samson, Roch. *Fishermen and Merchants in 19th Century Gaspé*. Ottawa: Parks Canada, 1984.
———. *Fishing at Grand Grave in the Early 1900s*. Ottawa: Parks Canada, 1980.
Sansom, Joseph. *Travels in Lower Canada*. Toronto: Coles Canadiana Collection, 1970.
Senior, Elinor Kyte. *British Regulars in Montreal: An Imperial Garrison, 1832-1854*. Montréal: McGill-Queen's University Press, 1981.
Scott, W.B. and Crossman, E.J. *Freshwater Fishes of Canada*. Bulletin 184. Ottawa: Fisheries Research Board of Canada, 1973.
Shaw, Gordon C. "St. Lawrence River," *The Canadian Encyclopedia*. Vol. 3: 1625-26.
Silverstone, P.H. *Warships of the Civil War Navies*. Annapolis: Naval Institute Press, 1988.
Smith, P.C. and Conover, R.J. "St. Lawrence, Gulf of," *The Canadian Encyclopedia*. Vol. 3: 1624.
Société de géographie de Québec. "L'honorable Pierre Fortin, fondateur de la Société de géographie de Québec," *Bulletin* (Québec), Vol. 4, No. 5 (1910): 347-50.
Stanley, George F.G. *New France: The Last Phase, 1744-1760*. Toronto: McClelland and Stewart, 1968.
———."The First Indian Reserves," *Revue d'histoire de l'Amérique française*, Vol. 4, No. 2 (September 1950): 178.

Steele, Ian K. *Guerillas and Grenadiers: The Struggle for Canada, 1689-1760.* Toronto: Ryerson, 1969.
Sulte, Benjamin. "Les Ancêtres du Ludger Duvernay," *Revue Canadienne* (Montréal), new series, Vol. 1 (April 1908): 349-58.
Tessier, Yves. "Ludger Duvernay et les débuts de la presse periodique aux Trois-Rivières." *Revue d'histoire de l'Amérique française*, Vol. 18, No. 3 (1964-65): 387-404.
Thwaites, Reuben Gold, ed. *The Jesuit Relations and Allied Documents.* 73 volumes in 36. New York: Pageant Book Company, 1959.
Trépanier, Pierre and Trépanier, Lise. "Archambeault, Louis," *Dictionary of Canadian Biography*, Vol. 11 (1982): 25-27.
Trofimenkoff, Susan Mann. *The Dream of a Nation: A Social and Intellectual History of Quebec.* Toronto: Macmillan, 1982.
United States Navy Department, Naval History Division. *Dictionary of American Naval Fighting Ships.* 8 volumes. Washington, 1959-81.
Upton, Leslie F.S. *Micmacs and Colonists: Indian-White Relations in the Maritime Provinces.* Vancouver: University of British Columbia Press, 1979.
Vachon, André. "Inventaire critique des notaires royaux 1663-1764." *Revue d'histoire de l'Amérique française.* Vol. 11, No. 1 (1957-58): 93-106.
———. "Lepailleur de Laferté, Michel," *Dictionary of Canadian Biography*, Vol. 2 (1969): 413.
Worthington, E.D. *Reminiscences of Student Life and Practices.* Sherbrooke: 1897.
Young, Brian and Dickinson, John A. *A Short History of Quebec: A Socio-economic Perspective.* Toronto: Copp Clark Pitman, 1988.

INDEX

PLACES AND TOPICS

Acadians, 49, 107, 169
Act of Union, 37, 78, 154
agriculture, 52, 141, 169
Algonquin,
  see Native Peoples
Allumettes, Île des, 17
America, 36-37, 62-63, 69-70, 115,
  140, 142, 153, 154, 168-76 passim,
  193
American rights in the Gulf, 1, 51, 56,
  58, 62-65,
  Fortin on, 70-73, 119, 126
American crime in the Gulf, 6, 54,
  63-69 passim,
  Fortin on, 10, 65-66, 69
Amherst, 51, 54, 59, 66, 80, 107, 120,
  122, 127
angler fish, 113-14
Anse-aux-Cousins, l', 54, 139
Anse-aux-Morts, l', 54, 139
Anse-aux-Griffons, l', 54, 76
Anticosti Island, 2, 47, 53, 57, 58, 83,
  175
Australia, 37, 108

Baie-Comeau, 1
Baie-de-Saint-Paul, 4
Barachois, 96
Barque, Île la, 122
Basques, 52, 125
Basques, Havre aux, 129
Batiscan, 17, 19
Batoche, 190
Bay of Fundy, 62, 71
Beauce, 133
Beauharnois, 37
Bermuda, 37
Bersimi, 53, 141
birds, 120, 168
  and Fortin, 114, 120-22, 167
Blanc-Sablon, 52, 53, 61, 81
Bleus, 153-62, 191, 193
  and Fortin, 153-54

  see also Conservatives
Bois, Île à, 81
Bonaventure, 4, 54, 93, 167, 176-77
Bonne-Espérance, 119
Brador, 52, 61, 62, 126
Brazil, 187
British Admiralty, 115
British North America, 47, 63, 73
British North America Act, 159

Cabot Strait, 47
Campbellton, N.B., 118, 176
Canada, French, 14, 23, 37, 43, 154,
  158, 190
Canada, Lower, 22, 24-26, 36-37, 50,
  78, 82, 117, 120, 154, 171
Canada, Province of, 153-54, 159
Canada, Upper, 37, 78, 82, 142, 154
  and Fortin, 155
Canadian Pacific Railway, 160, 191
Canadien, Le, 174-75, 195
Candle Snuffers, War of, 105-06
  and Fortin, 43, 75-76, 106-07
Canso, 54, 175
Cap Chat, Pointe de, 1, 131
Cape Breton, 47, 87, 175
Caraquet, N.B., 5, 128-30
Caribbean trade, 187
Caribou, Îlets, 12, 53
Carleton, 48, 76, 179
Cascapédia, Baie de, 128
Cascapédia, Rivière, 48-49, 117, 139
Census, 25, 43
Central Canada Railway, 156
Chaleur Bay, 11, 47, 49, 53, 62, 71, 88,
  89, 116, 118, 126
Chaleur Bay Railway and Fortin, 177
Champlain Sea, 47
Channel Island companies
  see Jersey companies
Charles Robin & Co., 54, 82, 87-91
  passim, 106
  Fortin's relations with, 87, 91-98
Charles Savage and Co., 92
cholera, 31

Clercs de Saint-Viateur, 22
Coacoacho, 116, 120
Collas, J. & E. and Co., 92
colonization and Fortin, 49, 167, 168-71, 179, 181
Confederation, 153, 176, 196
    and Fortin, 154-55, 193
Conscription Crisis, 159
Conservatives, 96, 131-32, 153-62 passim, 178, 181, 191
Convention of 1818, 51, 62, 63, 64, 70
Cormoran, Cap, 100
Corps-Mort, le, 10
Courrier des États-Unis, Le, 193
crime and Fortin, 53, 76-79, 79-82
    see also American crime in the Gulf
crimps, 82
Crown Lands (Province of Canada), 145-47
    Fortin quits, 151
    Fortin v. Whitcher, 148-51
Crown Lands (Quebec), 170
    Fortin as Commissioner of, 96-98, 131-33, 159, 180
    Fortin as conservationist, 130-33, 181
    Fortin and corruption in, 167, 168, 170, 180
Customs and Excise and Fortin, 81

Dalhousie, N.S., 58, 118
deer, conservation of, 120
Dollier de Casson, François, 18
Dominion Board of Trade, 175
dual representation and Fortin, 153, 157, 160-61
Durham Report, 37

East Indies, 108
Eastern Townships, 120, 132, 169
education and Fortin, 43, 54, 105, 107
    see also Candle Snuffers, War of
Eggman Harbour, 122
Électeur, L', 191
elections, Canada, 154, 158, 161, 162, 191
elections, Committee on and Fortin, 168
elections, Quebec, 168, 181, 182
    Fortin's by-election, 182

England, 157, 161, 170, 171
Entrée, Île d', 50
Étamamiou, Rivière, 120, 121, 126
Europe, 47, 99, 108, 120, 168, 175, 176
Événment, L', 197

famine and Fortin, 52, 90, 99, 140, 179
fisheries, 7, 73, 117, 126
    Fortin on bounties, 172-73
    Fortin as conservationist, 126-27
    Fortin and policing of, 51, 81, 119-20
fishery, caplin, 98
fishery, cod, 99, 126
    and Fortin, 55-56, 125
fishery, herring, 98, 99, 108, 187-88
fishery, mackerel, 67, 98, 108
fishery, muskellunge, 117, 120
fishery, pike, 114
fishery, salmon, 116-18
    and Fortin, 116, 118, 171-72
    see also Native Peoples
fishery, seal, 59
    and Fortin, 115, 127
fishery, trout, 117
fishery, whale, 118
    and Fortin, 115, 118-19
Fisheries and Coal Mining Co., 167
Fisheries Committee, and Fortin, 5, 172
Fisheries Protection Service, 64, 100, 155
fishes of the Gulf and Fortin, 113-14
forestry
    see Crown Lands
Forteau Bay, 175
France, 20, 61, 115, 126, 132, 170
    and Fortin, 92, 193
    see also Saint-Pierre and Miquelon
Fundy, Bay of, 62

Gaspé, 2, 62, 69, 76-82 passim, 88, 94, 107, 117, 123, 153, 167, 171, 177, 182, 185, 186
    Fortin on free port of, 99
Gaspé Basin, 11, 54, 122, 128-30 passim
Gaspésie, 48-49, 106, 116, 119, 136, 137, 142, 150, 169, 176-79 passim, 197
    Fortin as booster, 48-50

Gazette, La, 44
Geographical Society of Quebec, 115
    and Fortin, 115
Godbout, 79, 139
Governor-General's salary and Fortin, 156-57
Grand Manan, 175
Grand-Étang, 68
Grande-Grave, 88
Grande-Rivière, 92, 94, 95
Grande-Vallée, 6, 68
Great Britain, 20, 36, 51, 73, 126, 136-38, 142, 174
    and Fortin, 71, 92, 109-10, 161, 162, 193
Great Lakes, 173
Grits, 153
    see also Liberals
Gros-Mécatina, Rivière du, 120, 121
Grosse-Île, 2, 31-35, 196
    and Fortin, 25, 32-33, 34-35
Gulf of St. Lawrence, ix, 1, 14, 47, 57, 64, 69-80 passim, 119, 173-75, 196

Halifax, 7, 107, 110, 121, 175
Havre-Aubert
    see Amherst
Havre-aux-Maisons, 59, 67, 107
Havre-Basque, 129
Havre-Saint-Pierre
    see Pointe aux Esquimaux
Holland, 18, 19, 187-88
horse hitching, 168
House of Commons,
    Fortin in the Gallery, 189-90
    Fortin's last question, 190
    Fortin quits, 161
    Fortin quits again, 191
    see also Elections, Canada
Hudson's Bay Co., 78
    Fortin criticizes, 100
Hunters' Lodges, 63
Hyman and Co., 88, 92
Îles-de-la-Madeleine, 2, 47, 50, 52, 54, 58, 62, 65, 67, 69, 81, 92, 98, 100, 107-08, 114, 127, 150, 163, 175-79 passim, 182
    and Fortin, 51-52, 94, 167, 168, 179-80
Indian
    see Native Peoples
Indien, Anse de l', 57
Indien, Pointe de l', 135
Intercolonial Railway and Fortin, 154, 156, 167, 176-77
International Fisheries Exhibition and Fortin, 188
Ireland, 31, 170
Isolated Risk Insurance Co., 187

Janvrin and Co., 88
Jacques-Cartier, Mont, 48
Jacques-Cartier, Rivière, 171
Jersey companies, 48, 52, 62, 87-90, 97-98, 105, 126, 194
    Fortin criticizes, 98-100, 101, 108
    Fortin's relations with, 87, 91-97
    and Fortin's election, 92, 153
Jersey, Fortin visits, 93
Jesuits, 18, 21-22
Joint Imperial-American Commission, 1
Journal de Québec, Le, 34
justice in the Gulf and Fortin, 157, 177-79

Kamouraska, 3, 120
King's Domain/Post, 100
Kingston, 145

labour laws and Fortin, 82-83, 91, 168
Labrador, 2, 47, 62, 81, 99, 136
Labrador Co., 97, 99
language and Fortin, 3
Laprairie, 21-22, 25, 34-35, 38-43 passim, 197
Laval, University of, 114
Leboutillier Bros. and Co., 54, 88
    and Fortin, 81, 92, 98
Liberals, 153, 155-62 passim
liquor laws and Fortin, 80
Lloyds of London, 12, 83, 174
Longue-Pointe, 4, 10, 57
Louisbourg, 20, 87
Loyalists, 48, 137

Magna Carta, 116
Magpie, 94, 98
Major Robinson Route
    see Intercolonial Railway
Malbaie, 77, 78, 175, 195
Manitoba, 191
Manitoba Act, 156, 158
Maria, 135
Maritime Exhibition, Le Havre, 92
Marmettes, Îles aux, 122
Matane, 179
Matapédia, 49, 133, 169, 177
McGill Medical School, 23-24
Memphramégog, 120
merchant marine and Fortin, 108-10
    see also Navigation School
Meules, Cap aux, 67, 127
Mexico, 187
Micmac
    see Native Peoples, Innu
Mille Vaches, 175
Minerve, La, 2, 36, 97, 197
Mingan, 4, 53, 57, 100, 140
Miquelon
    see Saint-Pierre and Miquelon
Miramichi, 58
Missisquoi, 37
Moisie, Rivière, 80, 116, 139
Moniteur Canadien, Le, 42
Montagnais
    see Native Peoples, Innu
Mont-Joli, 176
Mont-Louis, 6, 54
Montréal, 12, 18, 19, 20, 33, 35-36, 62, 76-77, 80, 111, 153, 173, 175, 180, 196
Montreal Gazette, 31-33 passim, 39-41, 42, 179, 197
Montréal General Hospital, 24
Montréal Riots and Fortin, 3, 35-43
Monts, Pointe des, 1, 12
Moore's Corners, 37
Morning Chronicle, 175
Mouton, Baie de, 52, 140
Moville, Ireland, 175

Naskapi
    see Native Peoples, Innu

Natashquan, 52, 79, 105, 107, 119, 139, 142
National Policy, Fortin on, 161, 162-63, 191, 194
Native Peoples, 17, 116, 137-38, 141, 190, 194
    and Fortin, 135-36, 139-40
    Innu, 52, 79, 119, 136-37, 140-43, 145
    Iroquois, 18-19, 136, 196
    Métis, 155, 158, 190-91
    Micmac, 2, 48, 117, 118, 135, 136-37, 145
navigation school and Fortin, 107-11
navigational aids and Fortin, 173-74
New Brunswick, 7, 64, 109, 118, 130, 136, 154, 155, 163, 172, 176
New Brunswick Schools Act, 193
    Fortin pilloried over, 158-59
New Carlisle, 177, 194
Newfoundland, 20, 50, 61, 62, 81, 87, 126, 163, 187
New France, 14, 17-21 passim, 126
    and Fortin, 196
New Richmond, 48, 128, 135, 139
North Africa, 133
North Shore, 2, 7, 12, 52-54 passim, 78, 94, 97-101 passim, 107, 108, 120-22, 126, 127, 131, 141, 142, 146, 163, 186
    Fortin and customs, 7
    Fortin's visits to, 53, 150
North Shore Railway, 181
North West River, 116
Nova Scotia, 7, 20, 50-52, 62, 63, 64, 71, 107-09 passim, 130, 136, 154, 155, 163, 172, 176, 191
    fishermen of, 56, 68, 81, 120-21, 140

Oblats, Father, 141
Oeufs, Île aux, 48
Oies, Îles aux, 122
Oiseaux, Île aux, 79, 121, 173
Oiseaux, Rochers aux, 174-75
Ontario, Province of, 88, 130, 133, 154, 155, 158, 162, 168-69, 170, 172, 176, 190, 191, 193
    see also Quebec-Ontario debt

INDEX 213

Opinion publique, L', 50, 192
Orléans, Île d', 2
Ottawa Valley, 18, 132, 169
oyster farming, 127
    Fortin's attempts, 127-29
    Lavoie's critique, 129-30

Pabos, 5, 54, 106
Paspébiac, 54, 90, 92, 94-98 passim, 173
Patrie, La, 197
Patriotes, 36,
Penouille, 76
Percé, 5, 53, 54, 58, 77, 79, 82, 83, 88, 91, 94, 95, 96, 106-07, 173, 178, 181, 186
Petit-Mécatina, Rivière du, 126
Petit séminaire de Montréal, 22-23
Pictou, N.S., 48, 178
Piles Railroad and Fortin, 131
Pilot, 42
Plaisance, Baie de, 67, 81
Pointe-aux-Esquimaux, 52, 107
Pointe-aux-Outardes, 78
Pointe-Saint-Charles, 25, 32, 34
Pointe-Saint-Pierre, 76, 180, 195
police, history of, 76-77
Port-Daniel, 116
Portugal, 125
Presse, La, 191, 197
Prince Edward Island, 54, 64, 69, 130, 172
    Fortin visits, 50-52, 169
Privy Council, 190
Proclamation of 1763, 137
Provincial Secretary and Fortin, 4, 35, 145
Public Works, 12, 145
Punch in Canada, 39, 41, 42

Québec (city of), 11, 17, 18, 20, 33, 62, 77, 81, 83, 100, 111, 145, 173, 175, 177, 197
Quebec Act, 50, 78
Quebec Association of Dentists, 168
Quebec Chronicle, 34
Quebec Fish and Game Club, 171

Quebec, Province of, 130, 153, 154, 155, 158, 167, 170, 172, 176, 191
Quebec-Ontario debt, 159-60, 156
    Fortin on, 159-60
Quebec Superior Court, 177, 182

Rebellion Losses Bill, 35, 37
Rebellion of, 1837-38, 36-37
    and Fortin, 37
reciprocity, 2, 64-65, 71
    and Fortin, 66, 70, 145
Reformers, 35, 37, 41, 153
    see also Liberals
Rekaska, 120
repatriation and Fortin, 168
Restigouche, 98
Rosiers, Cap des, 174
Richibucto, N.S., 58
Rimouski, 132, 181
Ristigouche River, 88, 117, 118, 136-37
Rio de Janeiro, 88
Rivière-au-Renard, 54, 68, 75-76, 83, 176
Rivière-au-Tonnère, 83
Rivière-de-Loup, 176
Rivière-Saint-Paul, 140
Roman Catholic Church, 90, 158, 161, 191
    and Fortin, 154, 157, 181
Rouges, 59-62 passim, 153-55 passim,
    and Fortin, 193
    see also Liberals *and* Grits
Royal Navy, 7, 63, 71-72
Rustico, P.E.I., 169

Saguenay, 132, 169
Saint John, N.B., 110
Saint-Cande le Jeune, Rouen, 17
Saint-Christophe, Île, 17-18
Saint-François-du-Lac, 19, 43
Saint-Jean Baptiste Society, 36
Saint-Jean, Rivière, 3, 11
Saint-Maurice, 132
Saint-Maurice, Rivière, 18
Saint-Michel Société ecclesiastique, 168
Saint-Ours, 20, 36
Saint-Pierre and Miquelon, 61, 62, 80-81
    Fortin visits, 193

Saint-Pierre-de-Rouen, Normandy, 20
Saint-Simon Bay, 128
Sainte-Anne-des-Monts, 79, 176, 181
Saskatchewan, 190
Saumon, Baie au, 107
Scotland, 116, 170
Sept-Îles, 11, 47, 52
Societé canadienne ltée, la, 133
South America, 99
South-West River, 116
sharpshooters, 10, 63
shipbuilding and Fortin, 8, 161
St. Lawrence Lowland, 47
St. Lawrence River, 1, 47, 115, 173, 176
St. Lawrence Valley, 36, 62, 168, 105
Statute of Westminster, 116
Strait of Belle Isle, 11, 47, 119
Studdard, Havre, 158
Sulpicians, 22
Sydney, N.S., 127

T.C. Lee and Co., 7-8, 13
Tanneries affair and Fortin, 180-81, 186
telegraph and Fortin, 94, 174-76
Témiscouata, 132
Terrebonne, 21
Tête-à-la-Vâche, 127
Tories, 35, 37, 41, 43, 153
    see also Conservatives
Toronto, 12
Toronto Agreement 1851, 7, 64
Treaty of Paris, 1763, 21, 61, 126
Treaty of Washington, 72, 194
    and Fortin, 72-73, 157, 168, 194, 197
Trois-Rivières, 17, 18, 19, 114, 162, 196
typhus, 32, 33-34

United States: see America

Varennes, 20
Verchères, 17, 19-22 passim
Vert, Île, 58, 62
Ville la Salle, 26

walrus, Fortin on, 115
Wapitigun, 121

Washeecootai, 120
West Indies, 98, 108, 187
wild animals, protection of, 120
Willam Fruing and Co., 81, 88, 92

PERSONS

Achintre, M.A., 27, 185
Allan, Sir Hugh A., 160
Amyot, Guillaume, 111
Archambeault, Louis, 159, 180
Aubé, Joseph, 116
Audobon, John J., 133
Austen, F.W.G., 113

Beaubien, Marie Louise, 25
Beauchesne, Arthur, 190
Beaudin, J.B., 79
Beausoleil, C., 159
Béchard, Auguste, 101, 106
    on Fortin, 87, 90, 102
Béique, Mme. L.-J., 26
Belleau, N.F., 149
Bellingham, S.R., 141
Bernier, Louis, 2, 6, 12, 66, 81, 106, 121, 128, 195
    and Fortin, 5-6, 7
Bisaillon, Beatrice:
    see Béique, Mme. L.-J.
Bisaillon, Joseph F.X., 26
Bisaillon, Suzanne, 25-27 passim
Bisson, Philippe, 4
Blais, Miss (of Mont-Louis), 54
Boilleau, Gauldrée, 62
Bonneau, Léonard, 25
Bonneau, Suzanne snr.
    see Racine, Suzanne
Bonneau, Suzanne jnr.
    see Bisaillon, Suzanne
Boucher, Jeanne, 19
Boucher, Pierre, 19
Boucherville, C.-É. Boucher de, 111, 181
Bourque, Joseph, 67
Bowell, Sir Mackenzie, 173
Bréaux, M. (Port Daniel), 116
Briard, M., (Paspébiac), 92
Brown, George, 153, 154, 155
Bruno, Commander Faà di, 62

INDEX   215

Campbell, Alexander, 149, 150-51
Cartier, Georges-Étienne, 23, 153, 157, 158
Cartier, Jacques, 47, 50, 52, 120
Cass, Lewis, 64
Champlain, Samuel de, 17, 18, 47, 126
   and Fortin, 13-14
Chapleau, Joseph-Adolphe, 131, 132
Chauveau, Pierre-Joseph-Olivier, 50, 106, 167
Christie, Robert, 50
Claude, Grand Chief, 137
Cloutier, Noel, 68
Coffin, Sir Isaac, 51, 180
Coffin, J.C., 51
Collins, John, 62, 69
Corbin, A., 139
Cosse, Commander, 61
Crevier, Antoine, 18
Crevier, Christophe, 17-18, 196
Crevier, Franciscus, 18
Crevier, Jean, 19, 43
Crevier, Jean-Baptiste:
   see Duvernay, Jean-Baptiste
Crevier, Jeanne Evard, 17-19 passim
Crevier, Jeanne
   see Boucher, Jeanne
Crevier, Marguerite
   see Fournier, Marguerite
Crossman, E.J., 114
Crowell, Paul, 63

Davidson, Captain, 83
Debien, Elie, 3-4
Delorme, Louis, 158
Dery, Pierre, 68
deVeulle, M. (Percé), 96-97
Dimock, R.W.H., 135-36
Dionne, Germain, 68
Domenique, Chief, 143
Dorion, Antoine-Aimé, 157
Douglas, George M., 32, 34, 35
Dugal, Narcisse, 68
Durham, Lord, 37
Duvernay, Jacques, 20
Duvernay, Jean-Baptiste, 17, 19
Duvernay, Joseph-Marie, 20
Duvernay, Ludger, 36-37

Duvernay, Julie
   see Fortin, Julie
Duvernay, Pierre sr, 19
Duvernay, Pierre jr, 20

Elgin, Lord, 35, 38
   on Fortin's troop, 42-43
Enwright, James, 96
Esperance, M., (Grand-Étang), 68

Fauvel, John, 88
Ferland, Abbé J.B.A., 88, 90, 105
Ferrier, James, 110
Flynn, Edmund James, 181, 182
Fontana, John, 65
Forster, J.R., 113
Fortier, Moise, 156n
Fortin, Angelique, 21
Fortin, Calixte, 11
Fortin, Catherine, 20
Fortin, Françoise, 20
Fortin, Francois-Herman, 21
Fortin, Julie, 17, 20, 21, 26, 36
Fortin, Pierre, 20
Fortin, Pierre (father of P.-É. Fortin), 20, 21, 22
Fortin, Pierre-Étienne, 1, 17
   aging of, 185, 187-88
   on aristocracy, 157
   and Assembly library, 115
   assumes command, 6-7
   on authority, 154, 192
   birth of, 21
   as a Canadien, 193
   a "concert of praise," 196
   as conservationist, 115, 125
   criticized by historians, 87
   in danger, 4
   death of, false report, 2
   death of, 197
   description of, 2, 185
   distrust of local government, 172
   as doctor in the Gulf, 54
   as doctor at Laprairie, 25, 43
   duties of in the Gulf, ix, 3-4
   education of, 22-25
   emergency in Montréal, 35
   eulogies for, 197

216 INDEX

finances of, 9, 187
honesty of, 191-92
and natural daughter, 25-27
as naturalist, 113-15
oppressor or champion? 193-95
in a painful love affair? 25
in partisan squabble, 170-71
and public relations, 4-5, 13, 66, 68, 76
patriot or vendu? 159, 191, 193
porpoise or shark? 188-89
proposes schooner, 7
quits Quebec politics, 182
and religion, 192-93
and scandals, 181-82, 192
and the Senate, 191
and social life, 27, 185
as Speaker, 160, 182
success or failure? x, 195
unseated, 181-82, 186
voting record of, 156-57
and the wilderness, 196-97
work habits of, 172
see also Bisaillon, Suzanne, and Racine, Suzanne
Fortin, Pierre-Nicolas, 20
Fortin, Suzanne:
  see Bisaillon, Suzanne
Fourgères, Fabien, 57
Fournier, Jacques, 19
Fournier, Louis, 83
Fournier, Marguerite, 19
Forster, J.R., 113
Freer, Deputy Sheriff, 76
Frontenac, Comte de, 19

Gauthier, Joseph, 77
Geistdoerfer, Aliette, 113
Gibaud, Moses, 92, 97
Gill, Théodore, 113
Gingras, Abbé Nerée, 89, 90, 169
Girard, George, 77
Gosford, Lord, 36
Grenier, Greg, 96
Groulx, Lionel, 23, 25

Haggart, John G, 188, 189
Hamilton, M.C., 167

Hardy, Charles, 48
Hodgetts, J.E., ix
Holiday, Mr. (Godbout), 139
Hunson, Joseph, 81-82
Huntsman, A.-G., 113

Johnson, Judge Francis J., 181
Johnson, R.B., 38, 43
Joly de Lotbinière, Henri-Gustave, 132
Joncas, François, 68
Jones, Captain, 52
Jones, Francis, 157

Kerr, Archie, 96
Kirke Brothers, the, 48

La Fontaine, Louis-Hippolite, 23, 37, 38, 40, 42
Langevin, Hector-Louis, 110, 158, 159
Langlois, Étienne, 37-38
Laurier, Wilfred, 179
Lavergne, G., 75
Lavoie, Napoléon, 186
Lavoie, René, 129-30
LeBlanc, Moise, 122
LeBoutillier, John, 88, 91, 92, 153
Lefebvre, Hubert, 25
Legras, Catherine
  see Fortin, Catherine
LePailleur, Catherine, 20
LePailleur, Françoise
  see Fortin, Françoise
LePailleur, Michel, 20
Lesperance, Michael, 149
Letellier de Saint-Just, Luc, 149

Macdonald, John A., 153, 158-62 passim, 172, 174, 179, 186, 191
  and Fortin, 70-72, 176
Mackenzie, Alexander, 160, 179
  and Fortin, 185
McLelan, Archibald W., 190
  and Fortin, 174, 188
Maisoneuve, Angelique
  see Fortin, Angelique
Manderson, H.A., 135-36
Mann, Edward Isaac, 137
Marault, Abbé O., 37

INDEX

Martel, Mr. (Gaspésie), 92
Marsh, George Perkins, 126, 128, 133
Mason, William, 40
Masson, Luc H., 157
Mercier, Honoré, 154, 159
Michel, Louis, jnr. 135-36
Michel, Louis, snr. 135-36
Middlemiss, John-Rollo, 181
   and Fortin, 186
Mitchell, Peter, 110
   and Fortin, 189
Moylan, W.W., 33
Myers, Alexander, 121

Nettle, Richard, 50, 148, 149

Obus, Frederick, 83
O'Reilly, Bernard, 32
O'Reilly, James, 159
Ouimet, Gédéon, 131, 181
   and Fortin, 180, 186

Papineau, Louis-Joseph, 36
Perley, M.H., 113
Petarhoo, Pierre, 79
Philippe, Captain, 140
Phips, William, 48
Potvin, Damase, 22, 23, 26, 27, 32, 35-36, 87, 155, 193
Powell, Mr. (of Natashquan), 142, 143
Price, D.E., 149-50
Price family, 131
Purdye, Captain, 192

Quigley Brothers, the, 79

Racine, Delphi, 26
Racine, Suzanne, 25-27 passim
Rail, Peter, 76
Richard, Auguste, 68
Richardson, J., 113
Richey, M.H., 173
Riel, 190-91
   Fortin's attitude to, 158, 196
   Fortin vilified over, 191, 193
Robin, Charles, 87-88
   see also Charles Robin and Co.
Robin, John, 87

Robin, Philip, 87, 105
Robin, Pipon Co., 87
Robitaille, Théodore, 92, 93, 97, 159
Russell, Andrew, 146, 148
Ryan, Michael P., 159

Saint-Pierre, M. (Montréal), 186
Scott, Captain (Grosse-Île), 35
Scott, Thomas, 158, 190
Seaton, William, 110
Seward, William Henry, 64
Shepherd, Dr., 24
Shepphard, Martin, 98
Sirois, Captain Phileas, 195-96
St. Croix, John de, 75
St. Croix, M. (Jersey), 178
Sulpicians, 22
Suddard, Captain, 119
Sutherland, Mr. (Îles-de-la-Madeleine), 80
Sweeney, John, 159

Talbot, Captain, 7
Talon, Jean, 126
Tarte, Israël, 161, 191-92, 197
   on Fortin, 2
Taschereau, Henri-Élzear, 154
Têtu, David H., 148
Têtu, Théophile, 129-30, 151, 186
Thoreau, Henry, 133
Thrasher, John, 137
Tilly (coroner), 77
Tilley, Sir Leonard, on Fortin, 162-63
Tremblay, P.-A., 131-32, 170-71, 180
Tully, John, 39

Uniacke, James B., 64

Vavin, Commander, 62

Wakeham, Dr., 175
Walker, Hovenden, 48
Webster, Daniel, 64
Wetherall, Charles, 38, 43
Whitcher, W.F., 146-51 passim
   see also Crown Lands Dept.
Winter, Peter, 195
Wolfe, James, 21, 48
Worthington, E.D., 24

VESSELS

Alliance, 7, 68
Arabian, 48
Atravida, 79

Bee, 57
Blanchard, 88-89

Canadienne, La, 3, 48, 57, 71, 83, 100, 128, 145, 195-96
  annual departure, 1-2
  and Captain Talbot, 7
  casualties on, 11
  costs of, 9, 12, 13
  damage to, 11, 12, 66, 92
  delivers mail, 54
  description of, 8-9
  discipline on, 5, 6
  and Fortin, 10, 67, 151, 188
  insurance of, 12
  and law and order, 2, 75, 136
  lost at sea, 185
  opposition to, 12-13, 155
  on North Shore, 150
  voyage of 1861 statistics, 53
  wreck of, 5, 11-12
Commerce, 68

Doris, 7
Druid, 71

Electra, 82

Fauvette, La, 61

Front of Chester, 68

Glendon, 186
George Mangham, 62, 69-70

Isa, 68

Lady Head, 48, 192
Lochmaben Castle, 79-80
Lucknow, 140

Mackerel, 88-89
Marceau, Le, 62
Marguerite, 195
Mary Jane, 57
Mouche, La, 61

Napoleon III, 6, 66, 99
North American, 58

Ocean Bride, 121-22

Princess, 4

Rowland Hill, 34
Royal Middy, 83

San Giovanni, 62
Sarah and Julie, 67
Seaflower, 87
Shylock, 80
Silver Key, 80
Stacey, 67
St. Lawrence, 67

Transit, 41

Victoria, 80
Village Belle, 67